GARFIELD
Livin' the Sweet Life

BY JIM DAVIS

Ballantine Books ● **New York**

A Ballantine Books Trade Paperback Original

Copyright © 2021 by PAWS, Inc. All Rights Reserved. "GARFIELD" and the GARFIELD characters are trademarks of PAWS, Inc. Based on the Garfield® characters created by Jim Davis

Published in the United States by Ballantine Books, an imprint of Random House, a division of Penguin Random House LLC, New York.

BALLANTINE and the HOUSE colophon are registered trademarks of Penguin Random House LLC.

NICKELODEON is a Trademark of Viacom International, Inc.

All of the comics in this work have been previously published.

ISBN 978-0-593-15646-9
Ebook ISBN 978-0-593-15647-6

Printed in China on acid-free paper

randomhousebooks.com

9 8 7 6 5 4 3 2 1

HAPPINESS IS...

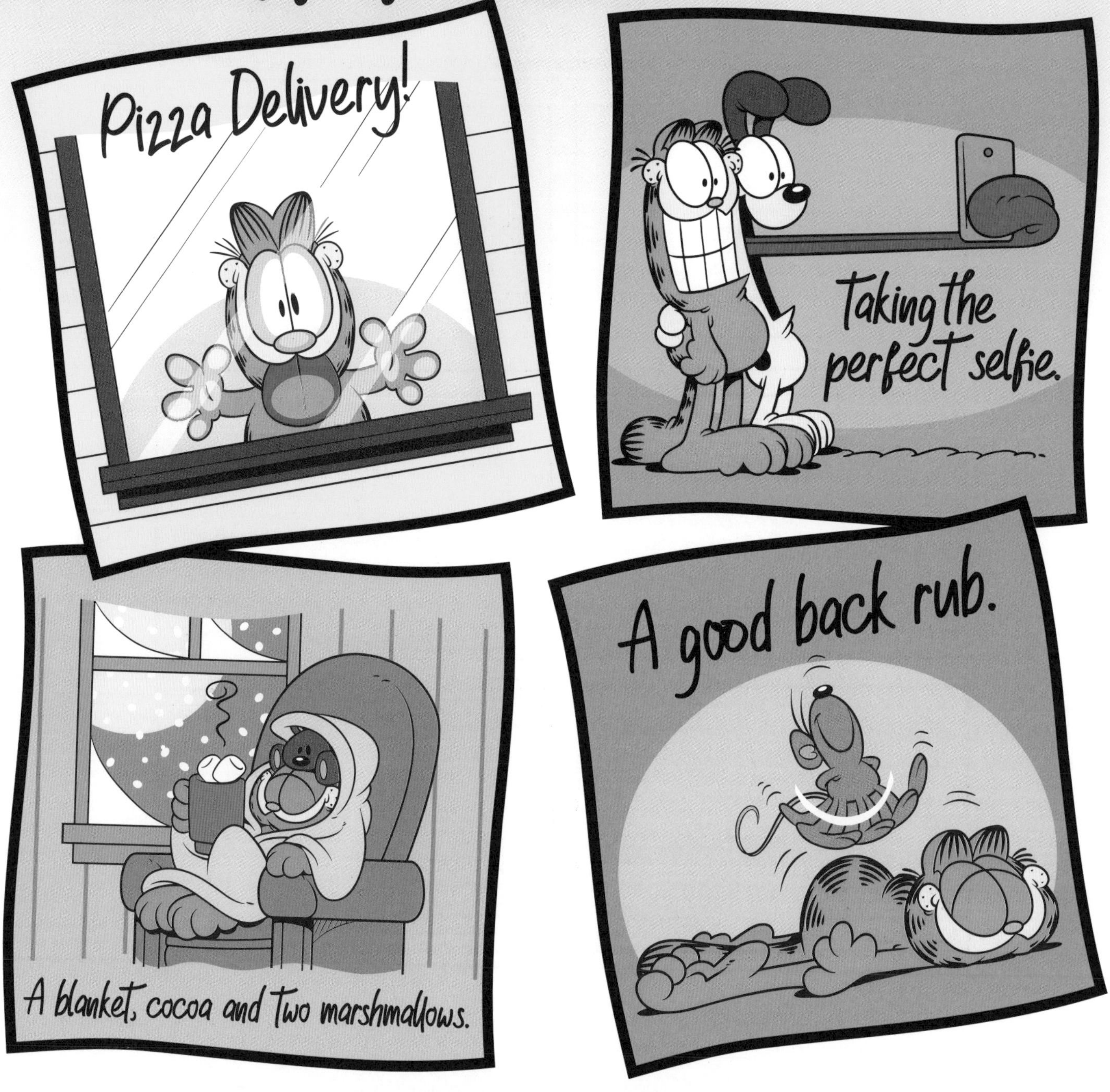
Pizza Delivery!
Taking the perfect selfie.
A blanket, cocoa and two marshmallows.
A good back rub.

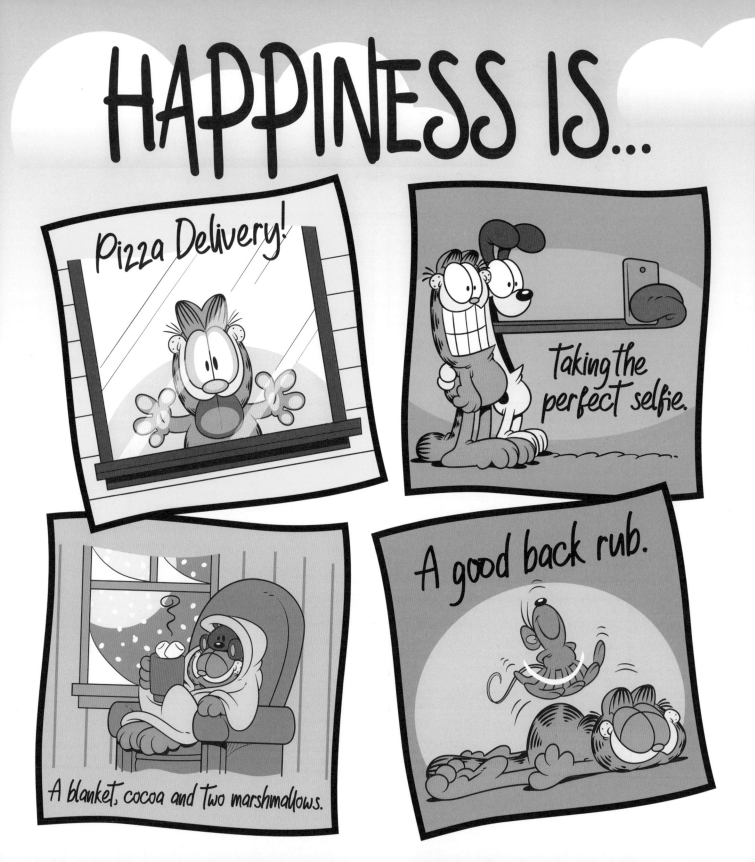

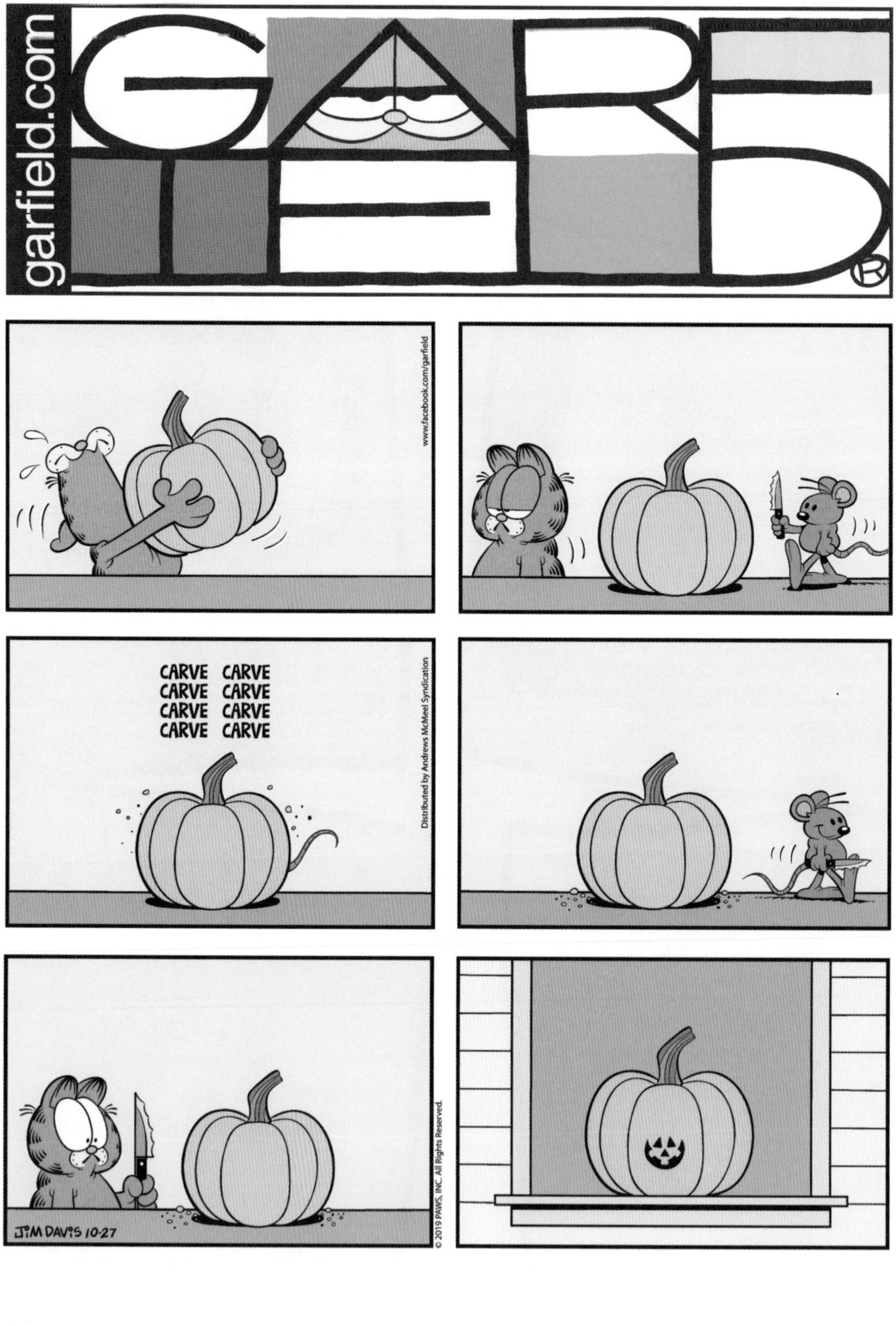
garfield.com
GARFIELD
www.facebook.com/garfield
CARVE CARVE
CARVE CARVE
CARVE CARVE
CARVE CARVE
Distributed by Andrews McMeel Syndication
JIM DAVIS 10-27
© 2019 PAWS, INC. All Rights Reserved.

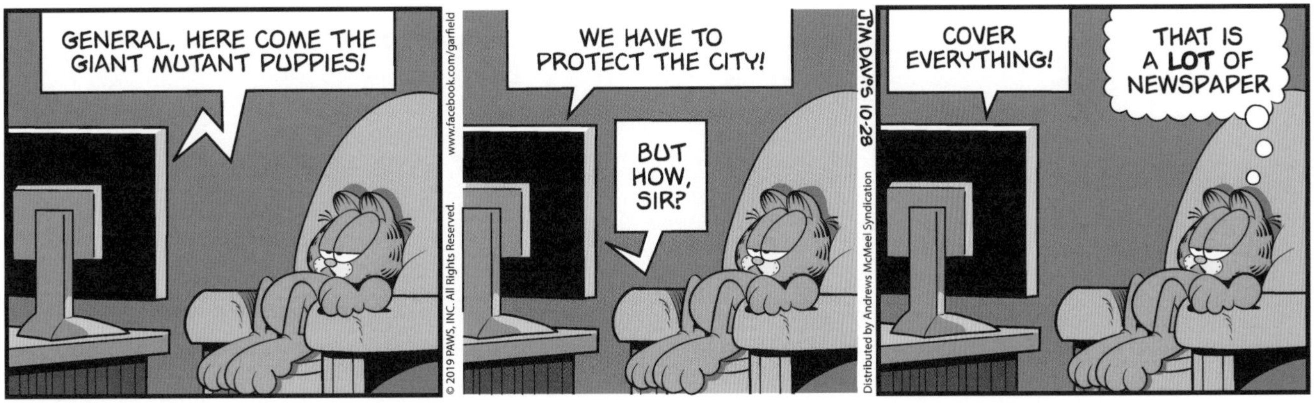
GENERAL, HERE COME THE GIANT MUTANT PUPPIES!
© 2019 PAWS, INC. All Rights Reserved. www.facebook.com/garfield
WE HAVE TO PROTECT THE CITY!
BUT HOW, SIR?
JIM DAVIS 10-28
Distributed by Andrews McMeel Syndication
COVER EVERYTHING!
THAT IS A **LOT** OF NEWSPAPER

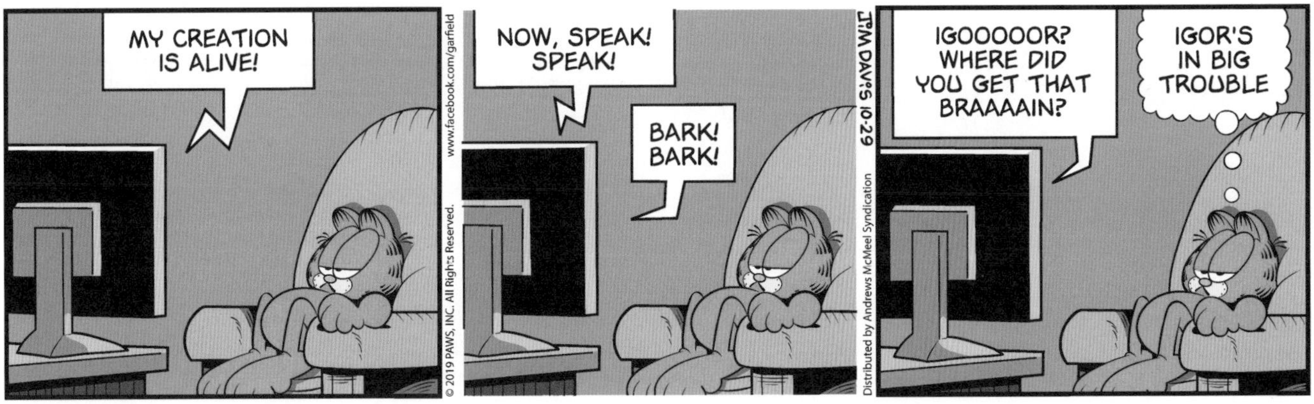
MY CREATION IS ALIVE!
© 2019 PAWS, INC. All Rights Reserved. www.facebook.com/garfield
NOW, SPEAK! SPEAK!
BARK! BARK!
JIM DAVIS 10-29
Distributed by Andrews McMeel Syndication
IGOOOOOR? WHERE DID YOU GET THAT BRAAAAIN?
IGOR'S IN BIG TROUBLE

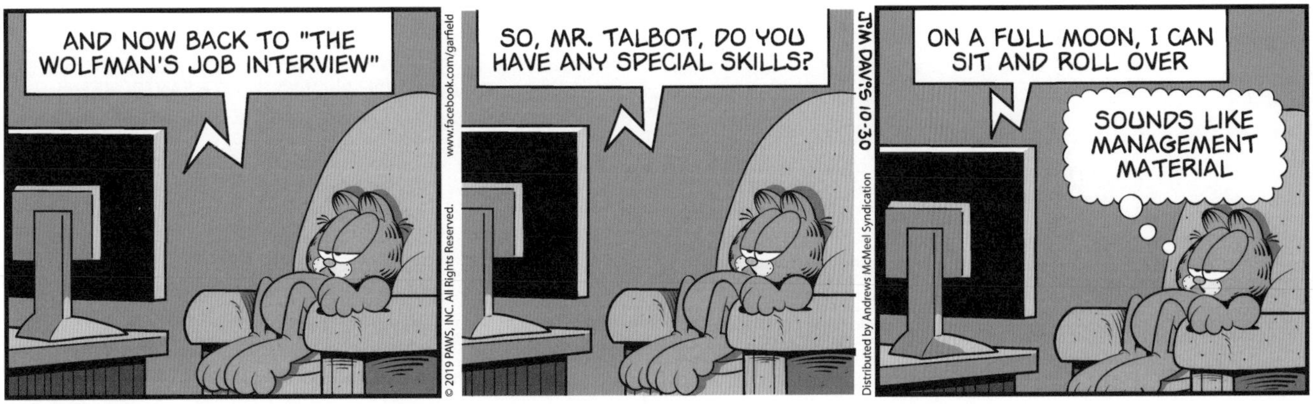
AND NOW BACK TO "THE WOLFMAN'S JOB INTERVIEW"
© 2019 PAWS, INC. All Rights Reserved. www.facebook.com/garfield
SO, MR. TALBOT, DO YOU HAVE ANY SPECIAL SKILLS?
JIM DAVIS 10-30
Distributed by Andrews McMeel Syndication
ON A FULL MOON, I CAN SIT AND ROLL OVER
SOUNDS LIKE MANAGEMENT MATERIAL

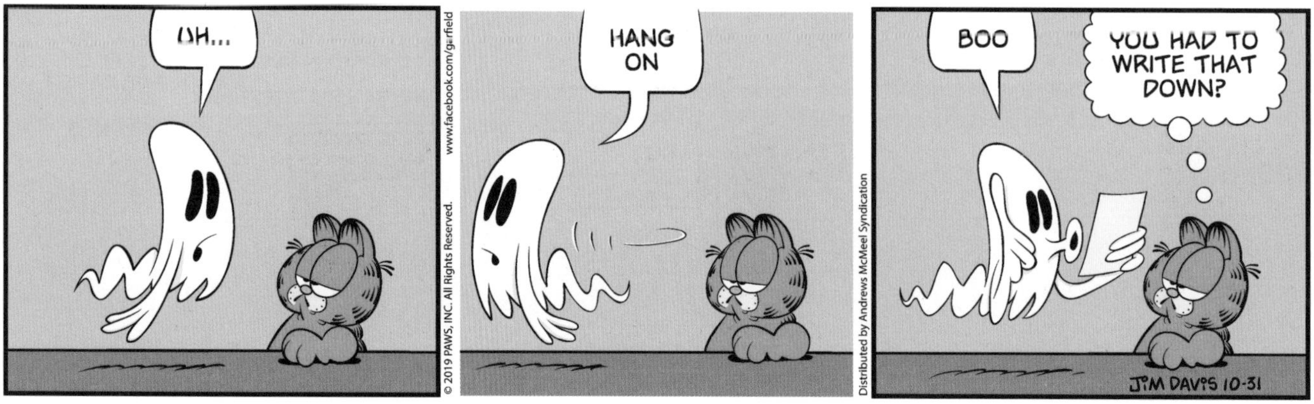
UH...
HANG ON
BOO
YOU HAD TO WRITE THAT DOWN?
© 2019 PAWS, INC. All Rights Reserved. www.facebook.com/garfield
Distributed by Andrews McMeel Syndication
JIM DAVIS 10-31

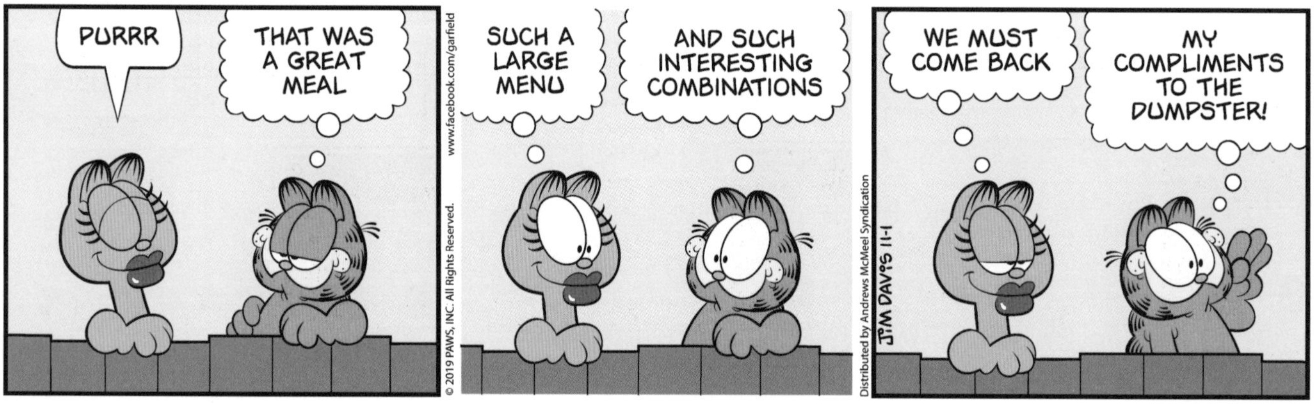
PURRR
THAT WAS A GREAT MEAL
SUCH A LARGE MENU
AND SUCH INTERESTING COMBINATIONS
WE MUST COME BACK
MY COMPLIMENTS TO THE DUMPSTER!
© 2019 PAWS, INC. All Rights Reserved. www.facebook.com/garfield
Distributed by Andrews McMeel Syndication
JIM DAVIS 11-1

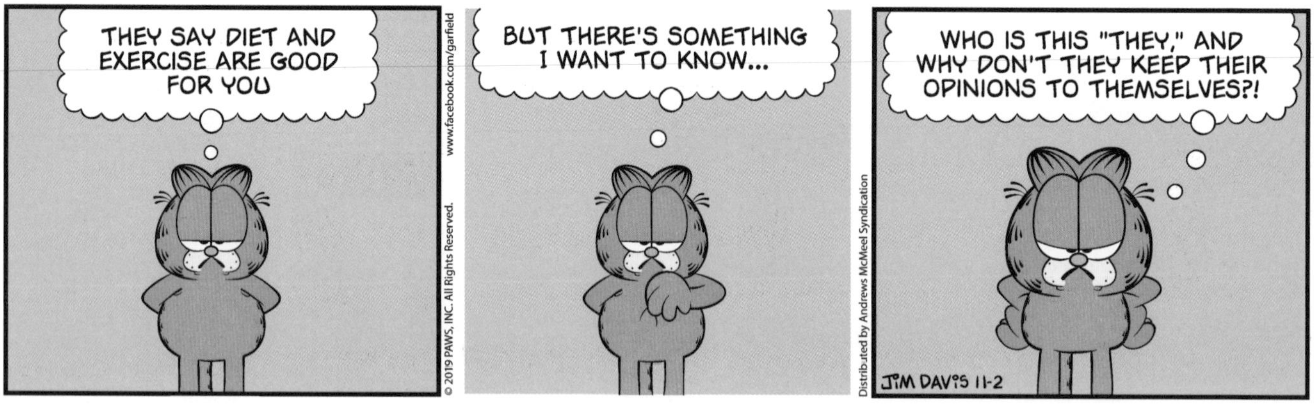
THEY SAY DIET AND EXERCISE ARE GOOD FOR YOU
BUT THERE'S SOMETHING I WANT TO KNOW...
WHO IS THIS "THEY," AND WHY DON'T THEY KEEP THEIR OPINIONS TO THEMSELVES?!
© 2019 PAWS, INC. All Rights Reserved. www.facebook.com/garfield
Distributed by Andrews McMeel Syndication
JIM DAVIS 11-2

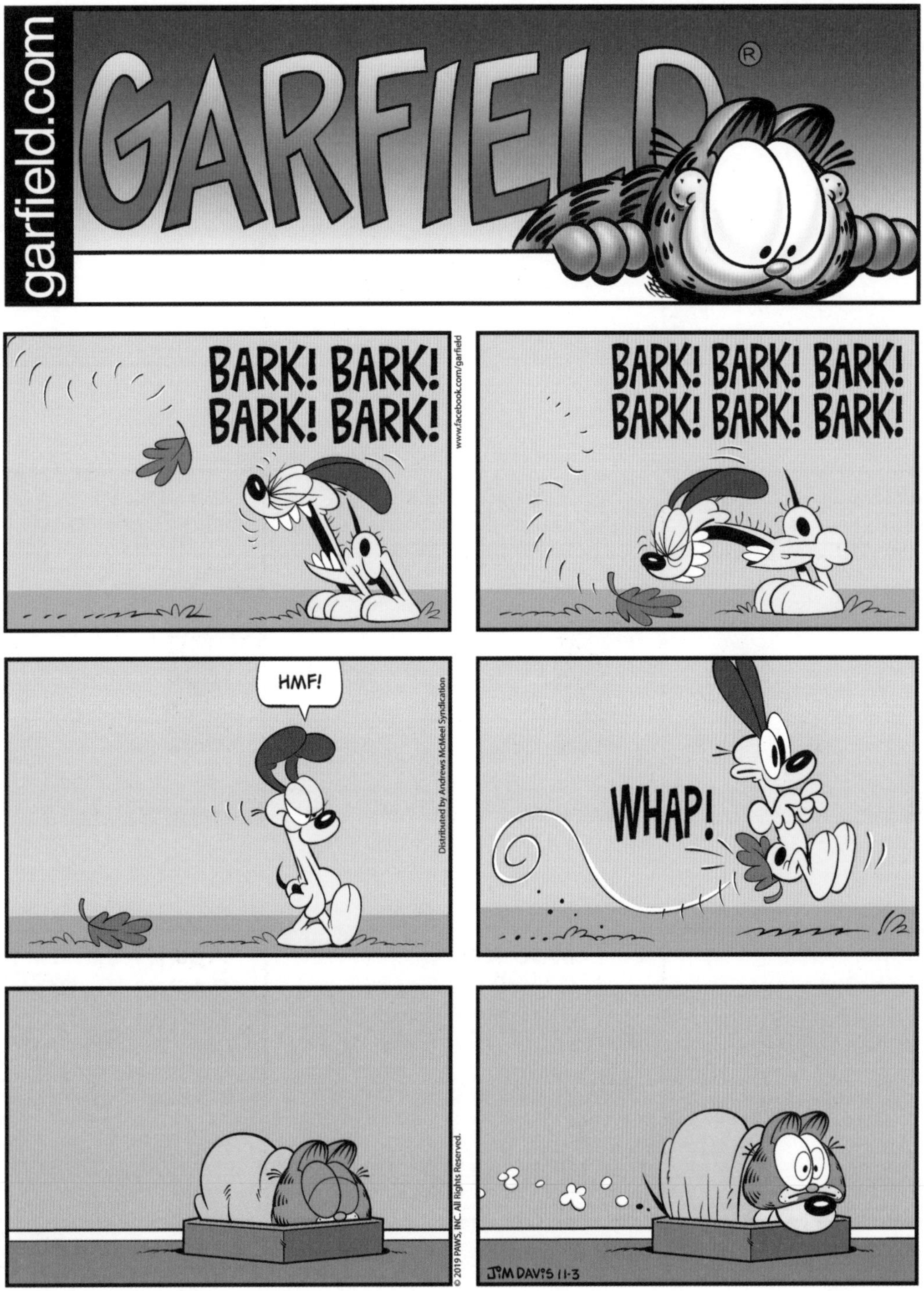
garfield.com
GARFIELD
BARK! BARK!
BARK! BARK!
www.facebook.com/garfield
BARK! BARK! BARK!
BARK! BARK! BARK!
HMF!
Distributed by Andrews McMeel Syndication
WHAP!
© 2019 PAWS, INC. All Rights Reserved.
JIM DAVIS 11-3

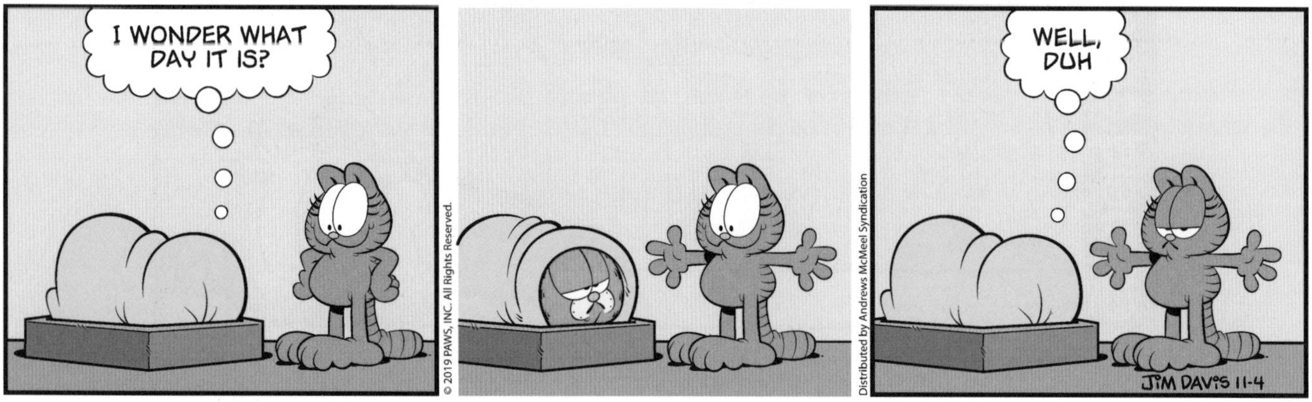
I WONDER WHAT DAY IT IS?
WELL, DUH
JIM DAVIS 11-4
© 2019 PAWS, INC. All Rights Reserved.
Distributed by Andrews McMeel Syndication

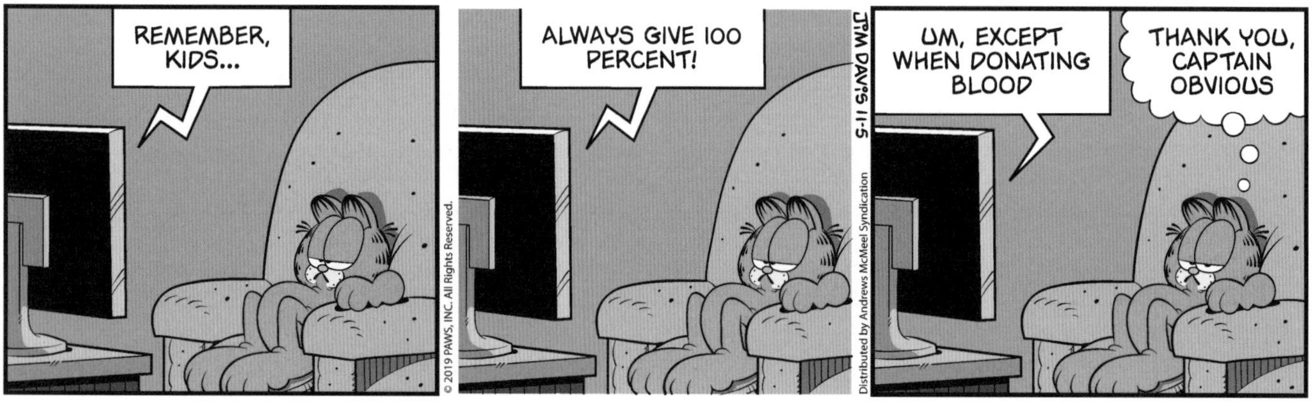
REMEMBER, KIDS...
ALWAYS GIVE 100 PERCENT!
UM, EXCEPT WHEN DONATING BLOOD
THANK YOU, CAPTAIN OBVIOUS
JIM DAVIS 11-5
© 2019 PAWS, INC. All Rights Reserved.
Distributed by Andrews McMeel Syndication

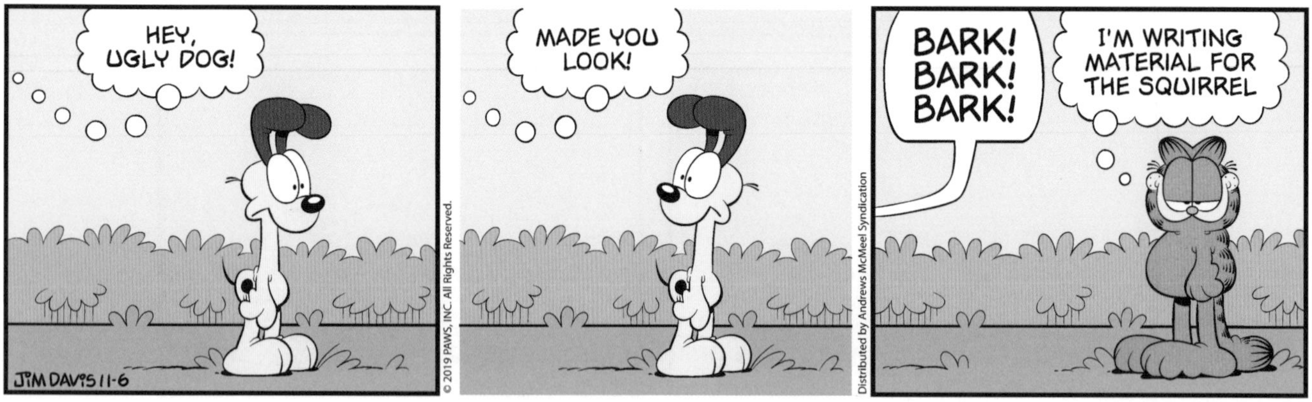
HEY, UGLY DOG!
MADE YOU LOOK!
BARK! BARK! BARK!
I'M WRITING MATERIAL FOR THE SQUIRREL
JIM DAVIS 11-6
© 2019 PAWS, INC. All Rights Reserved.
Distributed by Andrews McMeel Syndication

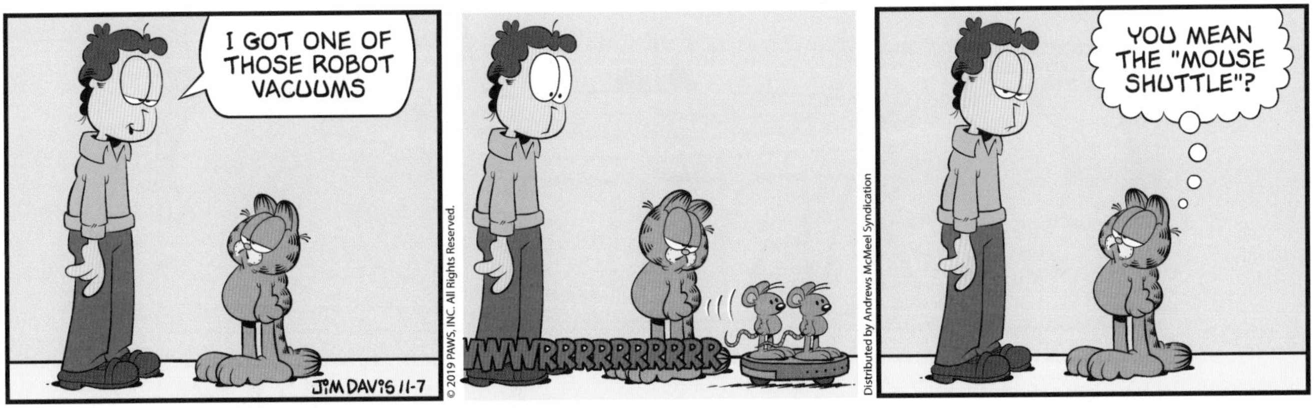
I GOT ONE OF THOSE ROBOT VACUUMS
JIM DAVIS 11-7
© 2019 PAWS, INC. All Rights Reserved.
VWWWRRRRRRRRRRR
Distributed by Andrews McMeel Syndication
YOU MEAN THE "MOUSE SHUTTLE"?

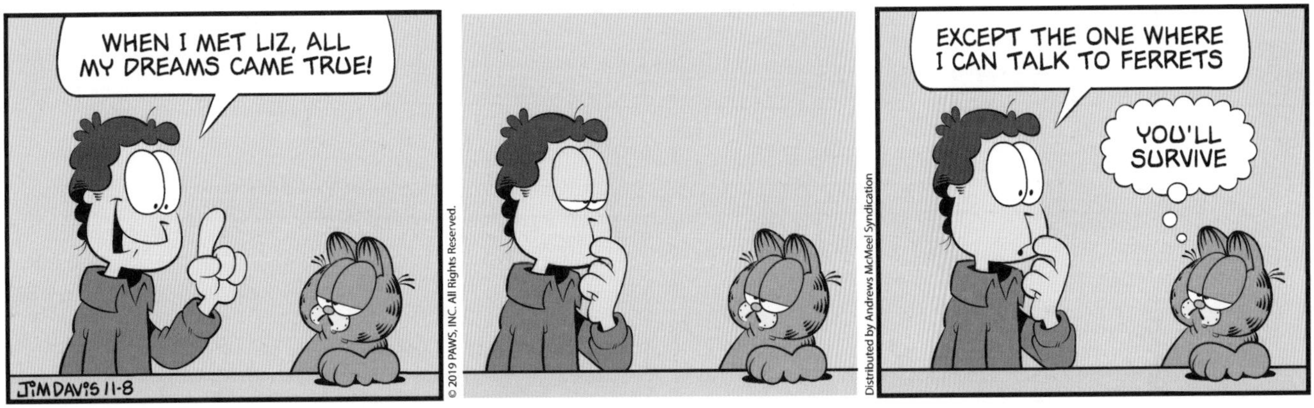
WHEN I MET LIZ, ALL MY DREAMS CAME TRUE!
JIM DAVIS 11-8
© 2019 PAWS, INC. All Rights Reserved.
Distributed by Andrews McMeel Syndication
EXCEPT THE ONE WHERE I CAN TALK TO FERRETS
YOU'LL SURVIVE

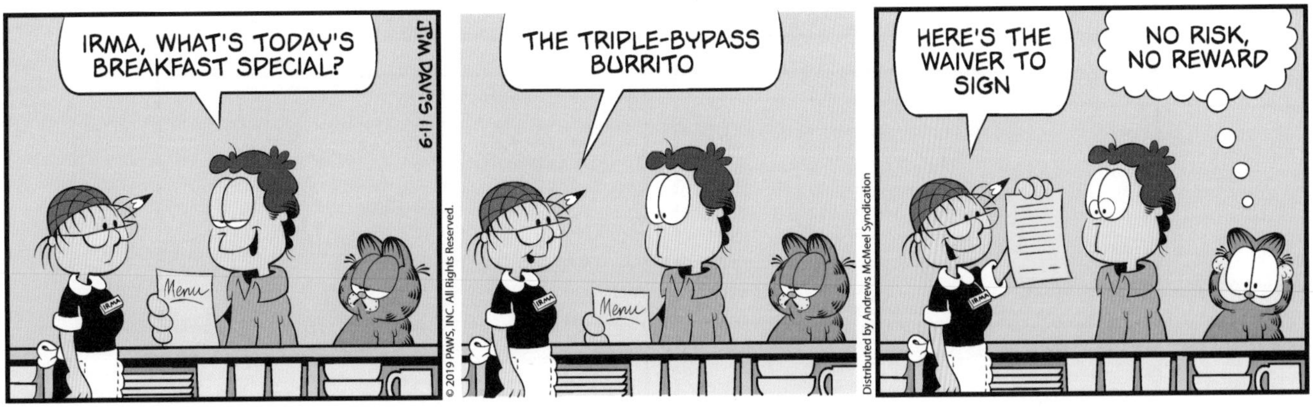
IRMA, WHAT'S TODAY'S BREAKFAST SPECIAL?
JIM DAVIS 11-9
Menu
© 2019 PAWS, INC. All Rights Reserved.
THE TRIPLE-BYPASS BURRITO
Distributed by Andrews McMeel Syndication
HERE'S THE WAIVER TO SIGN
NO RISK, NO REWARD

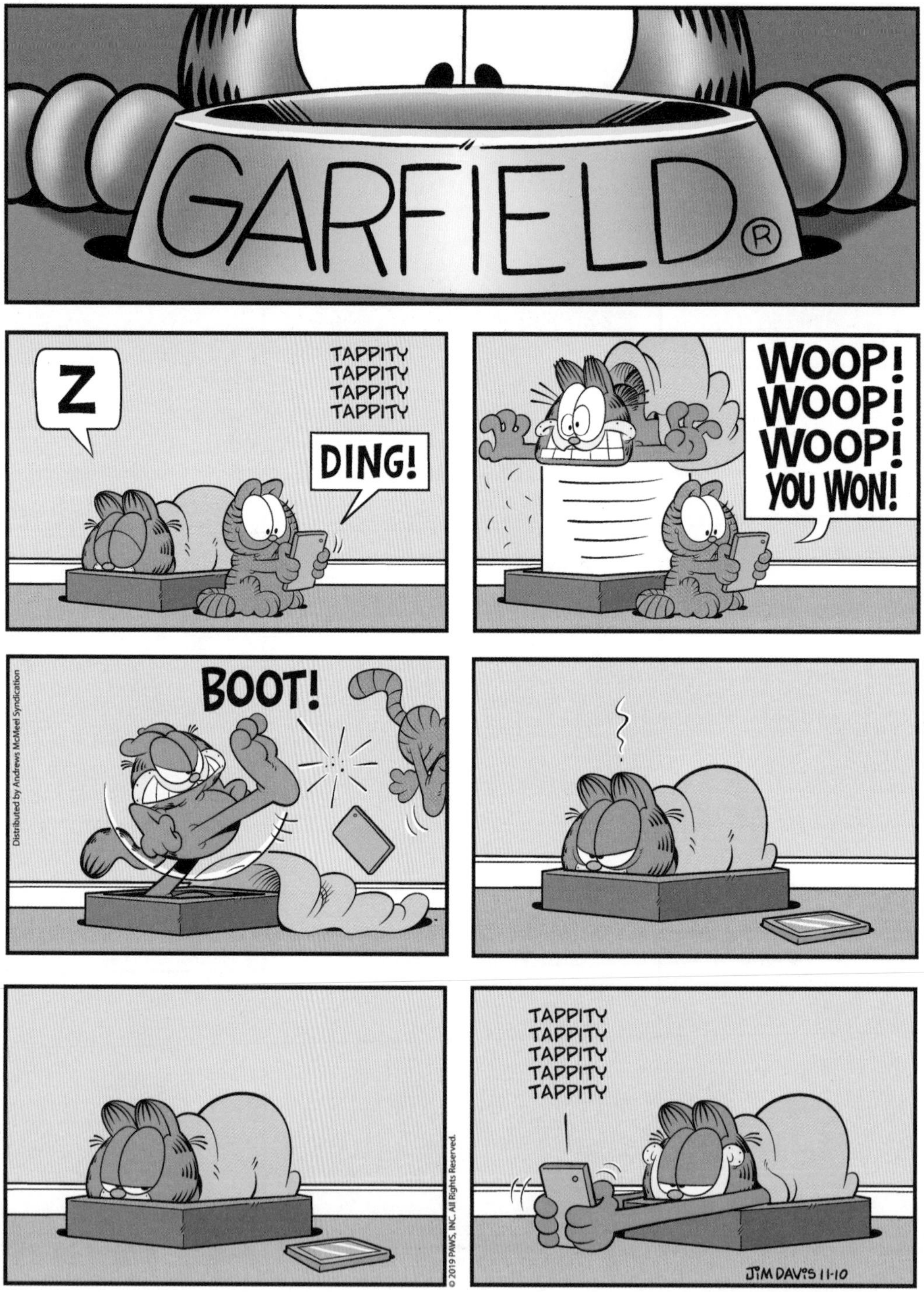
GARFIELD®
Z
TAPPITY
TAPPITY
TAPPITY
TAPPITY
DING!
WOOP!
WOOP!
WOOP!
YOU WON!
BOOT!
TAPPITY
TAPPITY
TAPPITY
TAPPITY
TAPPITY
JIM DAVIS 11-10
Distributed by Andrews McMeel Syndication
© 2019 PAWS, INC. All Rights Reserved.

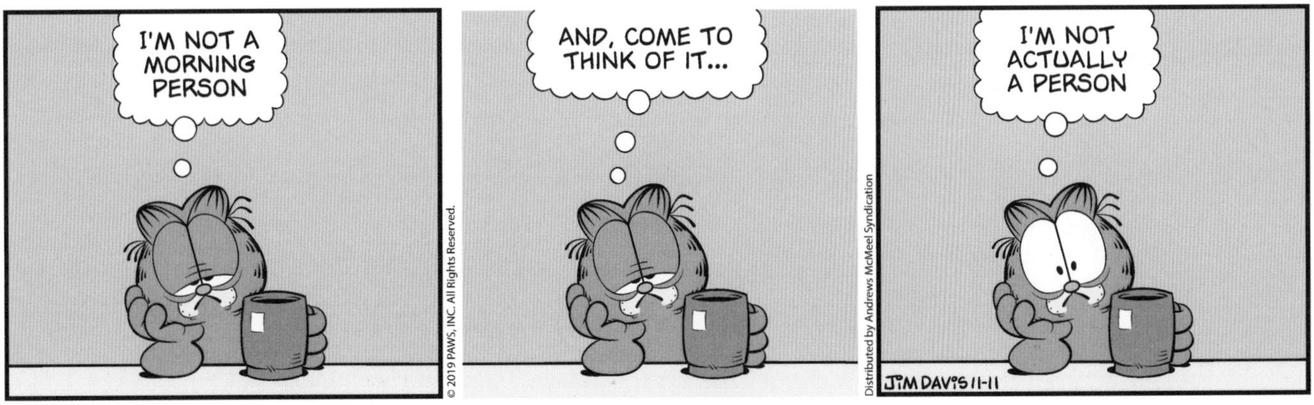
I'M NOT A MORNING PERSON
AND, COME TO THINK OF IT...
I'M NOT ACTUALLY A PERSON
© 2019 PAWS, INC. All Rights Reserved.
Distributed by Andrews McMeel Syndication
JIM DAVIS 11-11

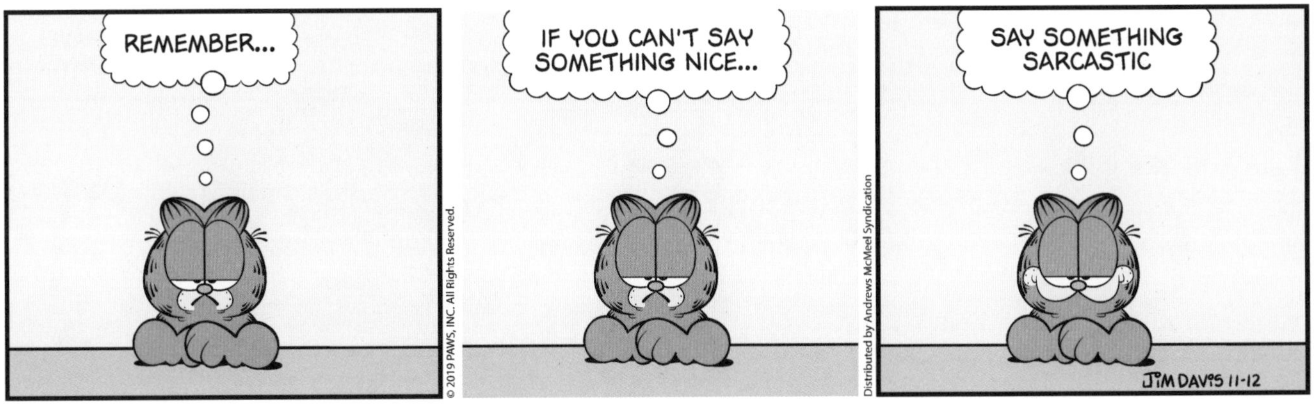
REMEMBER...
IF YOU CAN'T SAY SOMETHING NICE...
SAY SOMETHING SARCASTIC
© 2019 PAWS, INC. All Rights Reserved.
Distributed by Andrews McMeel Syndication
JIM DAVIS 11-12

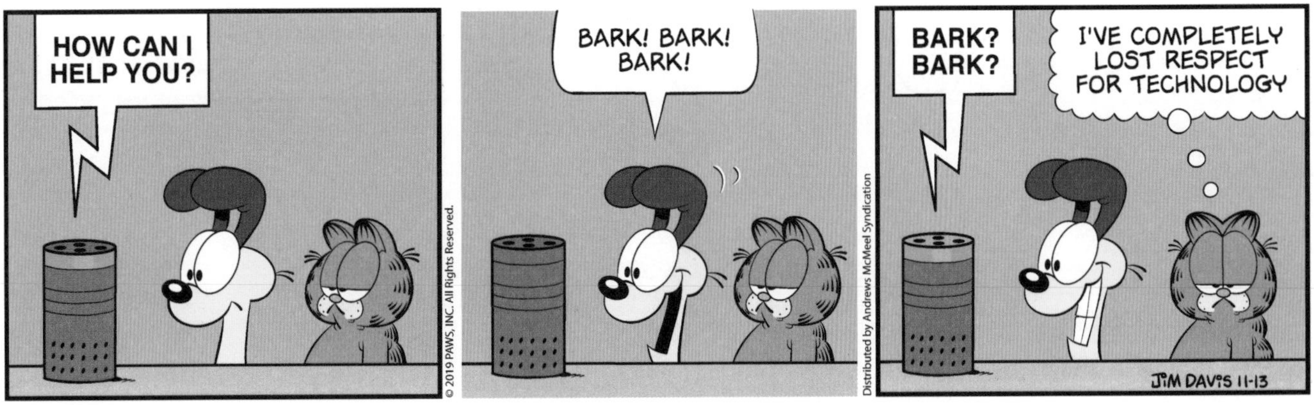
HOW CAN I HELP YOU?
BARK! BARK! BARK!
BARK? BARK?
I'VE COMPLETELY LOST RESPECT FOR TECHNOLOGY
© 2019 PAWS, INC. All Rights Reserved.
Distributed by Andrews McMeel Syndication
JIM DAVIS 11-13

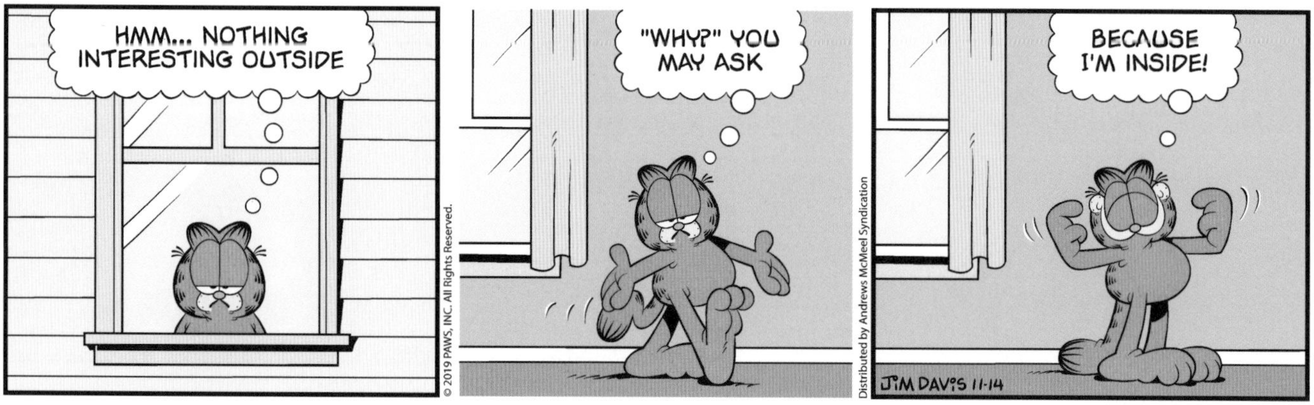
HMM... NOTHING INTERESTING OUTSIDE
"WHY?" YOU MAY ASK
BECAUSE I'M INSIDE!
JIM DAVIS 11-14
© 2019 PAWS, INC. All Rights Reserved.
Distributed by Andrews McMeel Syndication

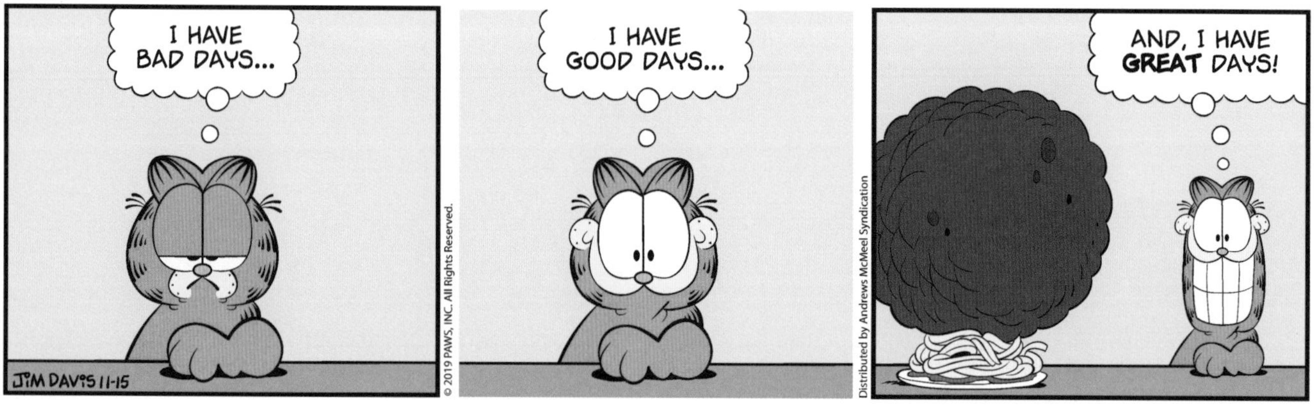
I HAVE BAD DAYS...
I HAVE GOOD DAYS...
AND, I HAVE **GREAT** DAYS!
JIM DAVIS 11-15
© 2019 PAWS, INC. All Rights Reserved.
Distributed by Andrews McMeel Syndication

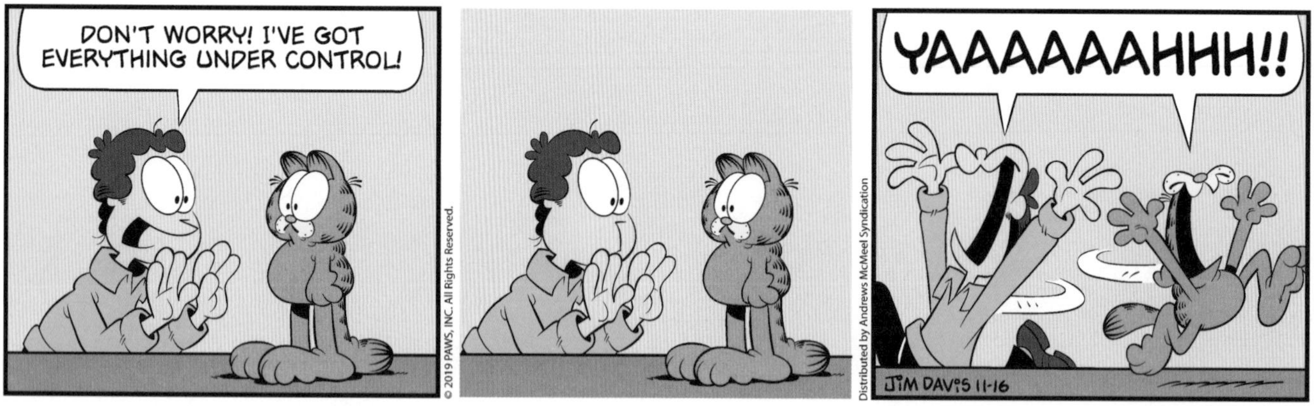
DON'T WORRY! I'VE GOT EVERYTHING UNDER CONTROL!
YAAAAAAHHH!!
JIM DAVIS 11-16
© 2019 PAWS, INC. All Rights Reserved.
Distributed by Andrews McMeel Syndication

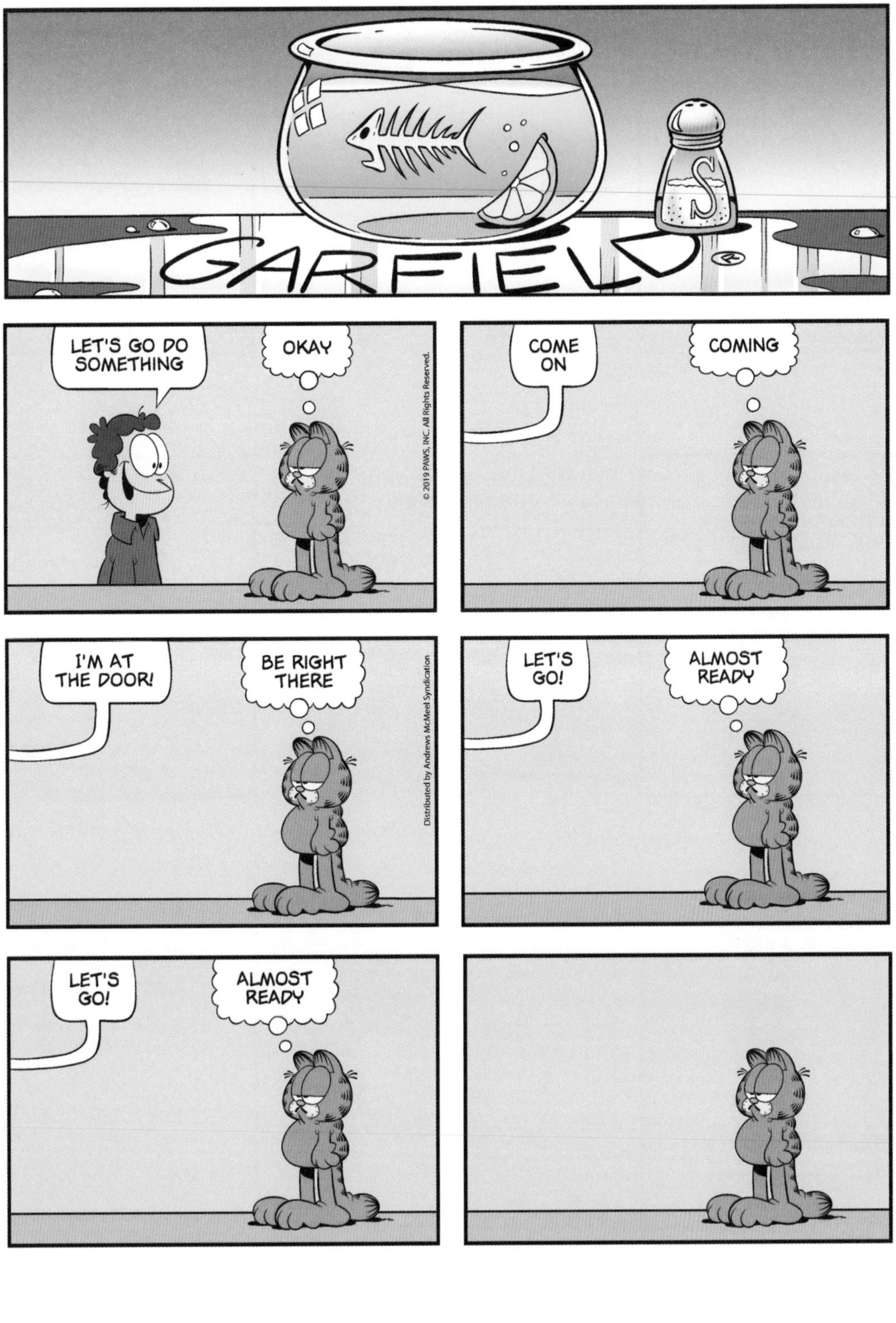
GARFIELD®
LET'S GO DO SOMETHING
OKAY
© 2019 PAWS, INC. All Rights Reserved.
COME ON
COMING
I'M AT THE DOOR!
BE RIGHT THERE
Distributed by Andrews McMeel Syndication
LET'S GO!
ALMOST READY
LET'S GO!
ALMOST READY

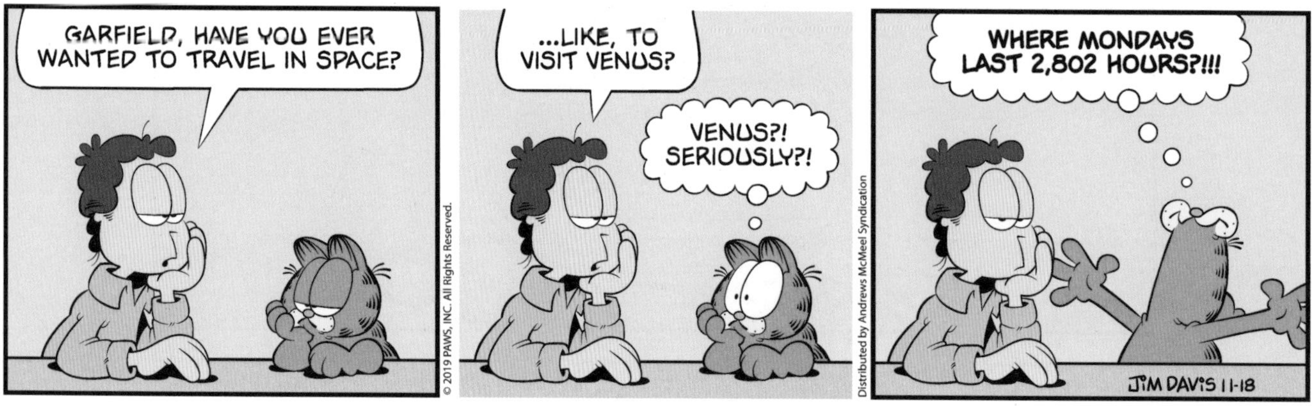
GARFIELD, HAVE YOU EVER WANTED TO TRAVEL IN SPACE?
...LIKE, TO VISIT VENUS?
VENUS?! SERIOUSLY?!
WHERE MONDAYS LAST 2,802 HOURS?!!!
© 2019 PAWS, INC. All Rights Reserved.
Distributed by Andrews McMeel Syndication
JIM DAVIS 11-18

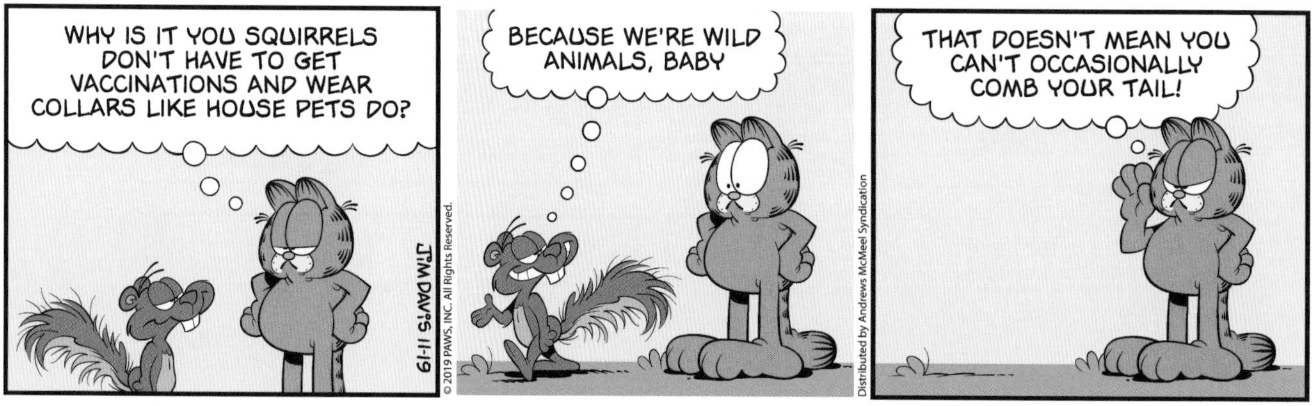
WHY IS IT YOU SQUIRRELS DON'T HAVE TO GET VACCINATIONS AND WEAR COLLARS LIKE HOUSE PETS DO?
BECAUSE WE'RE WILD ANIMALS, BABY
THAT DOESN'T MEAN YOU CAN'T OCCASIONALLY COMB YOUR TAIL!
JIM DAVIS 11-19
© 2019 PAWS, INC. All Rights Reserved.
Distributed by Andrews McMeel Syndication

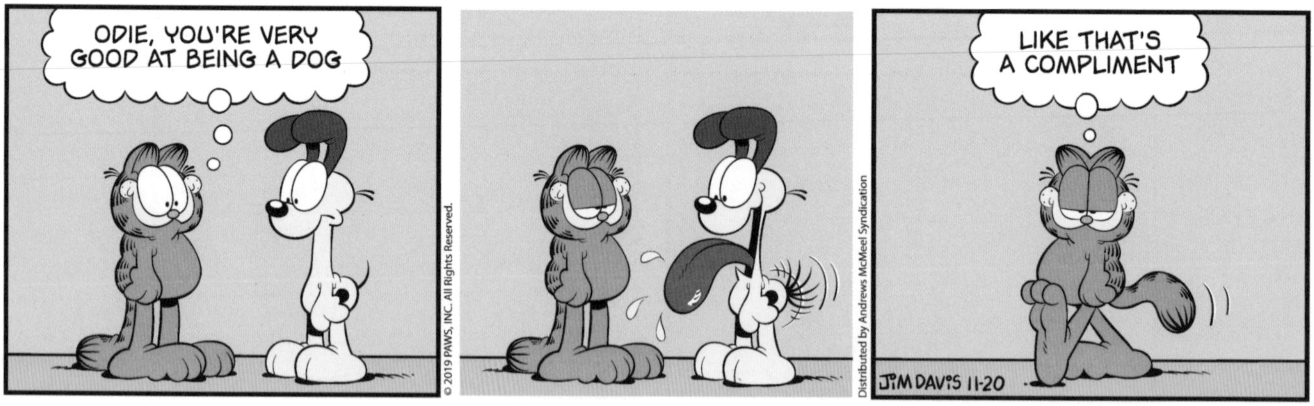
ODIE, YOU'RE VERY GOOD AT BEING A DOG
LIKE THAT'S A COMPLIMENT
© 2019 PAWS, INC. All Rights Reserved.
Distributed by Andrews McMeel Syndication
JIM DAVIS 11-20

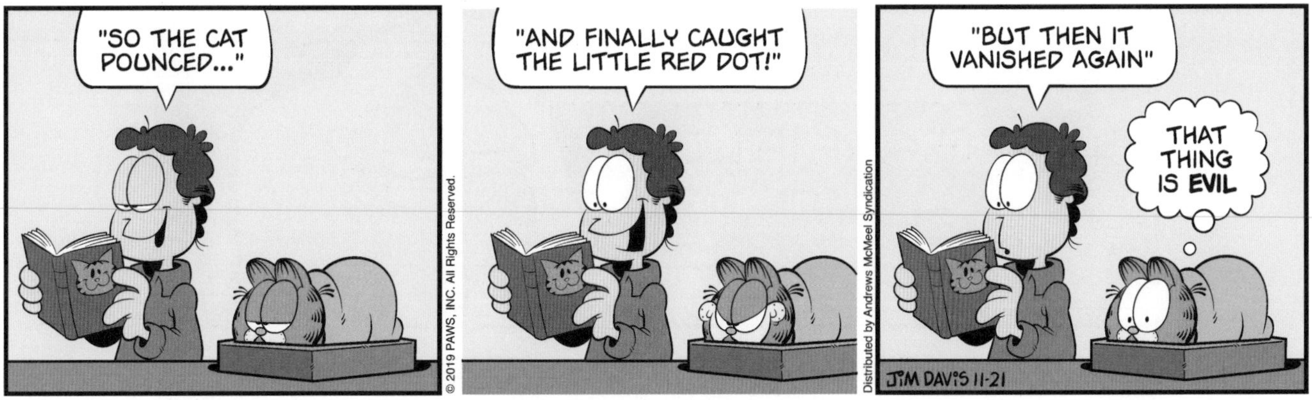
"SO THE CAT POUNCED..."
"AND FINALLY CAUGHT THE LITTLE RED DOT!"
"BUT THEN IT VANISHED AGAIN"
THAT THING IS **EVIL**
JIM DAVIS 11-21
© 2019 PAWS, INC. All Rights Reserved.
Distributed by Andrews McMeel Syndication

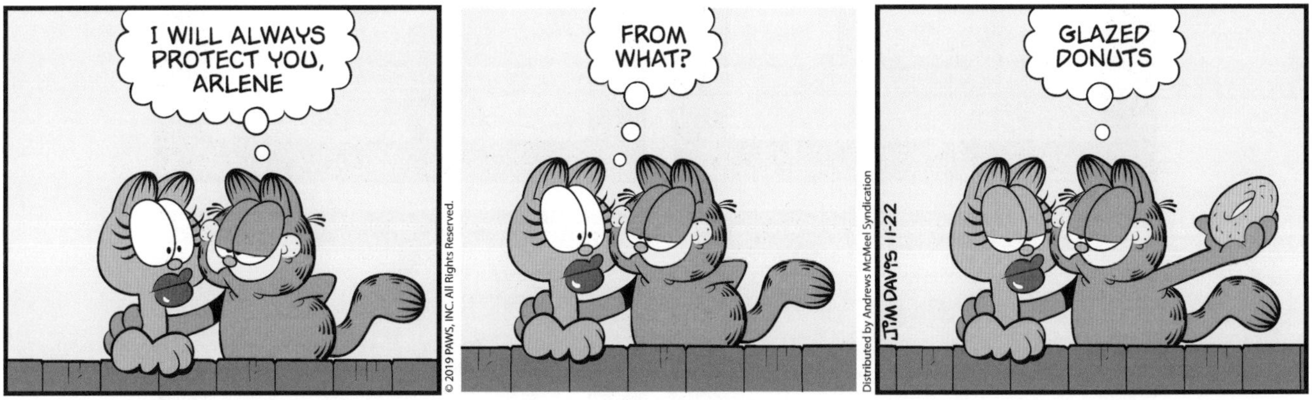
I WILL ALWAYS PROTECT YOU, ARLENE
FROM WHAT?
GLAZED DONUTS
JIM DAVIS 11-22
© 2019 PAWS, INC. All Rights Reserved.
Distributed by Andrews McMeel Syndication

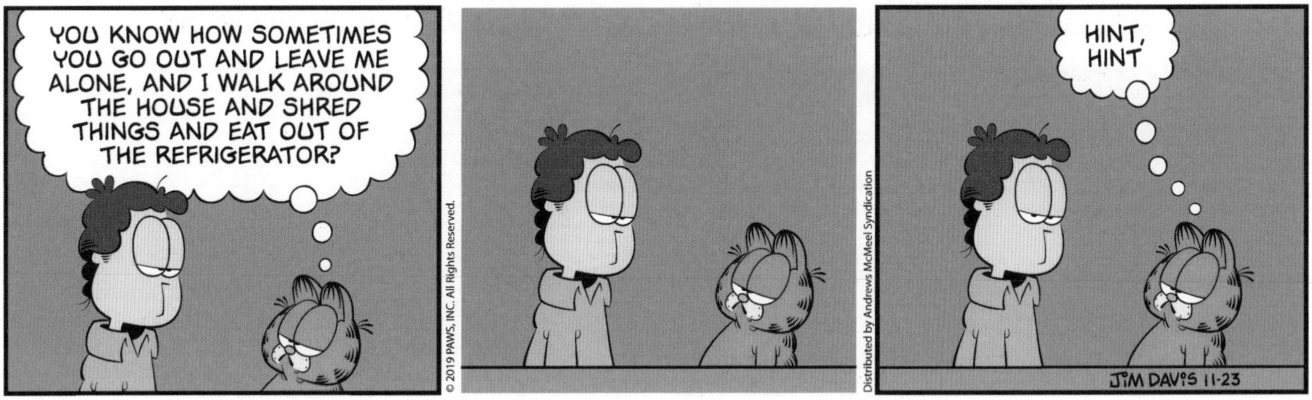
YOU KNOW HOW SOMETIMES YOU GO OUT AND LEAVE ME ALONE, AND I WALK AROUND THE HOUSE AND SHRED THINGS AND EAT OUT OF THE REFRIGERATOR?
HINT, HINT
JIM DAVIS 11-23
© 2019 PAWS, INC. All Rights Reserved.
Distributed by Andrews McMeel Syndication

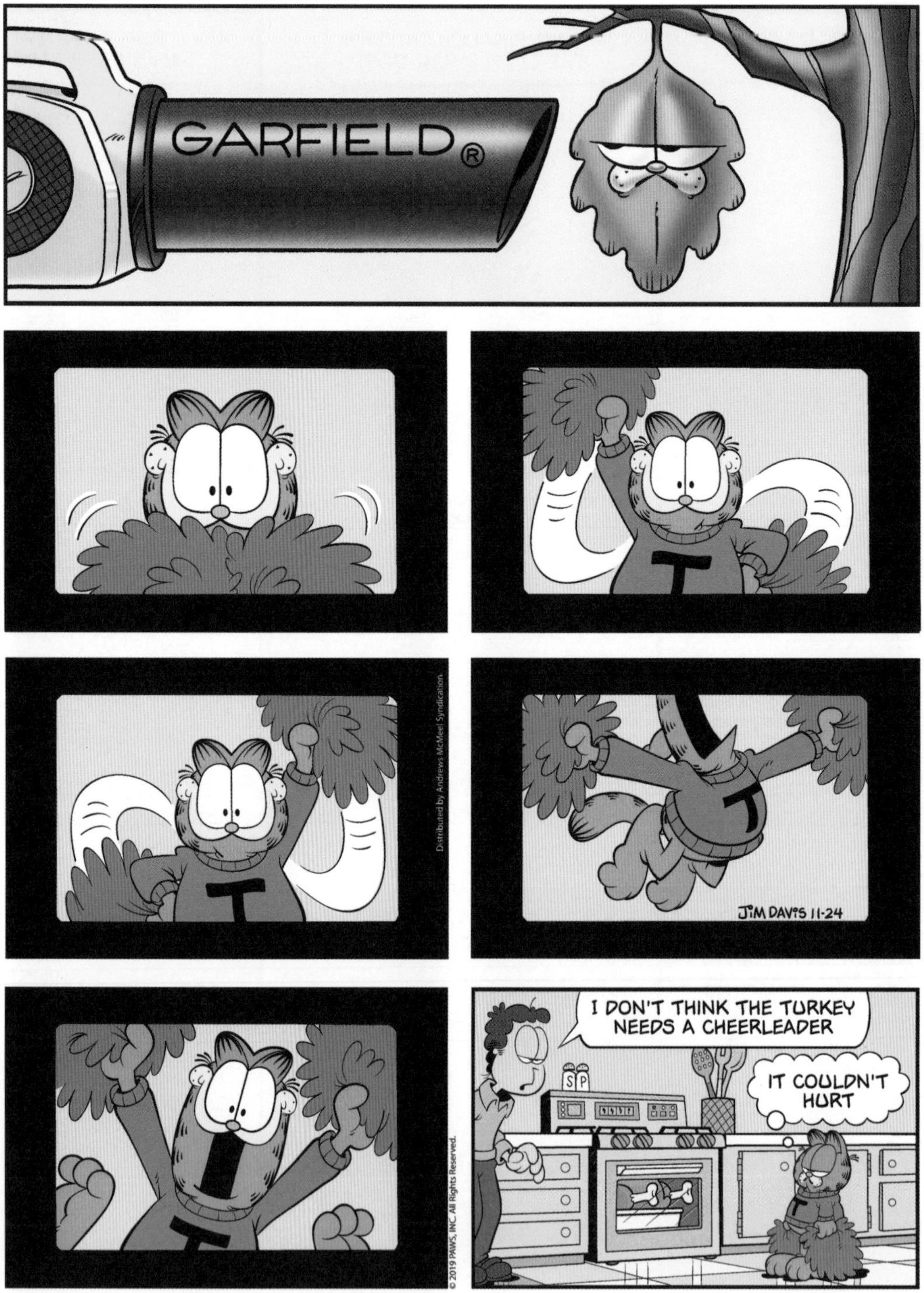
GARFIELD®
JIM DAVIS 11-24
I DON'T THINK THE TURKEY NEEDS A CHEERLEADER
IT COULDN'T HURT

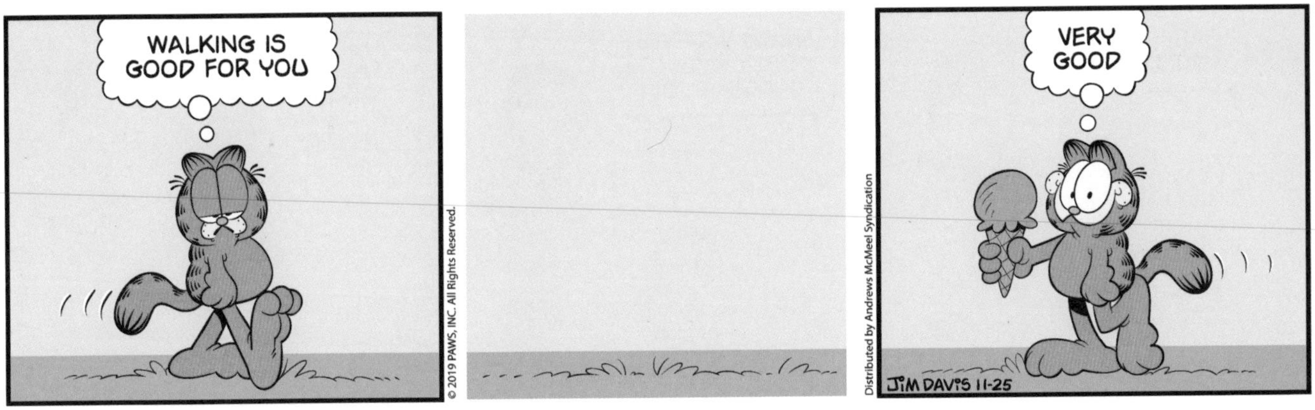

WALKING IS GOOD FOR YOU
VERY GOOD
JIM DAVIS 11-25
© 2019 PAWS, INC. All Rights Reserved.
Distributed by Andrews McMeel Syndication

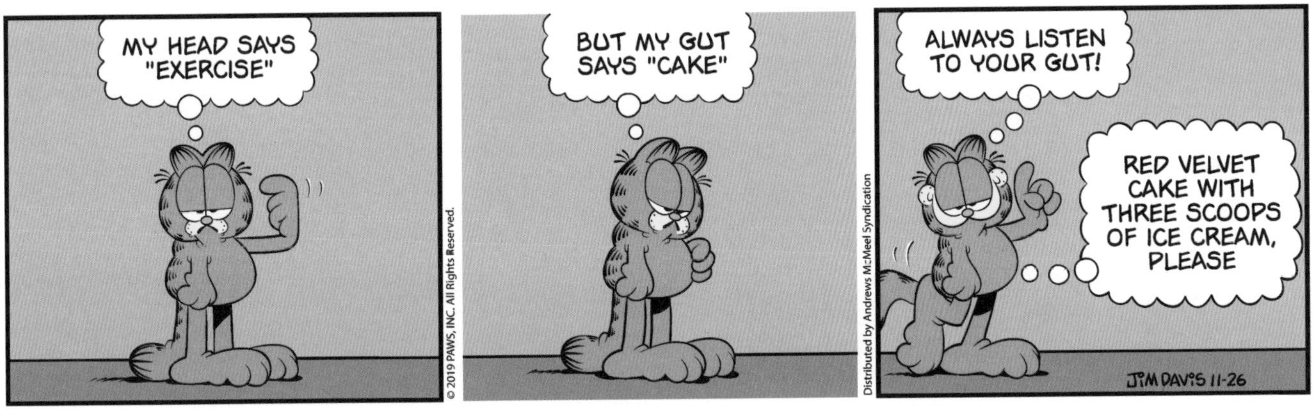

MY HEAD SAYS "EXERCISE"
BUT MY GUT SAYS "CAKE"
ALWAYS LISTEN TO YOUR GUT!
RED VELVET CAKE WITH THREE SCOOPS OF ICE CREAM, PLEASE
JIM DAVIS 11-26
© 2019 PAWS, INC. All Rights Reserved.
Distributed by Andrews McMeel Syndication

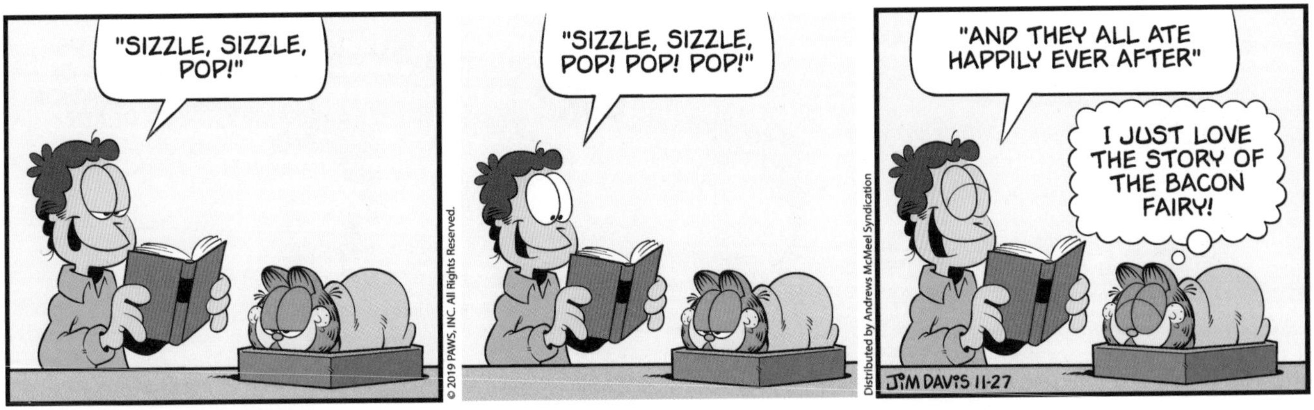

"SIZZLE, SIZZLE, POP!"
"SIZZLE, SIZZLE, POP! POP! POP!"
"AND THEY ALL ATE HAPPILY EVER AFTER"
I JUST LOVE THE STORY OF THE BACON FAIRY!
JIM DAVIS 11-27
© 2019 PAWS, INC. All Rights Reserved.
Distributed by Andrews McMeel Syndication

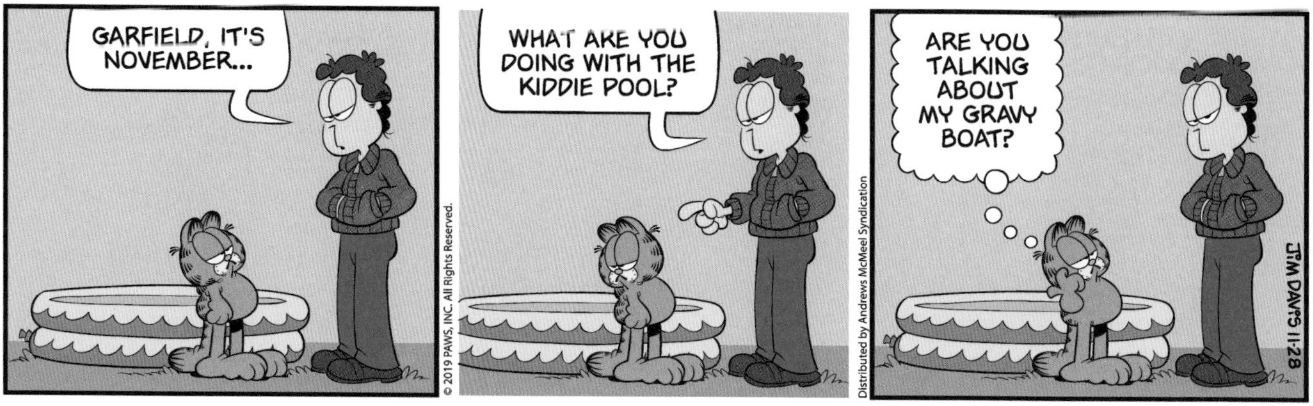
GARFIELD, IT'S NOVEMBER...
WHAT ARE YOU DOING WITH THE KIDDIE POOL?
ARE YOU TALKING ABOUT MY GRAVY BOAT?
JIM DAVIS 11-28
© 2019 PAWS, INC. All Rights Reserved.
Distributed by Andrews McMeel Syndication

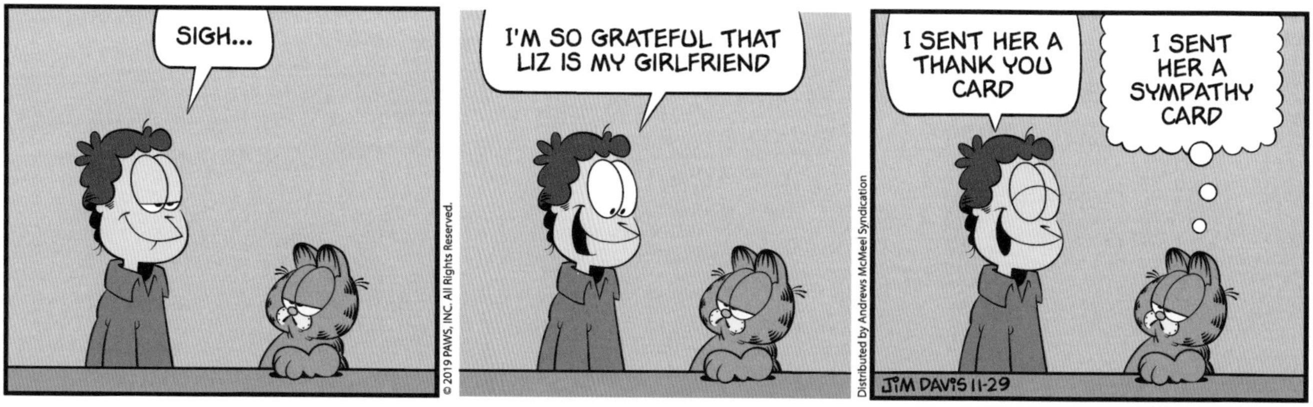
SIGH...
I'M SO GRATEFUL THAT LIZ IS MY GIRLFRIEND
I SENT HER A THANK YOU CARD
I SENT HER A SYMPATHY CARD
JIM DAVIS 11-29
© 2019 PAWS, INC. All Rights Reserved.
Distributed by Andrews McMeel Syndication

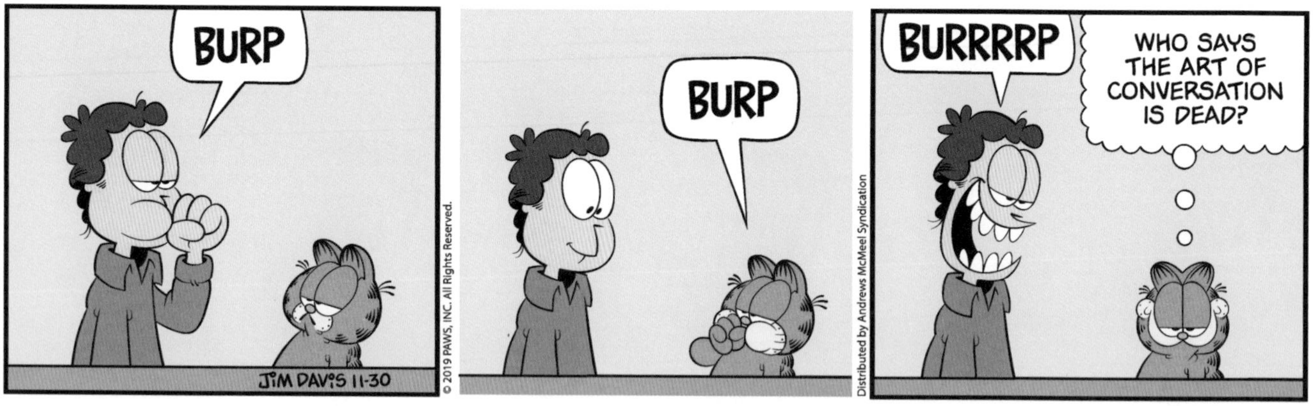
BURP
JIM DAVIS 11-30
BURP
BURRRRP
WHO SAYS THE ART OF CONVERSATION IS DEAD?
© 2019 PAWS, INC. All Rights Reserved.
Distributed by Andrews McMeel Syndication

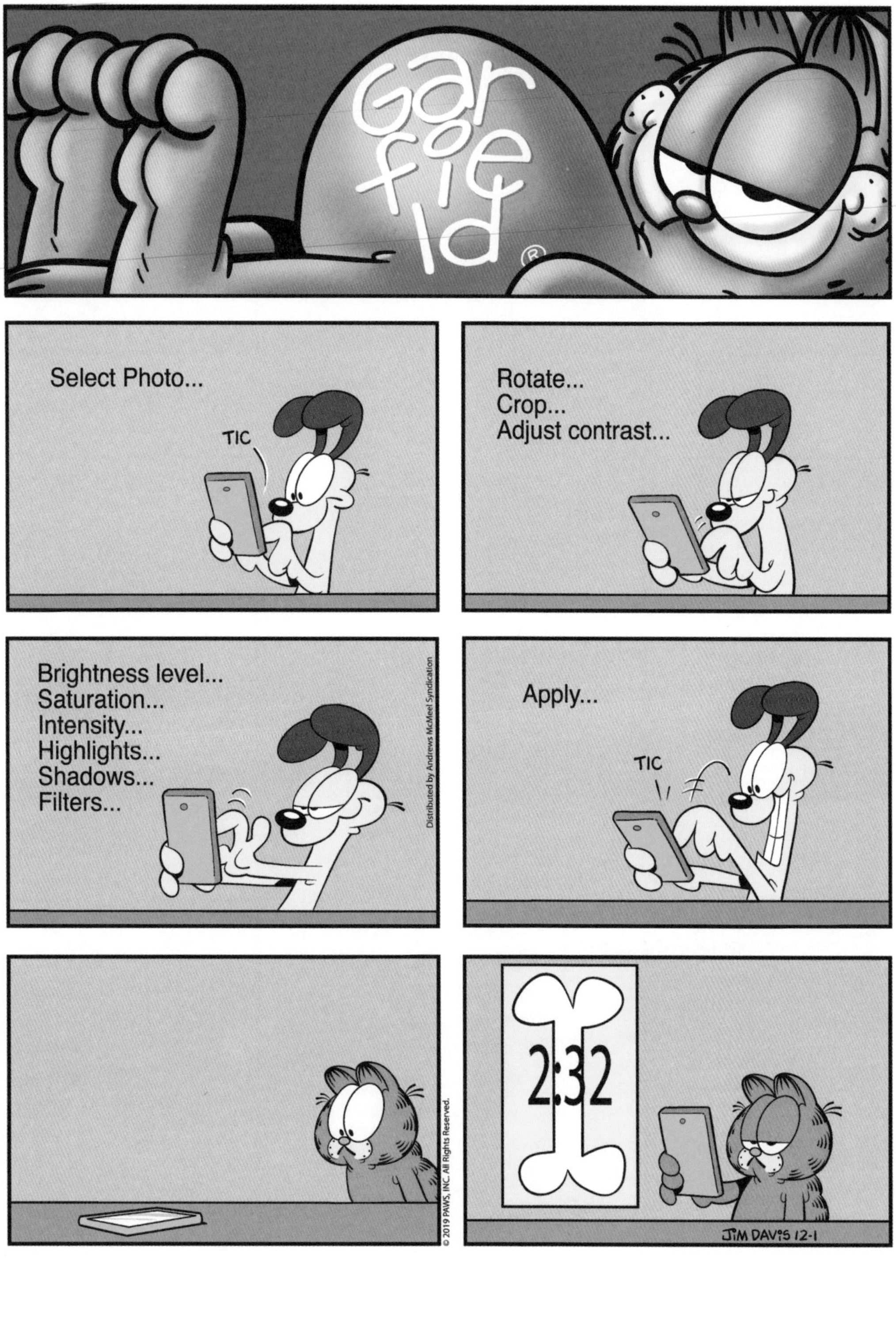

Garfield®
Select Photo...
TIC
Rotate...
Crop...
Adjust contrast...
Brightness level...
Saturation...
Intensity...
Highlights...
Shadows...
Filters...
Distributed by Andrews McMeel Syndication
Apply...
TIC
© 2019 PAWS, INC. All Rights Reserved.
2:32
JIM DAVIS 12-1

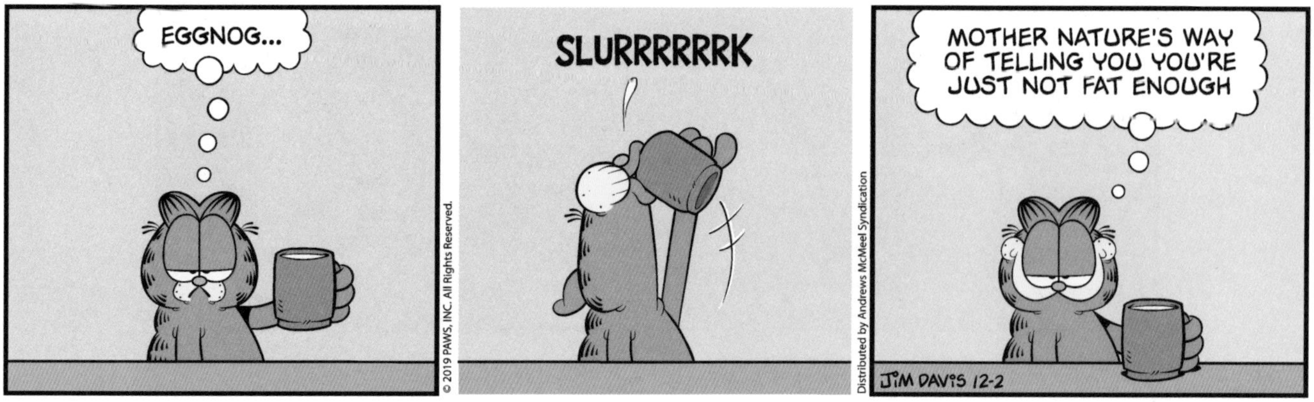
EGGNOG...
SLURRRRRRK
© 2019 PAWS, INC. All Rights Reserved.
MOTHER NATURE'S WAY OF TELLING YOU YOU'RE JUST NOT FAT ENOUGH
Distributed by Andrews McMeel Syndication
JIM DAVIS 12-2

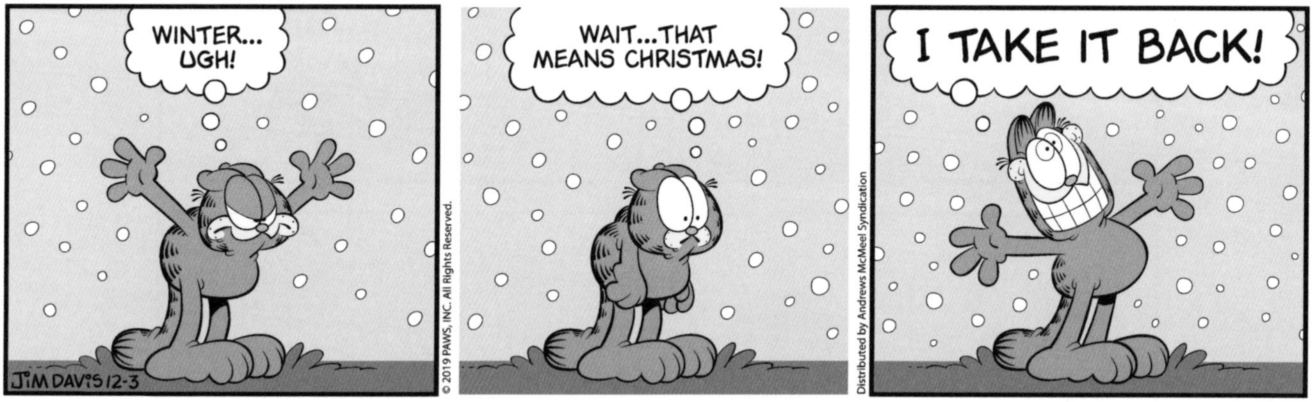
WINTER... UGH!
JIM DAVIS 12-3
© 2019 PAWS, INC. All Rights Reserved.
WAIT...THAT MEANS CHRISTMAS!
Distributed by Andrews McMeel Syndication
I TAKE IT BACK!

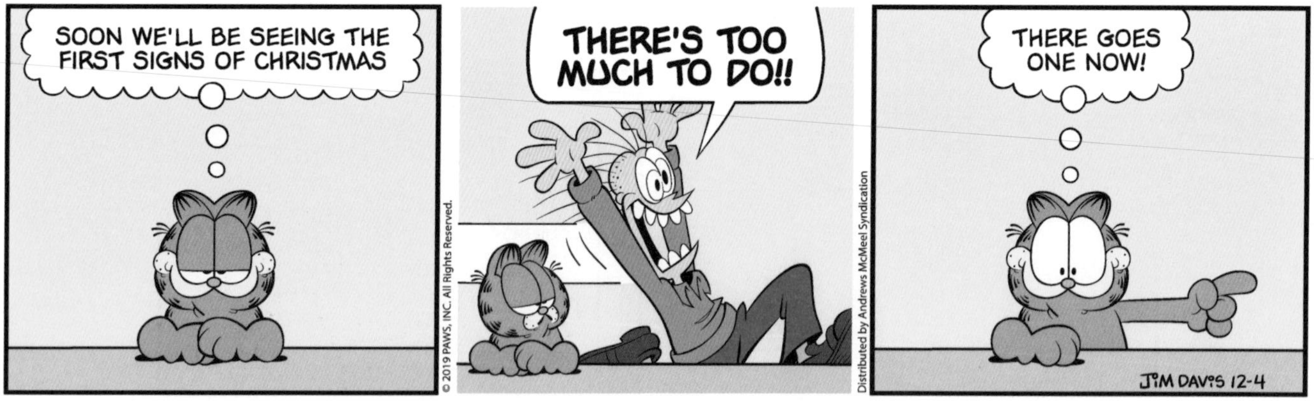
SOON WE'LL BE SEEING THE FIRST SIGNS OF CHRISTMAS
© 2019 PAWS, INC. All Rights Reserved.
THERE'S TOO MUCH TO DO!!
Distributed by Andrews McMeel Syndication
THERE GOES ONE NOW!
JIM DAVIS 12-4

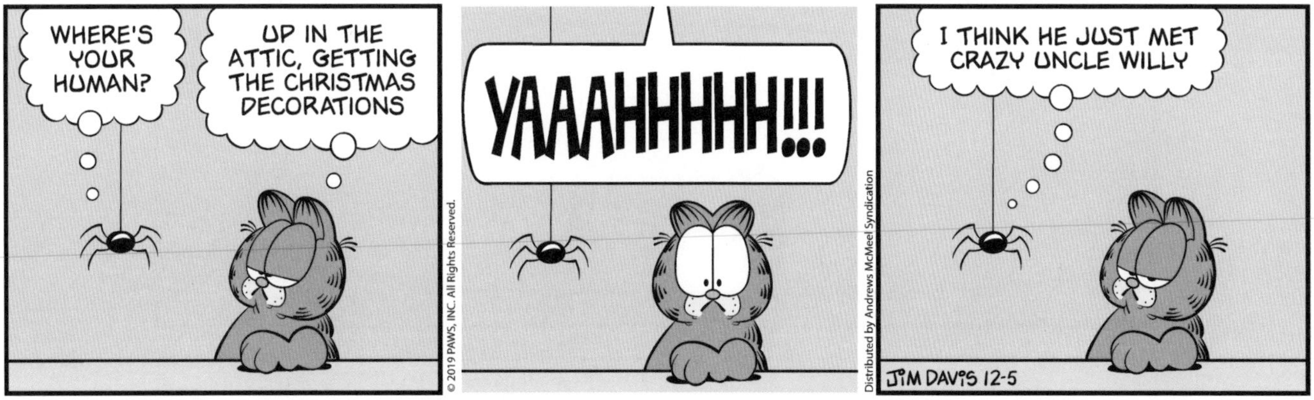
WHERE'S YOUR HUMAN?
UP IN THE ATTIC, GETTING THE CHRISTMAS DECORATIONS
YAAAHHHHH!!!...
I THINK HE JUST MET CRAZY UNCLE WILLY
JIM DAVIS 12-5
© 2019 PAWS, INC. All Rights Reserved.
Distributed by Andrews McMeel Syndication

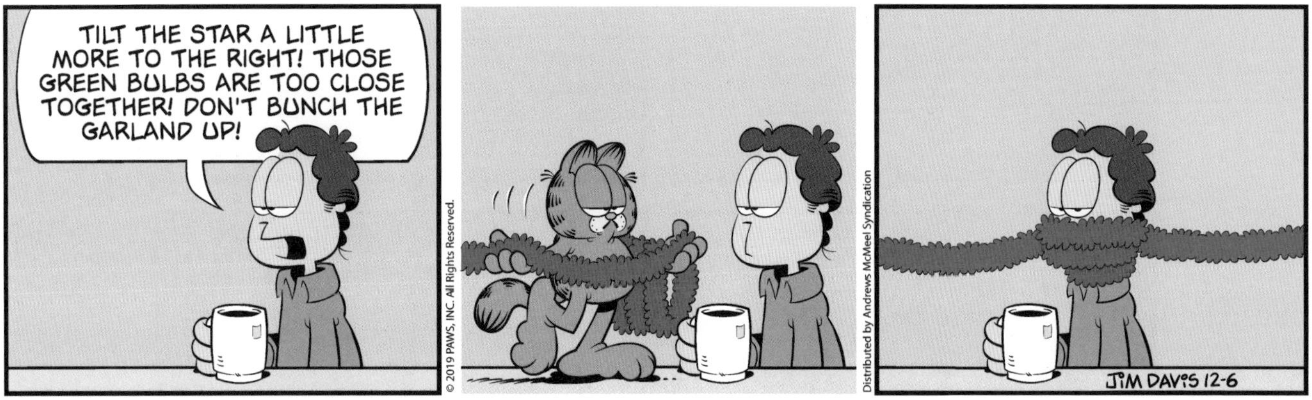
TILT THE STAR A LITTLE MORE TO THE RIGHT! THOSE GREEN BULBS ARE TOO CLOSE TOGETHER! DON'T BUNCH THE GARLAND UP!
JIM DAVIS 12-6
© 2019 PAWS, INC. All Rights Reserved.
Distributed by Andrews McMeel Syndication

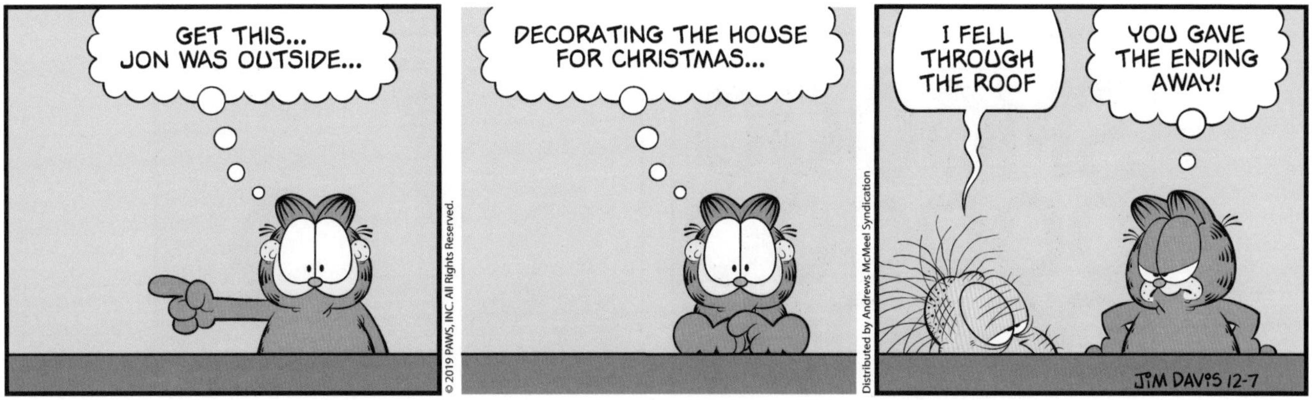
GET THIS... JON WAS OUTSIDE...
DECORATING THE HOUSE FOR CHRISTMAS...
I FELL THROUGH THE ROOF
YOU GAVE THE ENDING AWAY!
JIM DAVIS 12-7
© 2019 PAWS, INC. All Rights Reserved.
Distributed by Andrews McMeel Syndication

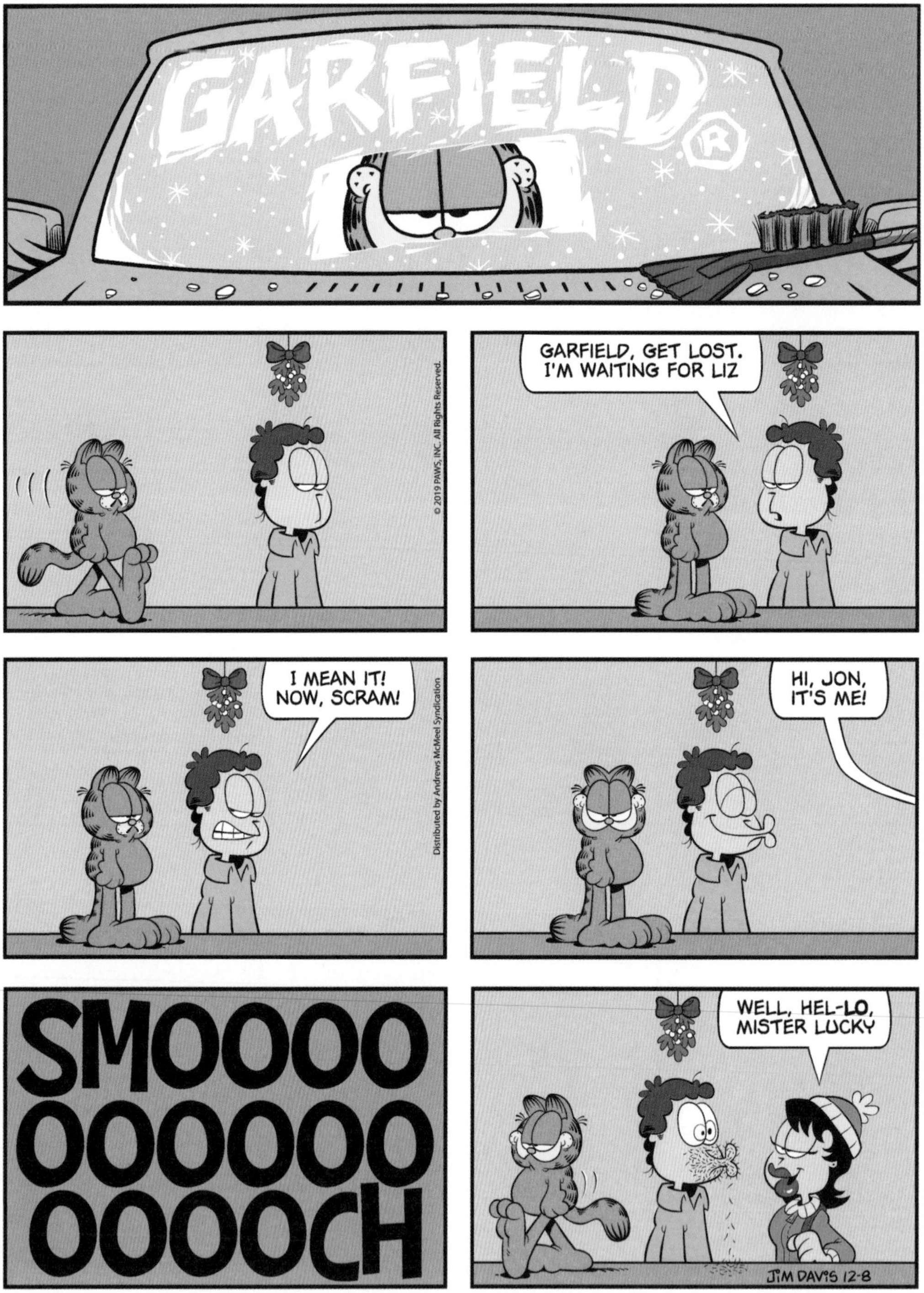
GARFIELD®
© 2019 PAWS, INC. All Rights Reserved.
GARFIELD, GET LOST. I'M WAITING FOR LIZ
I MEAN IT! NOW, SCRAM!
Distributed by Andrews McMeel Syndication
HI, JON, IT'S ME!
SMOOOO OOOOOO OOOOCH
WELL, HEL-LO, MISTER LUCKY
JIM DAVIS 12-8

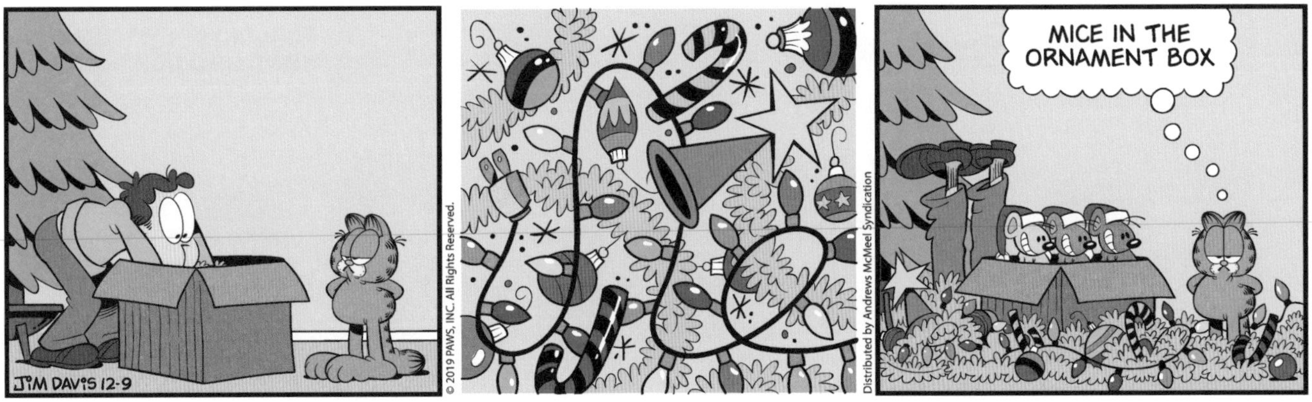
JIM DAVIS 12-9
© 2019 PAWS, INC. All Rights Reserved.
Distributed by Andrews McMeel Syndication
MICE IN THE ORNAMENT BOX

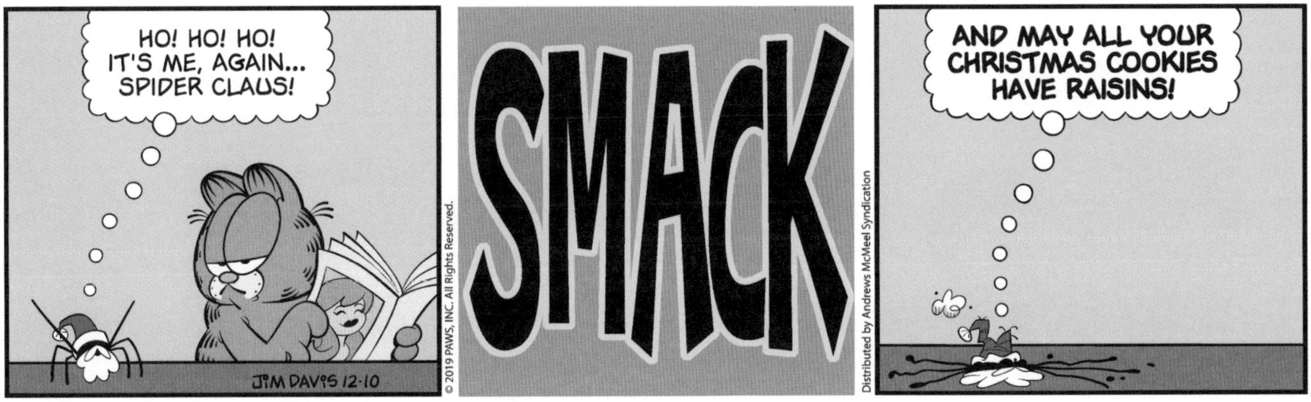
HO! HO! HO! IT'S ME, AGAIN... SPIDER CLAUS!
JIM DAVIS 12-10
© 2019 PAWS, INC. All Rights Reserved.
SMACK
Distributed by Andrews McMeel Syndication
AND MAY ALL YOUR CHRISTMAS COOKIES HAVE RAISINS!

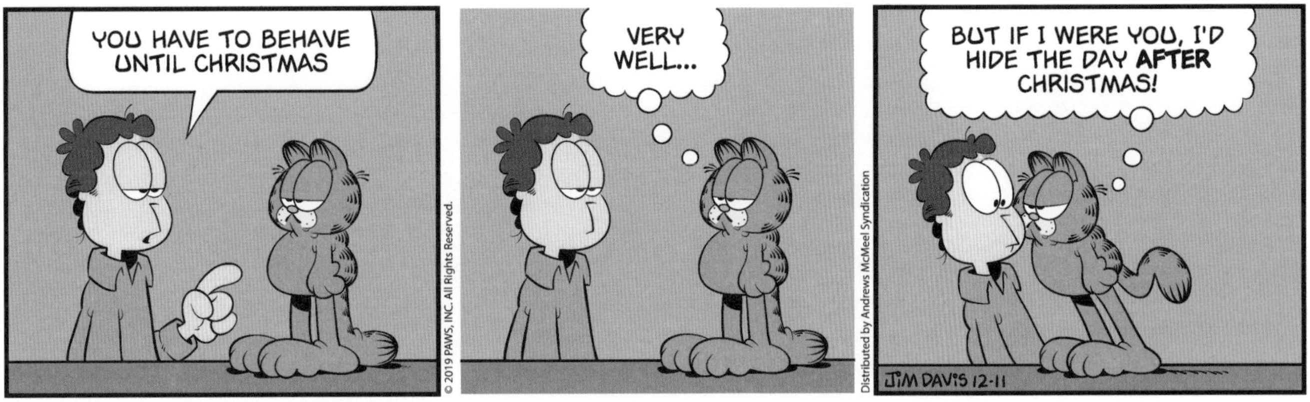
YOU HAVE TO BEHAVE UNTIL CHRISTMAS
© 2019 PAWS, INC. All Rights Reserved.
VERY WELL...
Distributed by Andrews McMeel Syndication
BUT IF I WERE YOU, I'D HIDE THE DAY **AFTER** CHRISTMAS!
JIM DAVIS 12-11

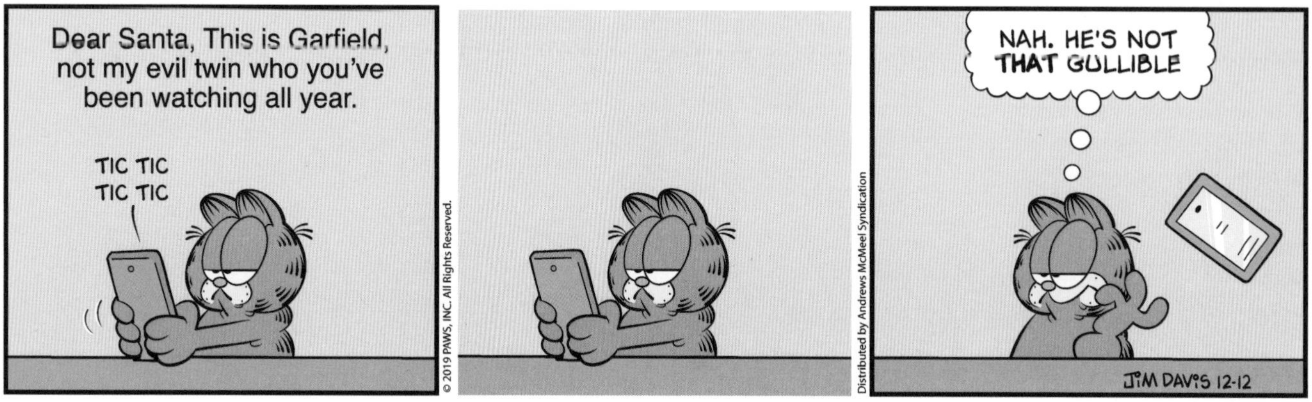
Dear Santa, This is Garfield, not my evil twin who you've been watching all year.
TIC TIC
TIC TIC
© 2019 PAWS, INC. All Rights Reserved.
Distributed by Andrews McMeel Syndication
NAH. HE'S NOT **THAT** GULLIBLE
JIM DAVIS 12-12

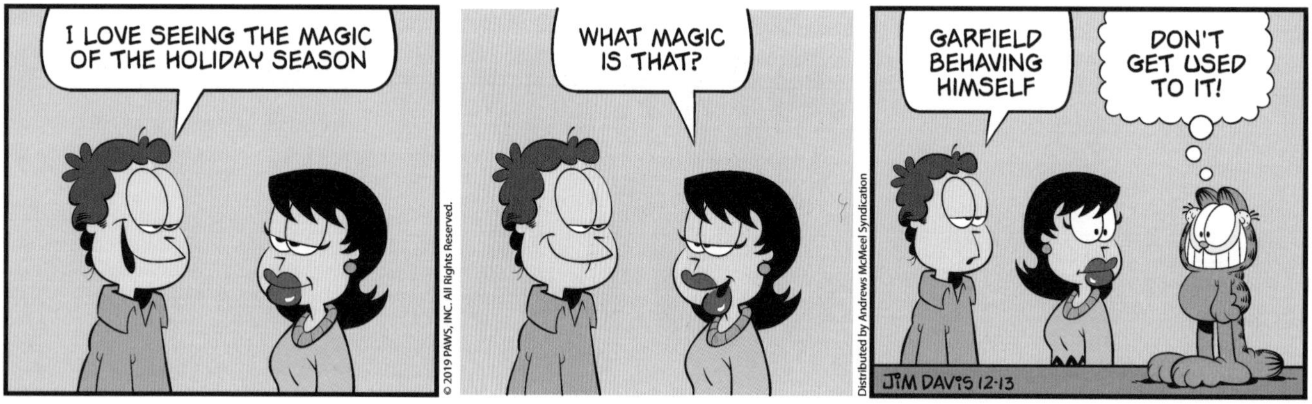
I LOVE SEEING THE MAGIC OF THE HOLIDAY SEASON
© 2019 PAWS, INC. All Rights Reserved.
WHAT MAGIC IS THAT?
Distributed by Andrews McMeel Syndication
GARFIELD BEHAVING HIMSELF
DON'T GET USED TO IT!
JIM DAVIS 12-13

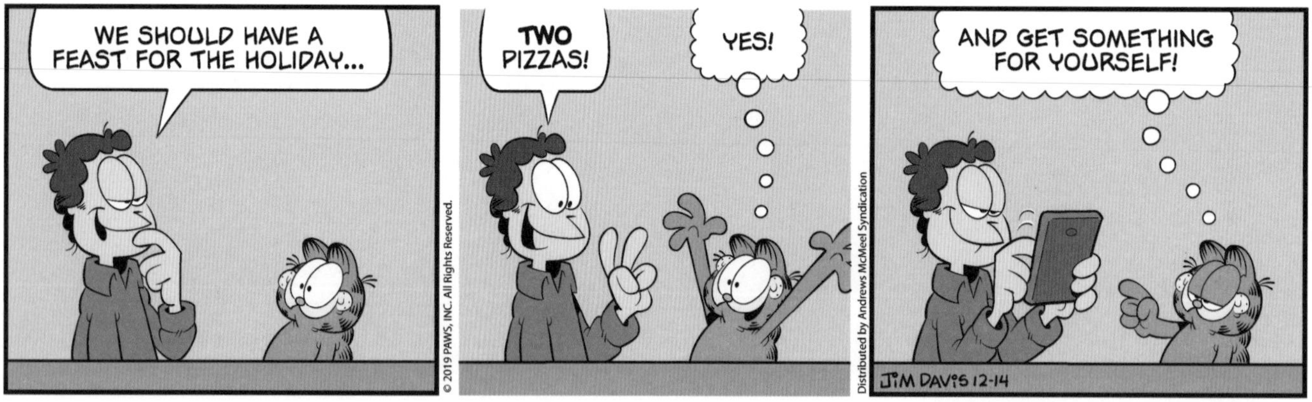
WE SHOULD HAVE A FEAST FOR THE HOLIDAY...
© 2019 PAWS, INC. All Rights Reserved.
TWO PIZZAS!
YES!
Distributed by Andrews McMeel Syndication
AND GET SOMETHING FOR YOURSELF!
JIM DAVIS 12-14

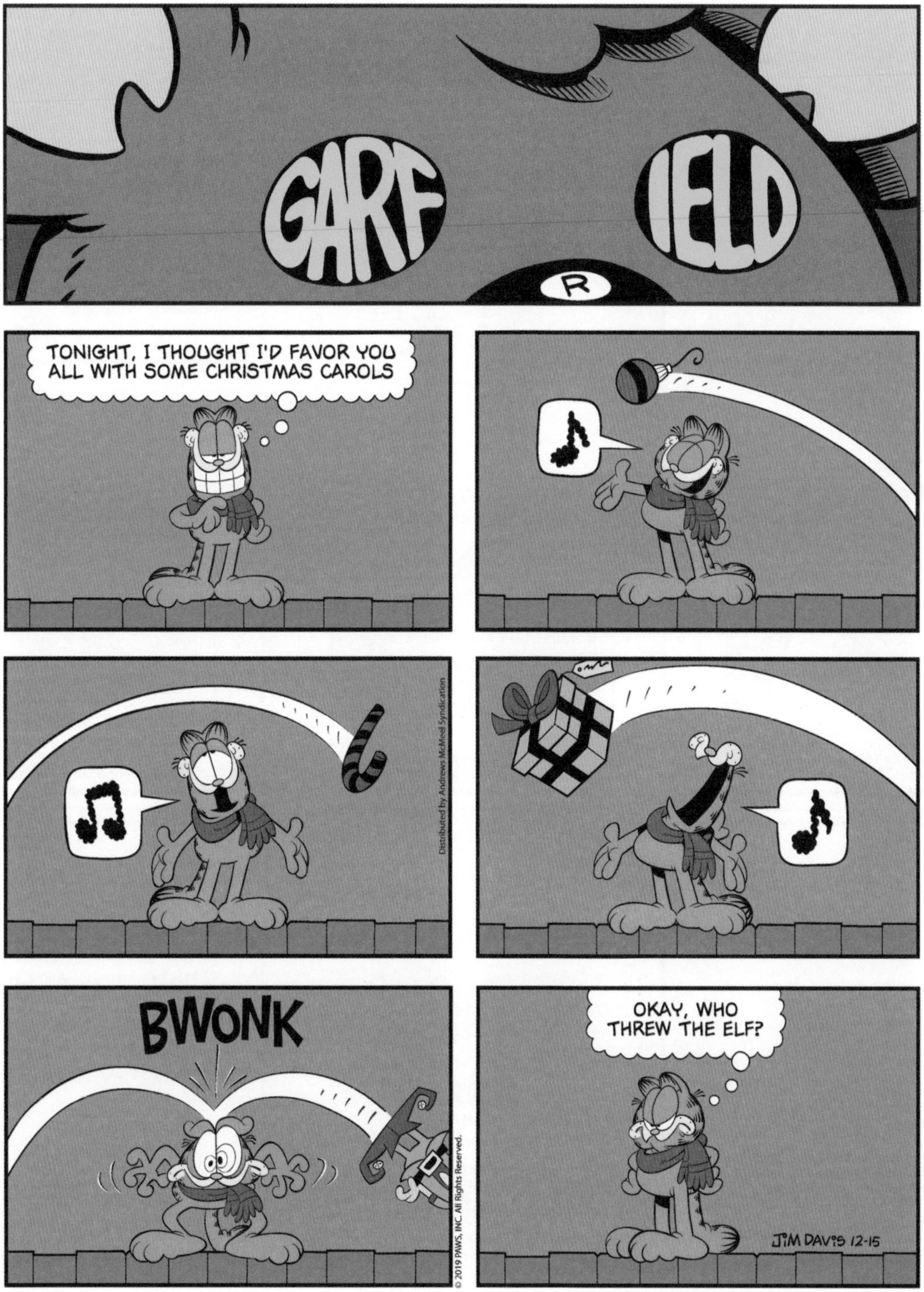
GARFIELD
TONIGHT, I THOUGHT I'D FAVOR YOU ALL WITH SOME CHRISTMAS CAROLS
Distributed by Andrews McMeel Syndication
BWONK
© 2019 PAWS, INC. All Rights Reserved.
OKAY, WHO THREW THE ELF?
JIM DAVIS 12-15

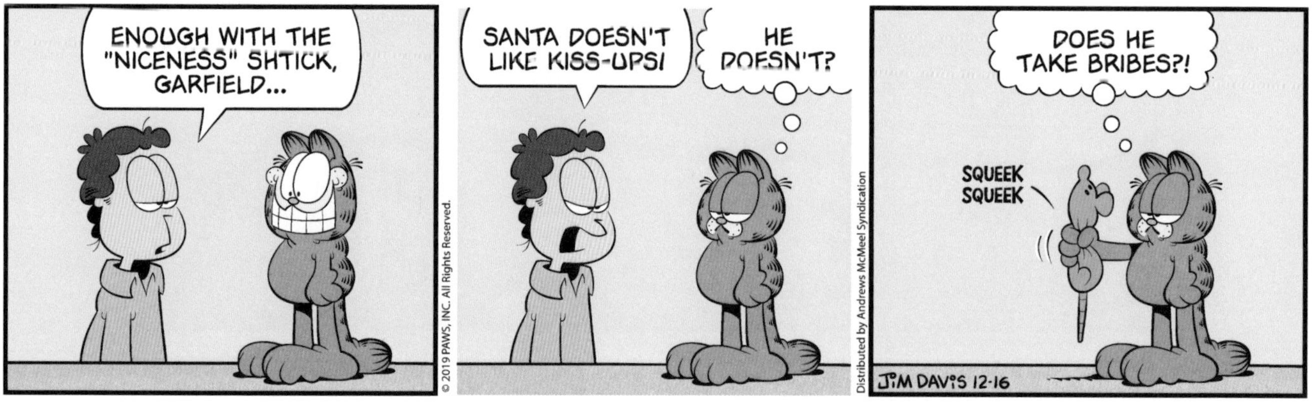
ENOUGH WITH THE "NICENESS" SHTICK, GARFIELD...
SANTA DOESN'T LIKE KISS-UPS!
HE DOESN'T?
DOES HE TAKE BRIBES?!
SQUEEK SQUEEK
© 2019 PAWS, INC. All Rights Reserved.
Distributed by Andrews McMeel Syndication
JIM DAVIS 12-16

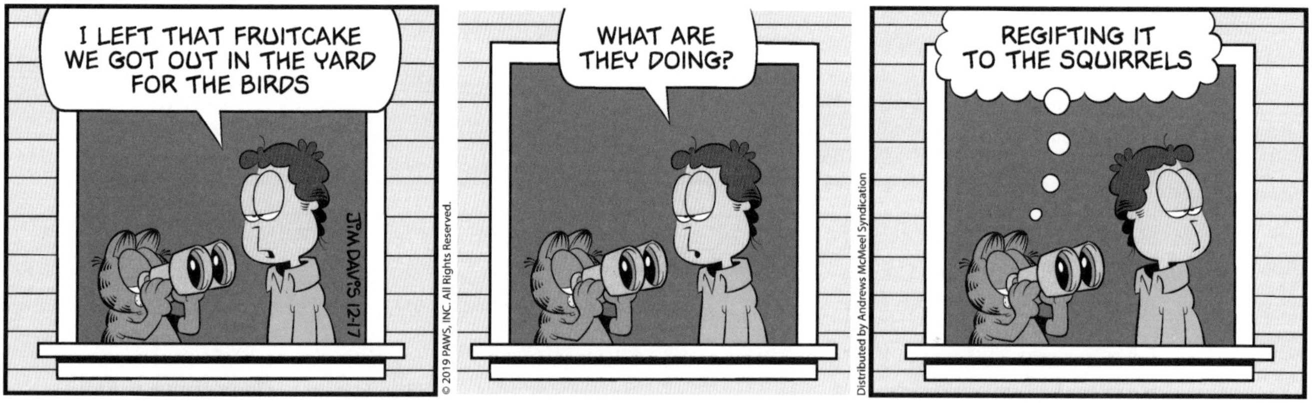
I LEFT THAT FRUITCAKE WE GOT OUT IN THE YARD FOR THE BIRDS
JIM DAVIS 12-17
WHAT ARE THEY DOING?
REGIFTING IT TO THE SQUIRRELS
© 2019 PAWS, INC. All Rights Reserved.
Distributed by Andrews McMeel Syndication

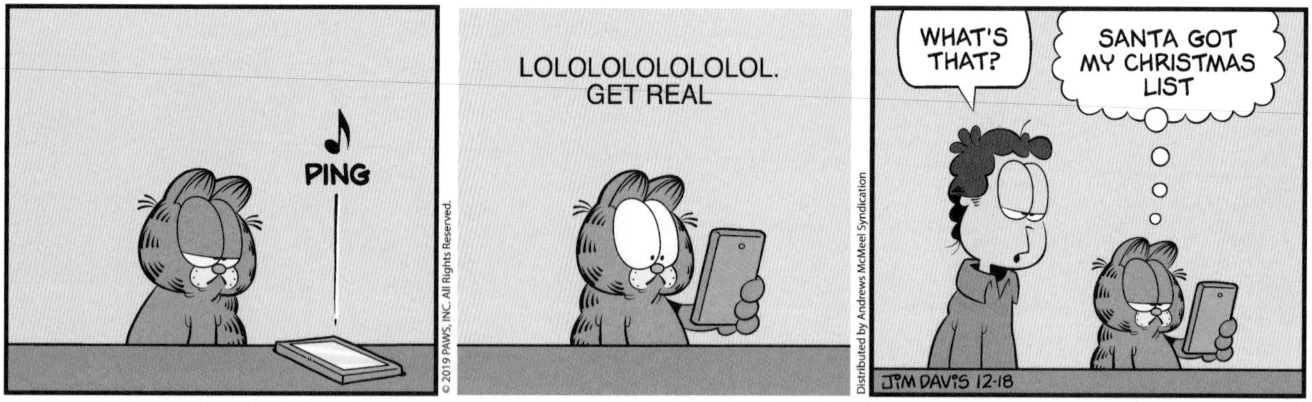
PING
LOLOLOLOLOLOLOL. GET REAL
WHAT'S THAT?
SANTA GOT MY CHRISTMAS LIST
© 2019 PAWS, INC. All Rights Reserved.
Distributed by Andrews McMeel Syndication
JIM DAVIS 12-18

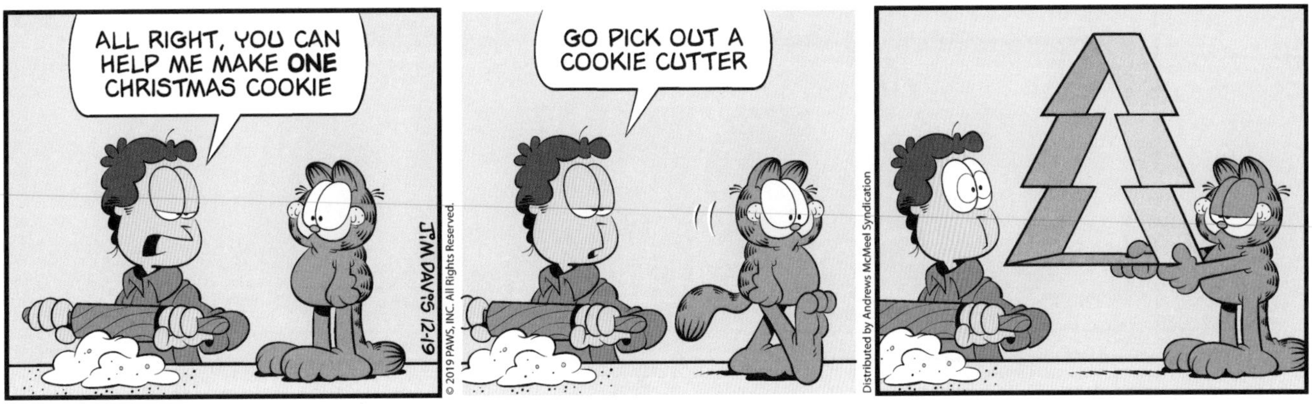
ALL RIGHT, YOU CAN HELP ME MAKE **ONE** CHRISTMAS COOKIE
JIM DAVIS 12-19
© 2019 PAWS, INC. All Rights Reserved.
GO PICK OUT A COOKIE CUTTER
Distributed by Andrews McMeel Syndication

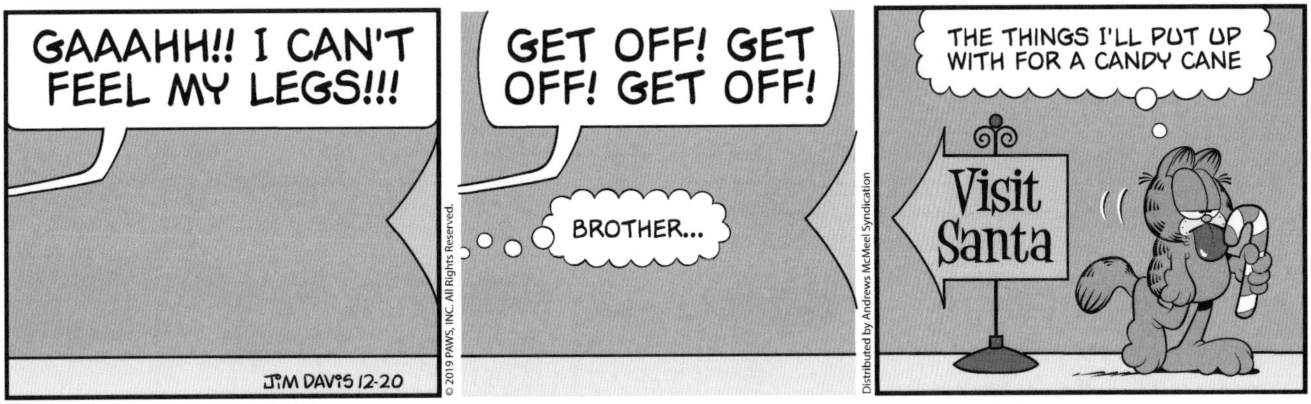
GAAAHH!! I CAN'T FEEL MY LEGS!!!
JIM DAVIS 12-20
© 2019 PAWS, INC. All Rights Reserved.
GET OFF! GET OFF! GET OFF! GET OFF!
BROTHER...
Distributed by Andrews McMeel Syndication
THE THINGS I'LL PUT UP WITH FOR A CANDY CANE
Visit Santa

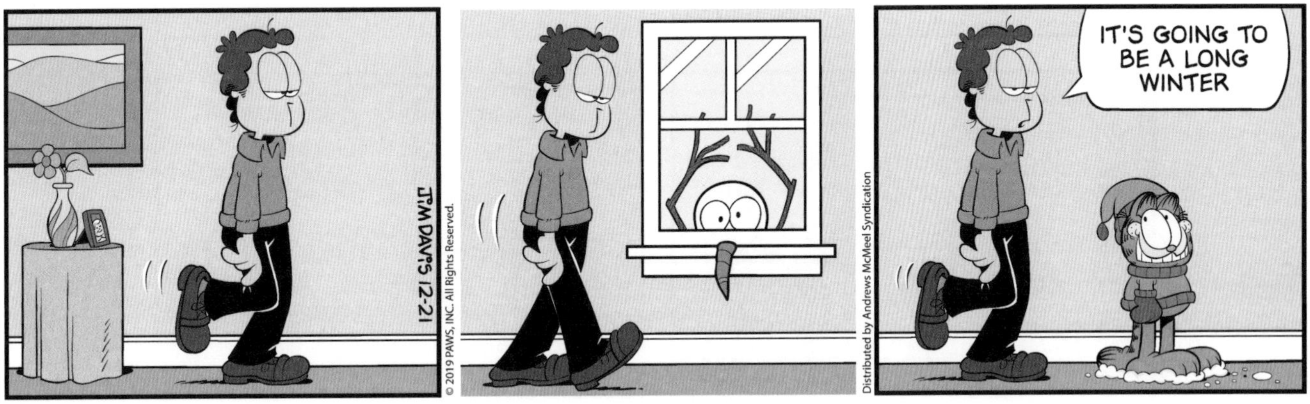
JIM DAVIS 12-21
© 2019 PAWS, INC. All Rights Reserved.
Distributed by Andrews McMeel Syndication
IT'S GOING TO BE A LONG WINTER

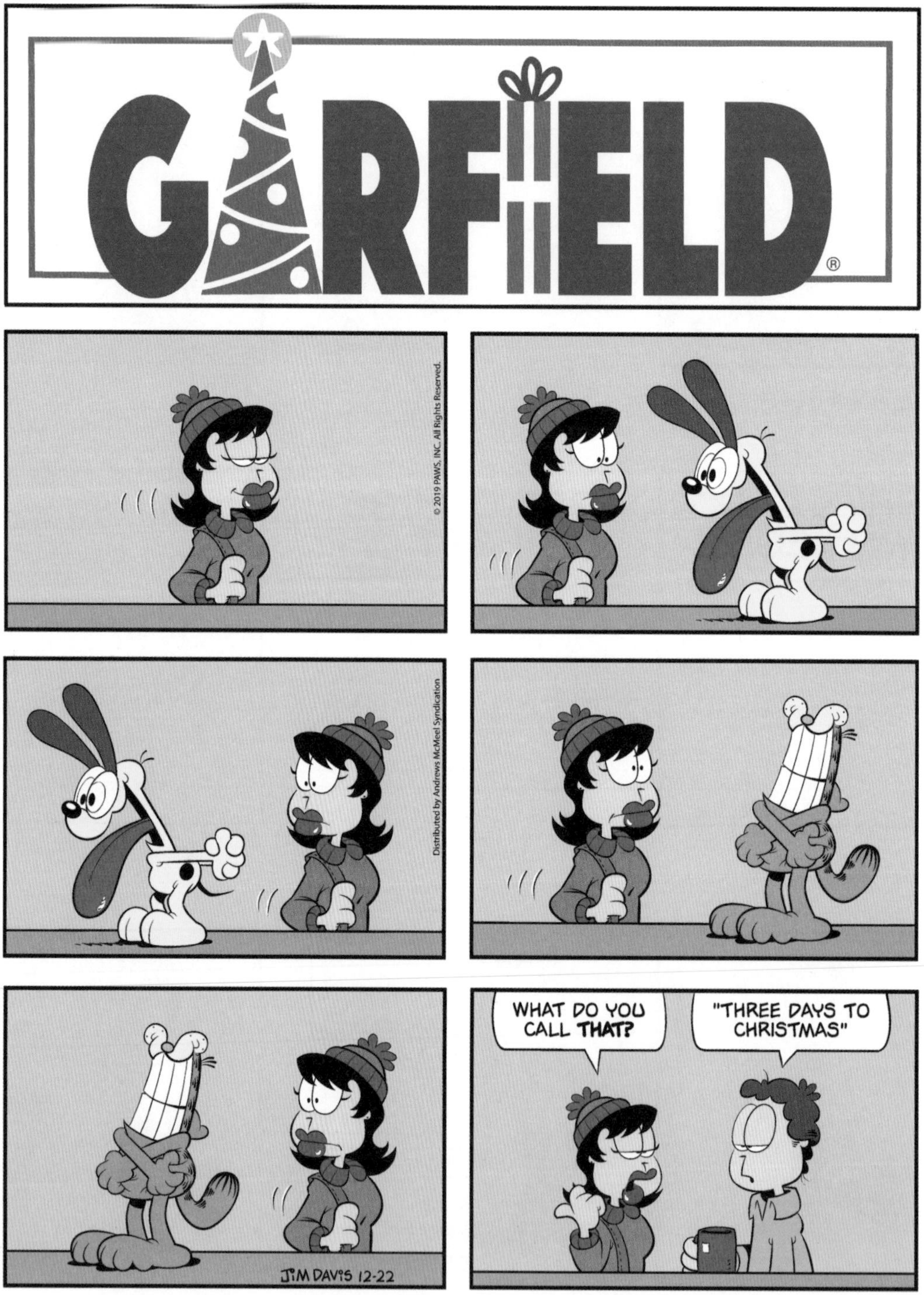
GARFIELD
© 2019 PAWS, INC. All Rights Reserved.
Distributed by Andrews McMeel Syndication
JIM DAVIS 12-22
WHAT DO YOU CALL **THAT?**
"THREE DAYS TO CHRISTMAS"

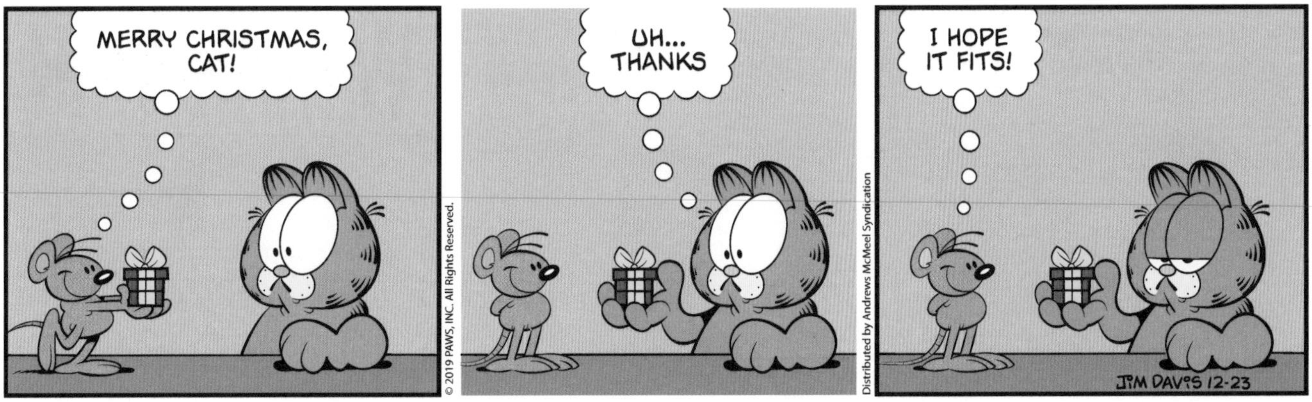
MERRY CHRISTMAS, CAT!
UH... THANKS
I HOPE IT FITS!
JIM DAVIS 12-23
© 2019 PAWS, INC. All Rights Reserved.
Distributed by Andrews McMeel Syndication

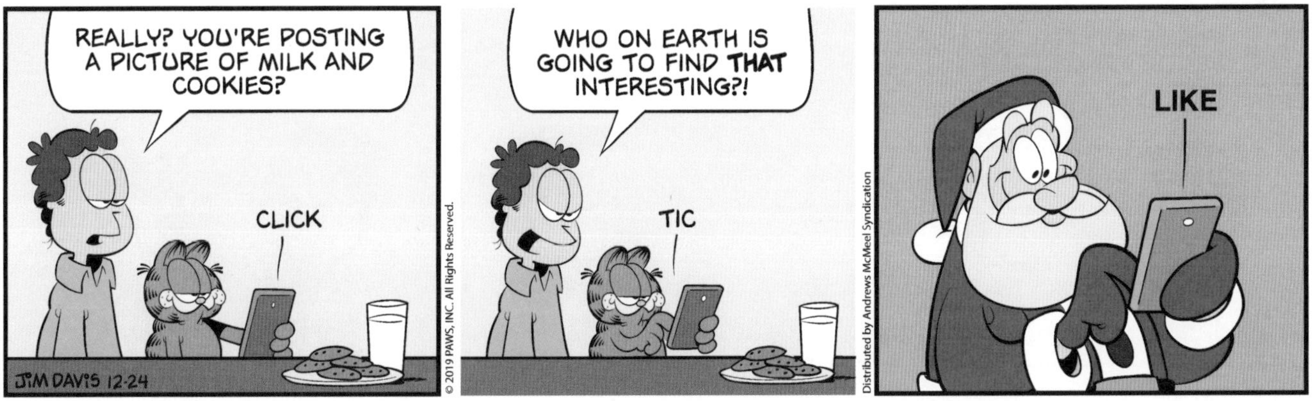
REALLY? YOU'RE POSTING A PICTURE OF MILK AND COOKIES?
CLICK
WHO ON EARTH IS GOING TO FIND **THAT** INTERESTING?!
TIC
LIKE
JIM DAVIS 12-24
© 2019 PAWS, INC. All Rights Reserved.
Distributed by Andrews McMeel Syndication

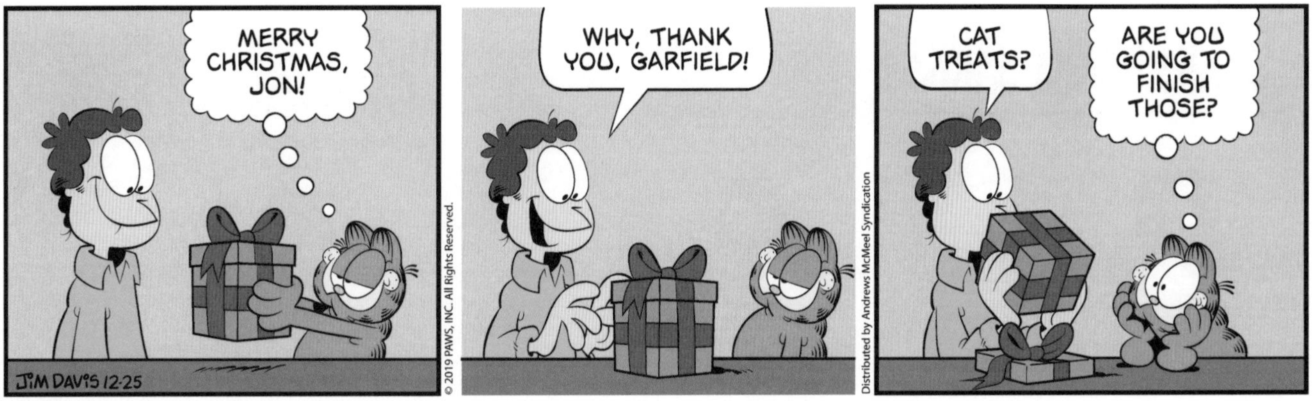
MERRY CHRISTMAS, JON!
WHY, THANK YOU, GARFIELD!
CAT TREATS?
ARE YOU GOING TO FINISH THOSE?
JIM DAVIS 12-25
© 2019 PAWS, INC. All Rights Reserved.
Distributed by Andrews McMeel Syndication

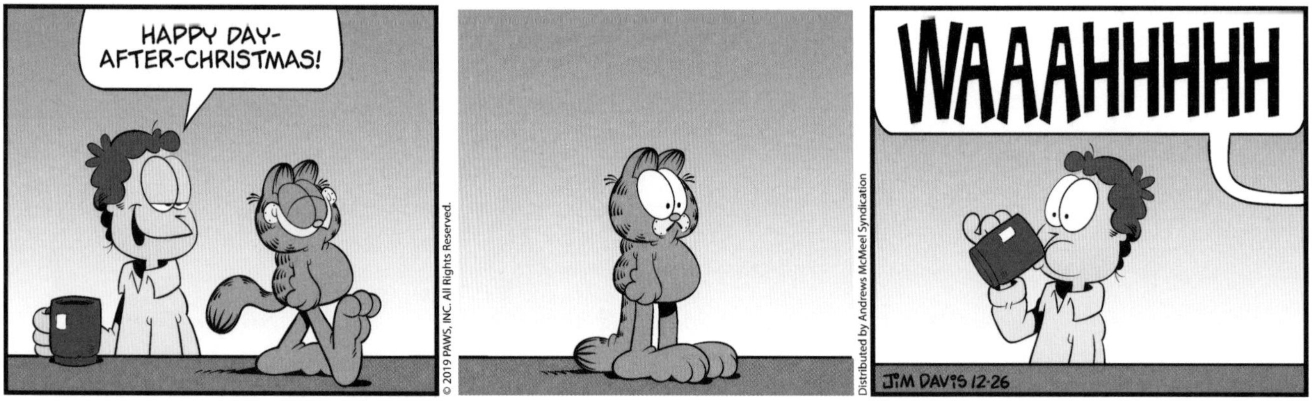
HAPPY DAY-AFTER-CHRISTMAS!
WAAAHHHHH
© 2019 PAWS, INC. All Rights Reserved.
Distributed by Andrews McMeel Syndication
JIM DAVIS 12-26

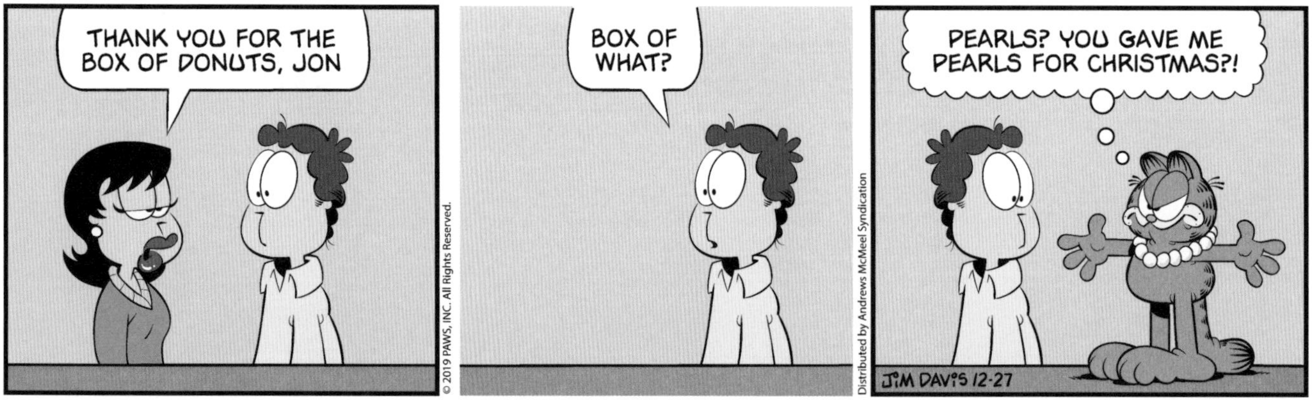
THANK YOU FOR THE BOX OF DONUTS, JON
BOX OF WHAT?
PEARLS? YOU GAVE ME PEARLS FOR CHRISTMAS?!
© 2019 PAWS, INC. All Rights Reserved.
Distributed by Andrews McMeel Syndication
JIM DAVIS 12-27

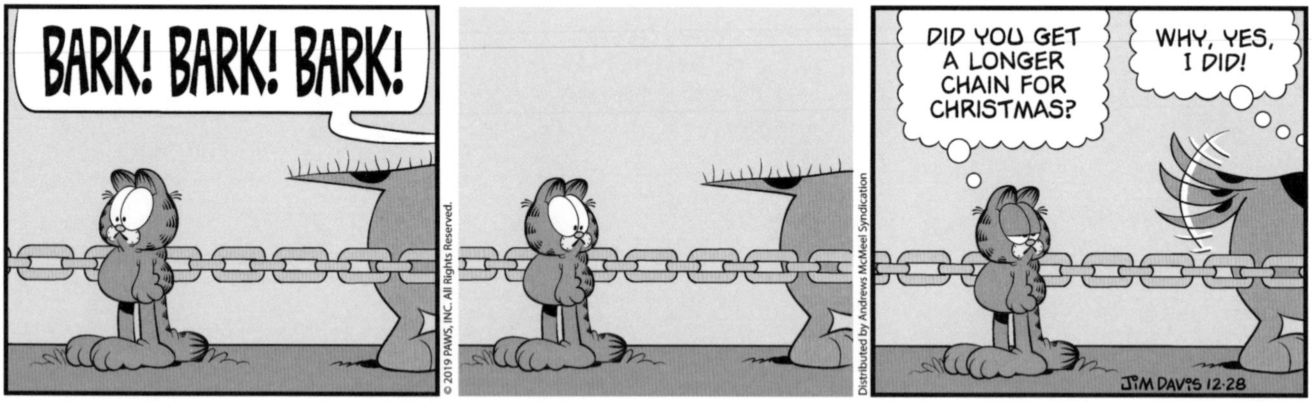
BARK! BARK! BARK!
DID YOU GET A LONGER CHAIN FOR CHRISTMAS?
WHY, YES, I DID!
© 2019 PAWS, INC. All Rights Reserved.
Distributed by Andrews McMeel Syndication
JIM DAVIS 12-28

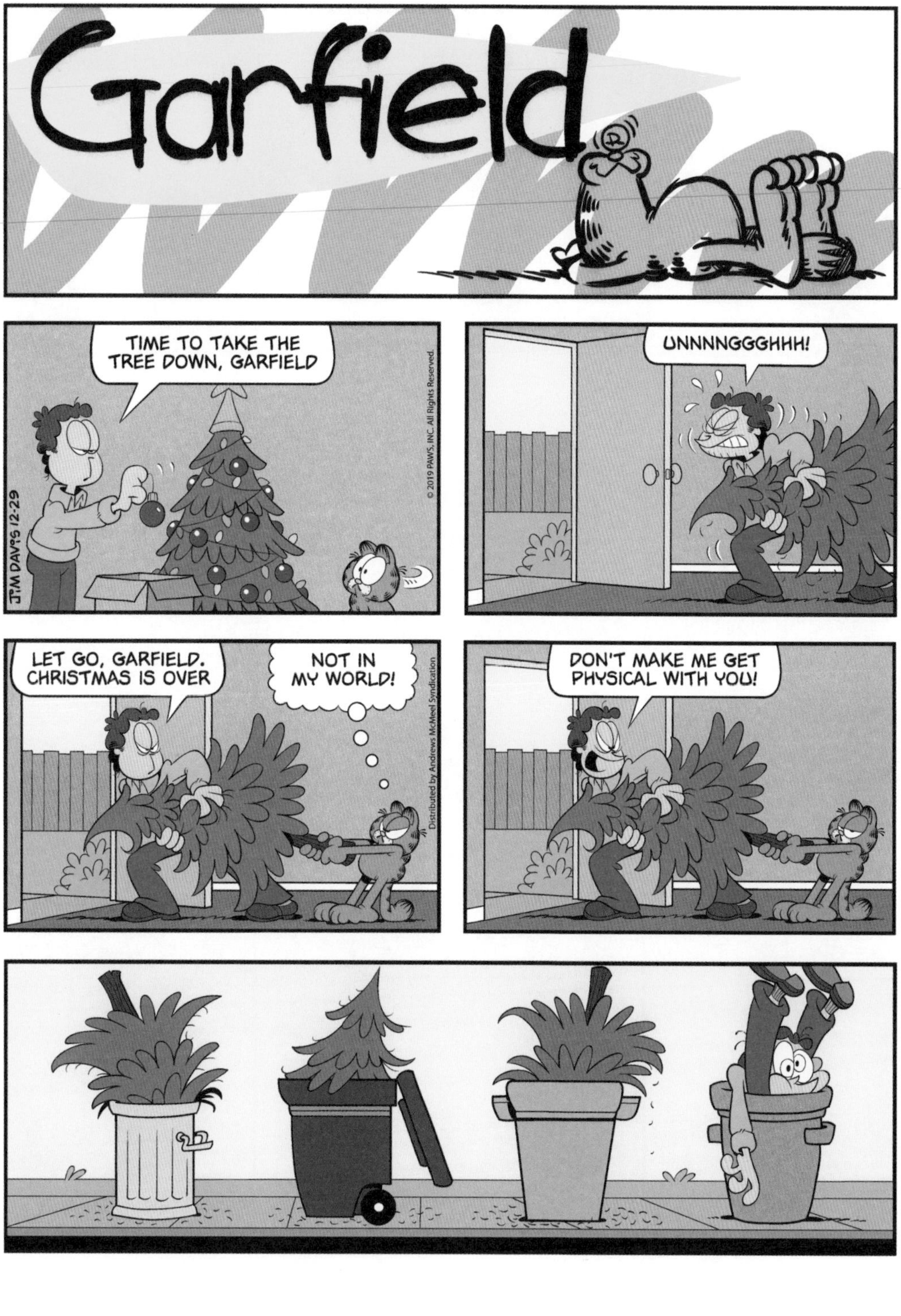
Garfield
TIME TO TAKE THE TREE DOWN, GARFIELD
JIM DAVIS 12-29
© 2019 PAWS, INC. All Rights Reserved.
UNNNNGGGHHH!
LET GO, GARFIELD. CHRISTMAS IS OVER
NOT IN MY WORLD!
Distributed by Andrews McMeel Syndication
DON'T MAKE ME GET PHYSICAL WITH YOU!

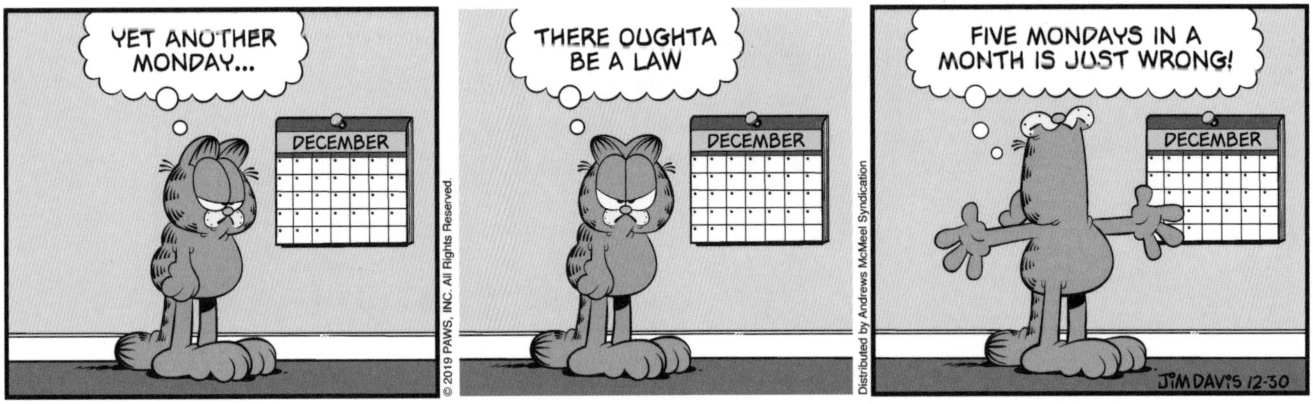
YET ANOTHER MONDAY...
DECEMBER
© 2019 PAWS, INC. All Rights Reserved.
THERE OUGHTA BE A LAW
DECEMBER
Distributed by Andrews McMeel Syndication
FIVE MONDAYS IN A MONTH IS JUST WRONG!
DECEMBER
JIM DAVIS 12-30

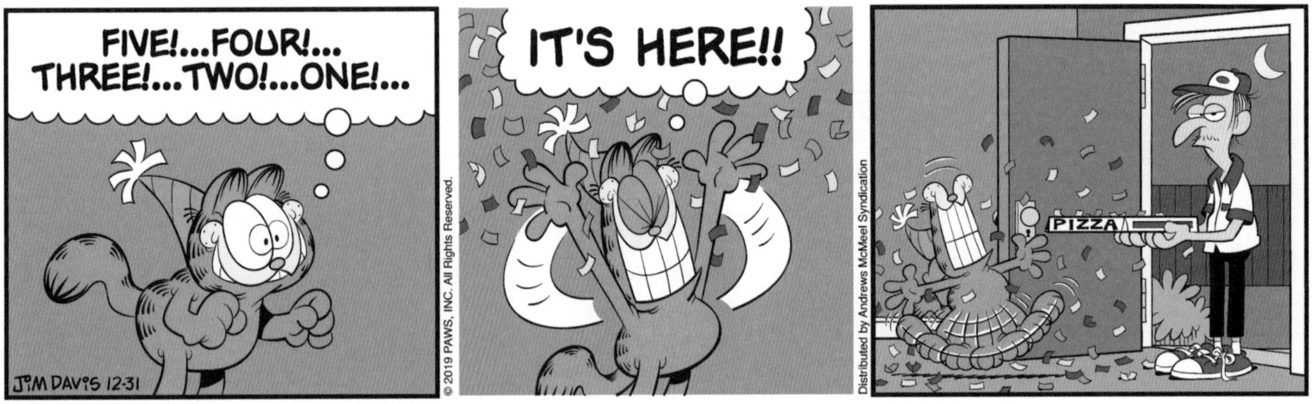
FIVE!...FOUR!... THREE!...TWO!...ONE!...
JIM DAVIS 12-31
© 2019 PAWS, INC. All Rights Reserved.
IT'S HERE!!
Distributed by Andrews McMeel Syndication
PIZZA

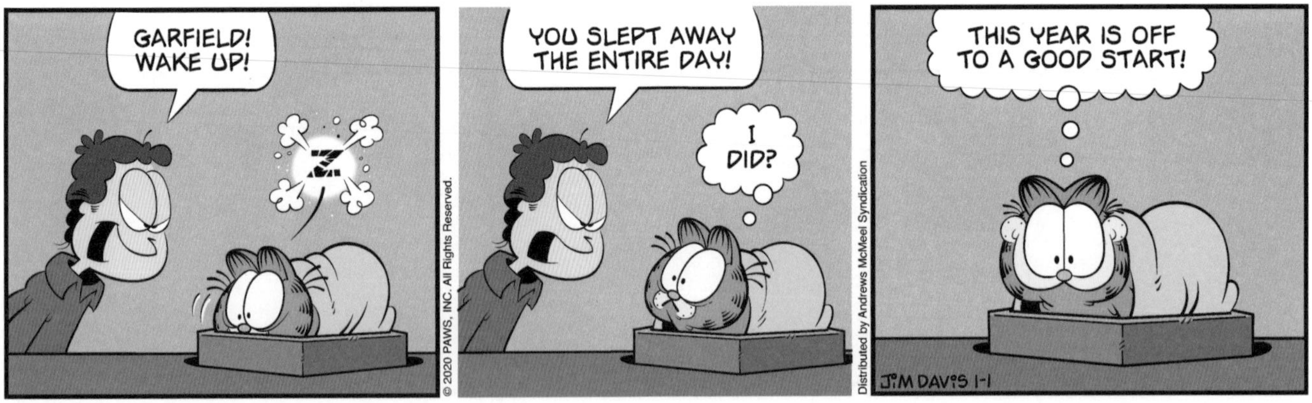
GARFIELD! WAKE UP!
Z
© 2020 PAWS, INC. All Rights Reserved.
YOU SLEPT AWAY THE ENTIRE DAY!
I DID?
Distributed by Andrews McMeel Syndication
THIS YEAR IS OFF TO A GOOD START!
JIM DAVIS 1-1

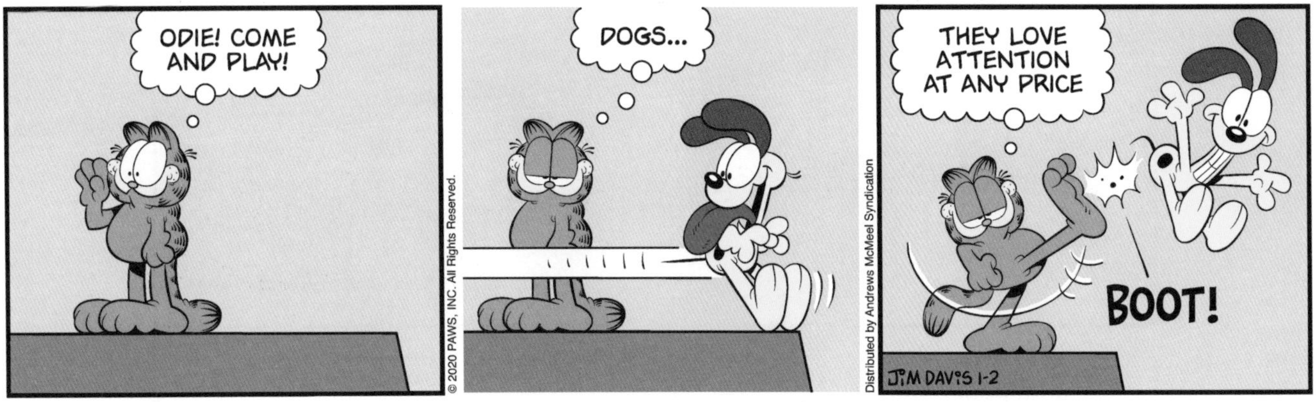
ODIE! COME AND PLAY!
DOGS...
THEY LOVE ATTENTION AT ANY PRICE
BOOT!
© 2020 PAWS, INC. All Rights Reserved.
Distributed by Andrews McMeel Syndication
JIM DAVIS 1-2

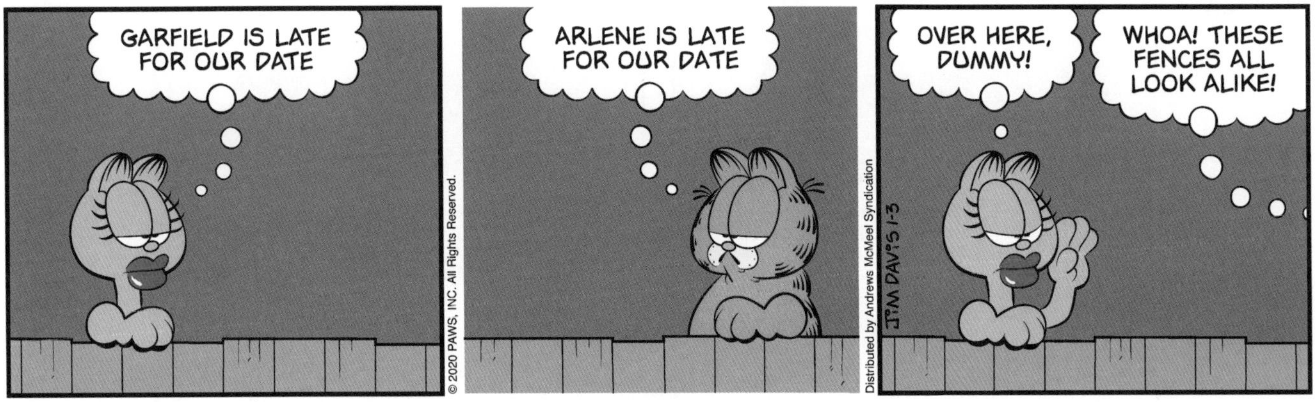
GARFIELD IS LATE FOR OUR DATE
ARLENE IS LATE FOR OUR DATE
OVER HERE, DUMMY!
WHOA! THESE FENCES ALL LOOK ALIKE!
© 2020 PAWS, INC. All Rights Reserved.
Distributed by Andrews McMeel Syndication
JIM DAVIS 1-3

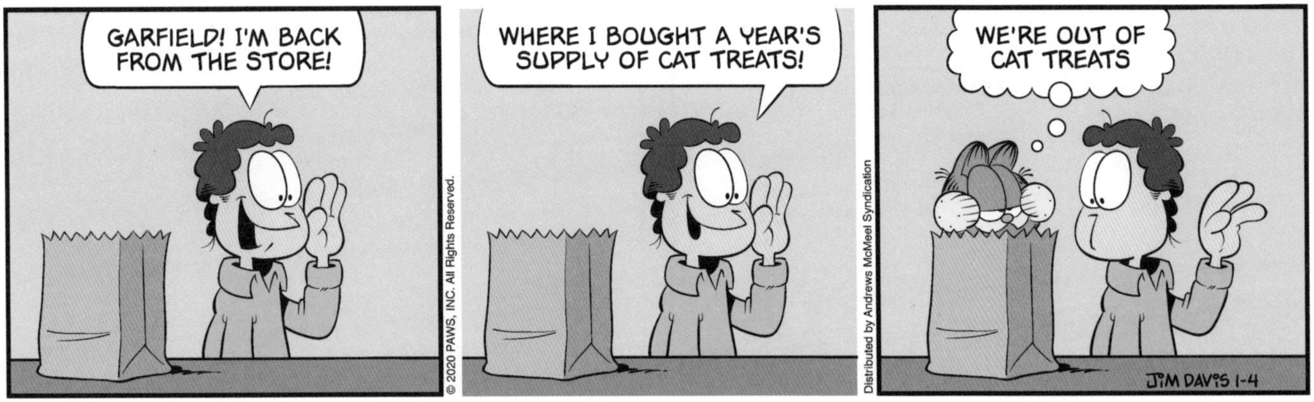
GARFIELD! I'M BACK FROM THE STORE!
WHERE I BOUGHT A YEAR'S SUPPLY OF CAT TREATS!
WE'RE OUT OF CAT TREATS
© 2020 PAWS, INC. All Rights Reserved.
Distributed by Andrews McMeel Syndication
JIM DAVIS 1-4

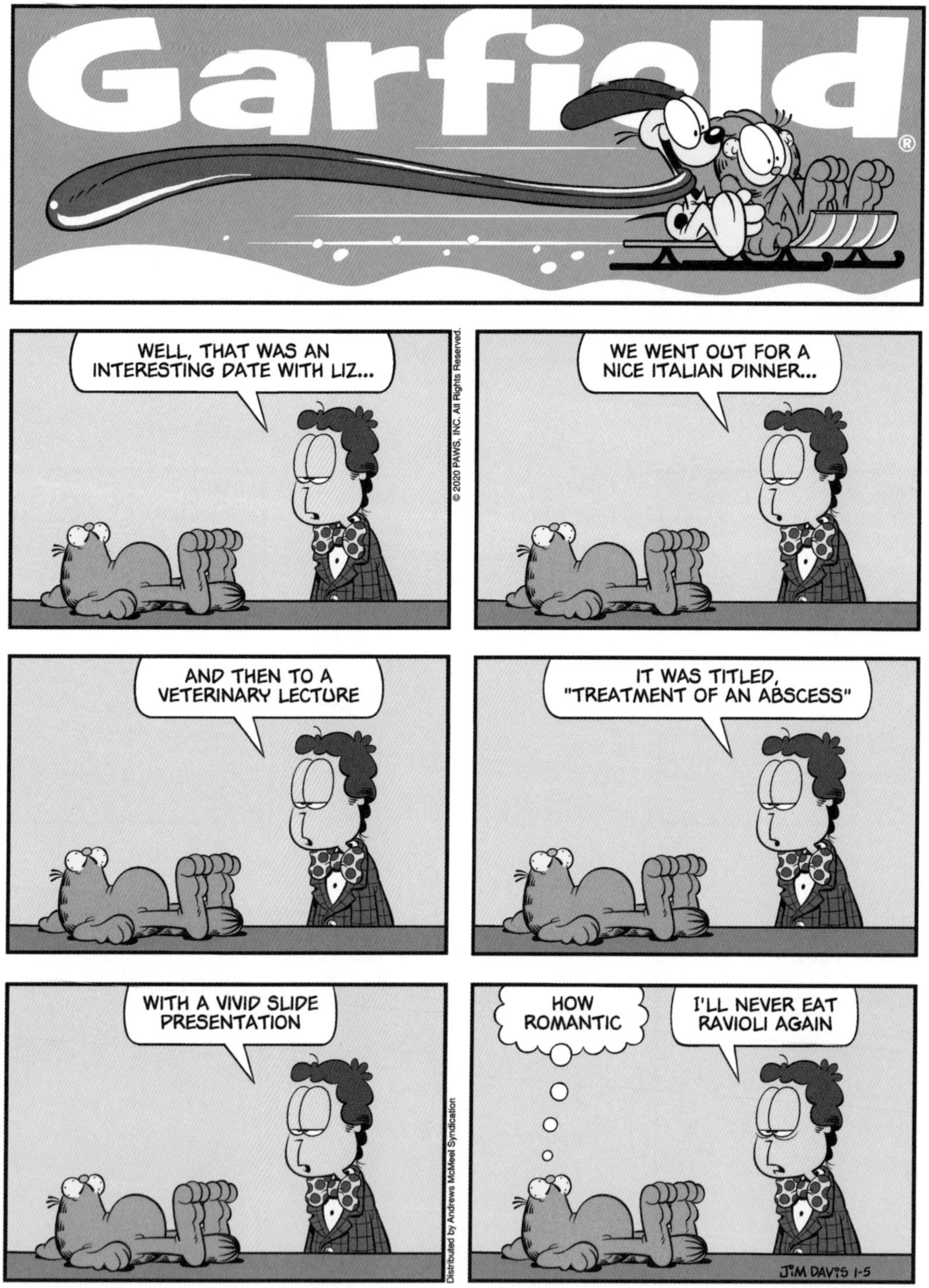
Garfield®
WELL, THAT WAS AN INTERESTING DATE WITH LIZ...
WE WENT OUT FOR A NICE ITALIAN DINNER...
AND THEN TO A VETERINARY LECTURE
IT WAS TITLED, "TREATMENT OF AN ABSCESS"
WITH A VIVID SLIDE PRESENTATION
HOW ROMANTIC
I'LL NEVER EAT RAVIOLI AGAIN
JIM DAVIS 1-5
© 2020 PAWS, INC. All Rights Reserved.
Distributed by Andrews McMeel Syndication

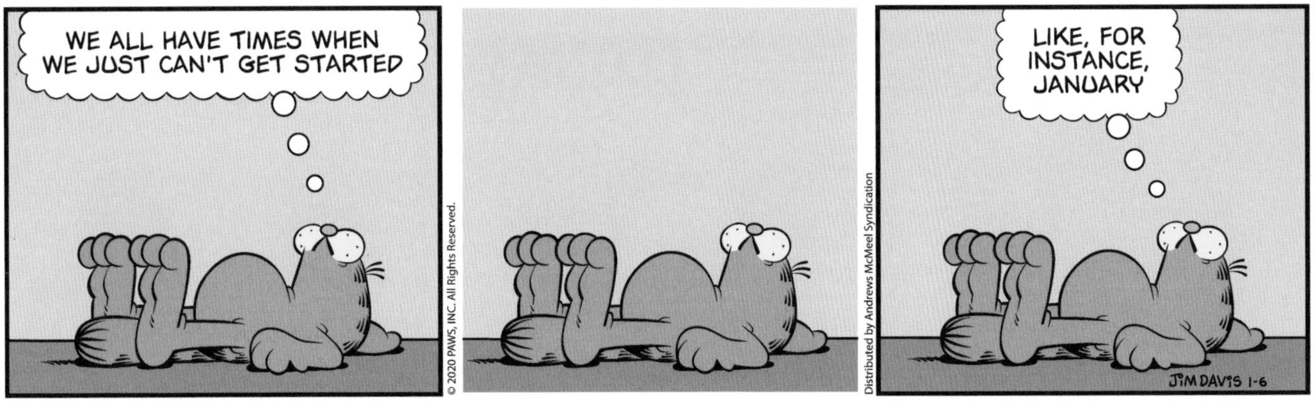
WE ALL HAVE TIMES WHEN WE JUST CAN'T GET STARTED
LIKE, FOR INSTANCE, JANUARY
JIM DAVIS 1-6
© 2020 PAWS, INC. All Rights Reserved.
Distributed by Andrews McMeel Syndication

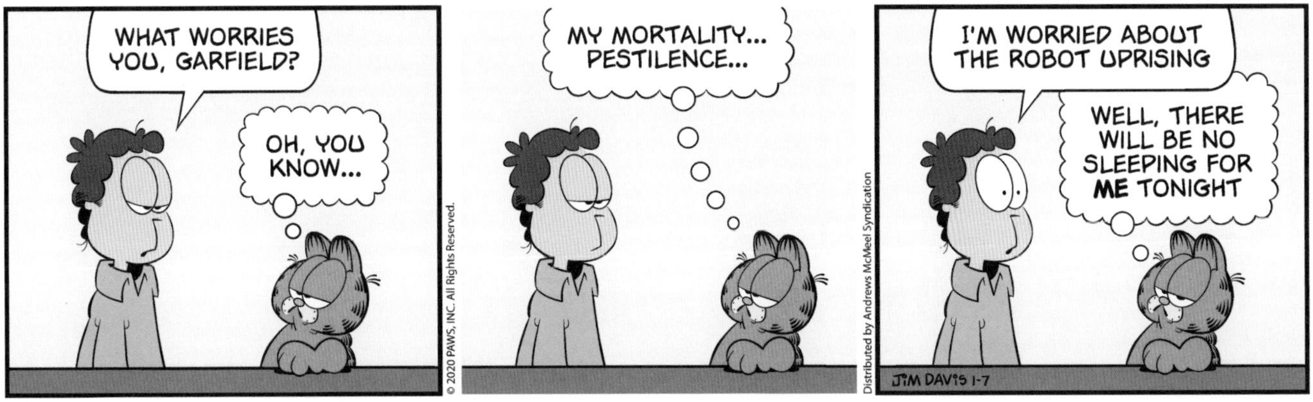
WHAT WORRIES YOU, GARFIELD?
OH, YOU KNOW...
MY MORTALITY... PESTILENCE...
I'M WORRIED ABOUT THE ROBOT UPRISING
WELL, THERE WILL BE NO SLEEPING FOR **ME** TONIGHT
JIM DAVIS 1-7
© 2020 PAWS, INC. All Rights Reserved.
Distributed by Andrews McMeel Syndication

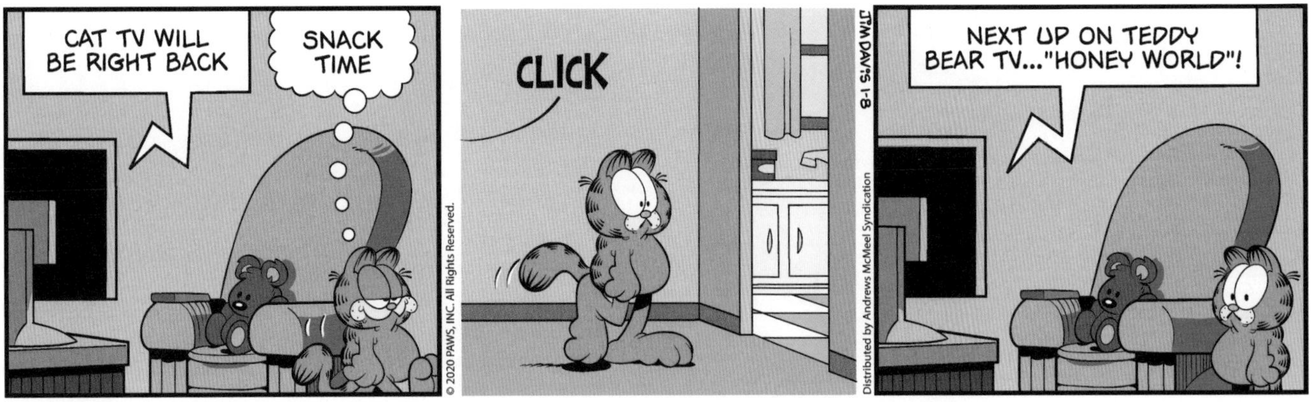
CAT TV WILL BE RIGHT BACK
SNACK TIME
CLICK
NEXT UP ON TEDDY BEAR TV..."HONEY WORLD"!
JIM DAVIS 1-8
© 2020 PAWS, INC. All Rights Reserved.
Distributed by Andrews McMeel Syndication

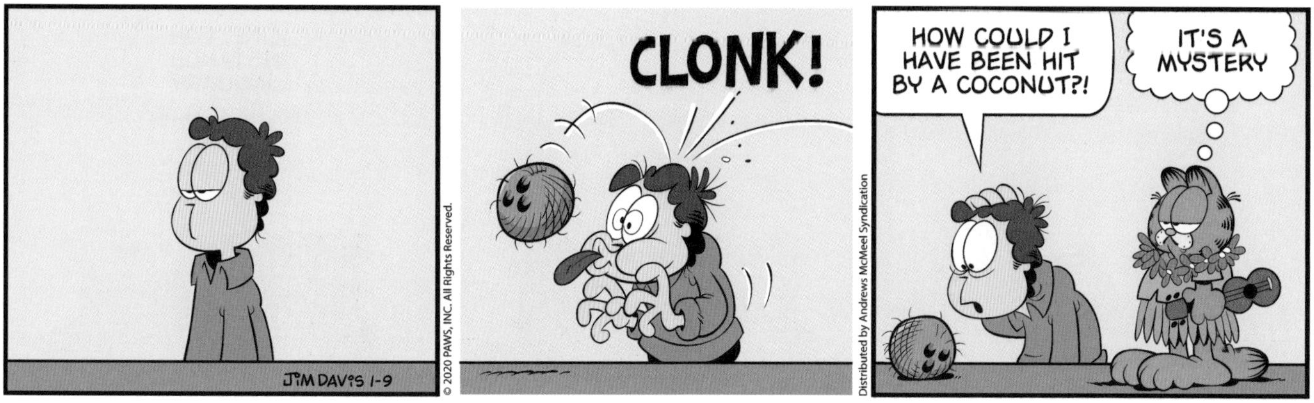
CLONK!
HOW COULD I HAVE BEEN HIT BY A COCONUT?!
IT'S A MYSTERY
JIM DAVIS 1-9
© 2020 PAWS, INC. All Rights Reserved.
Distributed by Andrews McMeel Syndication

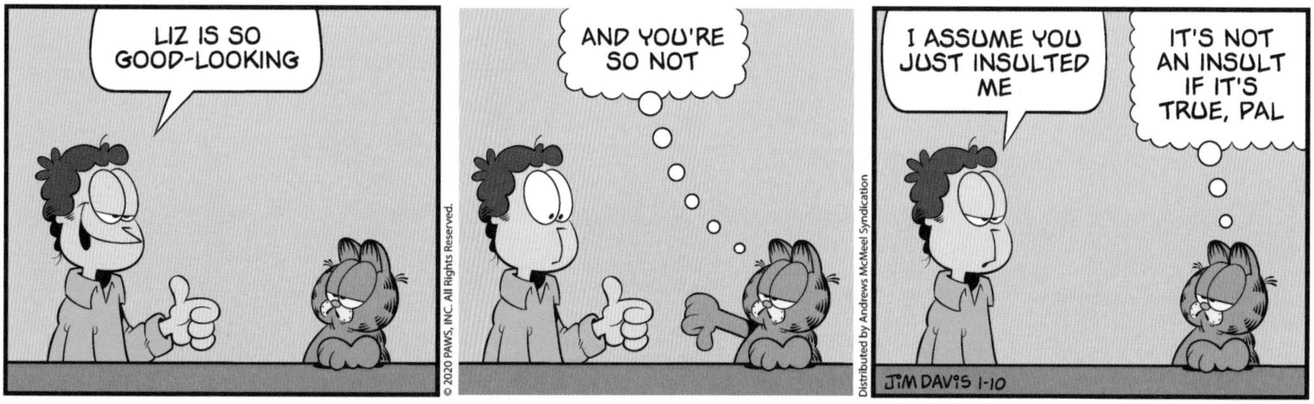
LIZ IS SO GOOD-LOOKING
AND YOU'RE SO NOT
I ASSUME YOU JUST INSULTED ME
IT'S NOT AN INSULT IF IT'S TRUE, PAL
JIM DAVIS 1-10
© 2020 PAWS, INC. All Rights Reserved.
Distributed by Andrews McMeel Syndication

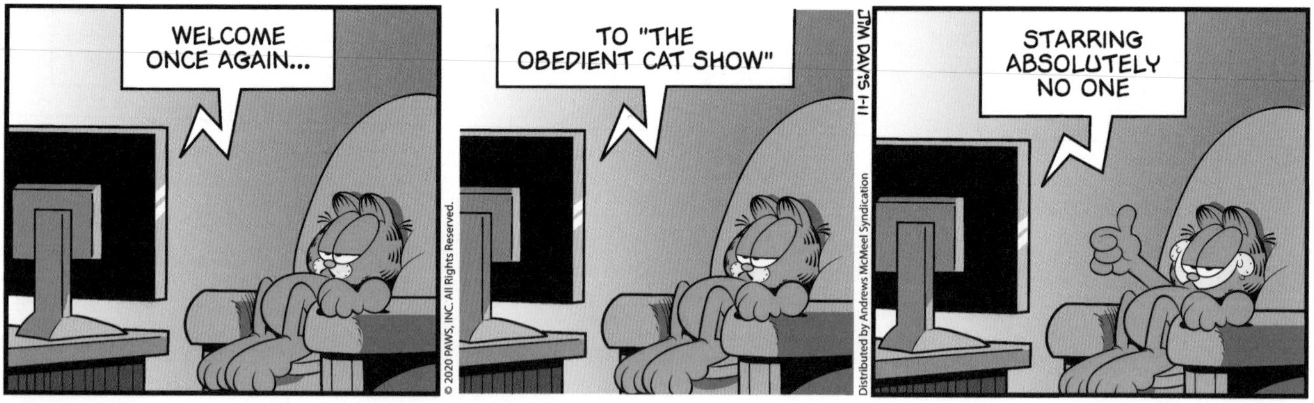
WELCOME ONCE AGAIN...
TO "THE OBEDIENT CAT SHOW"
STARRING ABSOLUTELY NO ONE
JIM DAVIS 1-11
© 2020 PAWS, INC. All Rights Reserved.
Distributed by Andrews McMeel Syndication

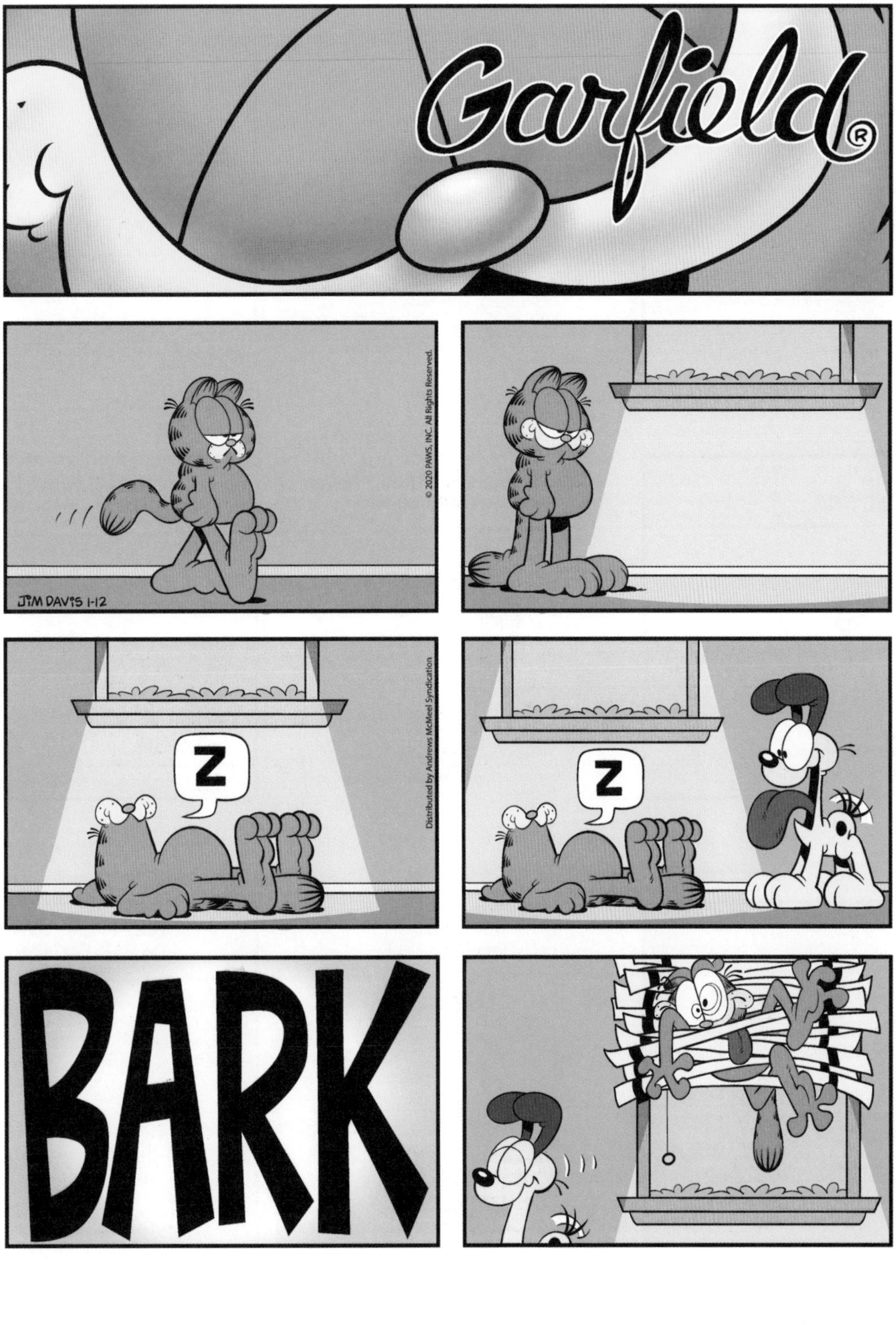
Garfield®
JIM DAVIS 1-12
© 2020 PAWS, INC. All Rights Reserved.
Distributed by Andrews McMeel Syndication
Z
Z
BARK

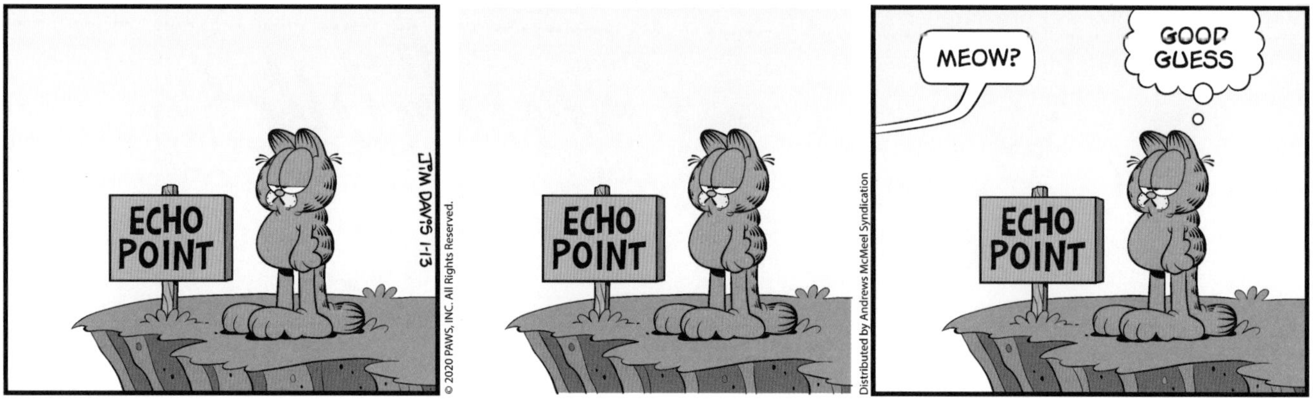
ECHO POINT
JIM DAVIS 1-13
© 2020 PAWS, INC. All Rights Reserved.
ECHO POINT
Distributed by Andrews McMeel Syndication
ECHO POINT
MEOW?
GOOD GUESS

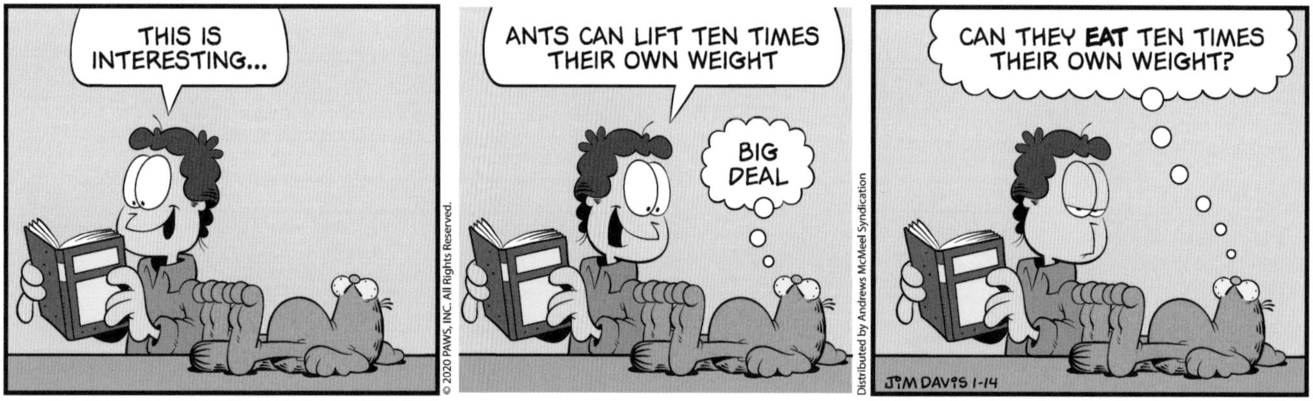
THIS IS INTERESTING...
© 2020 PAWS, INC. All Rights Reserved.
ANTS CAN LIFT TEN TIMES THEIR OWN WEIGHT
BIG DEAL
Distributed by Andrews McMeel Syndication
CAN THEY **EAT** TEN TIMES THEIR OWN WEIGHT?
JIM DAVIS 1-14

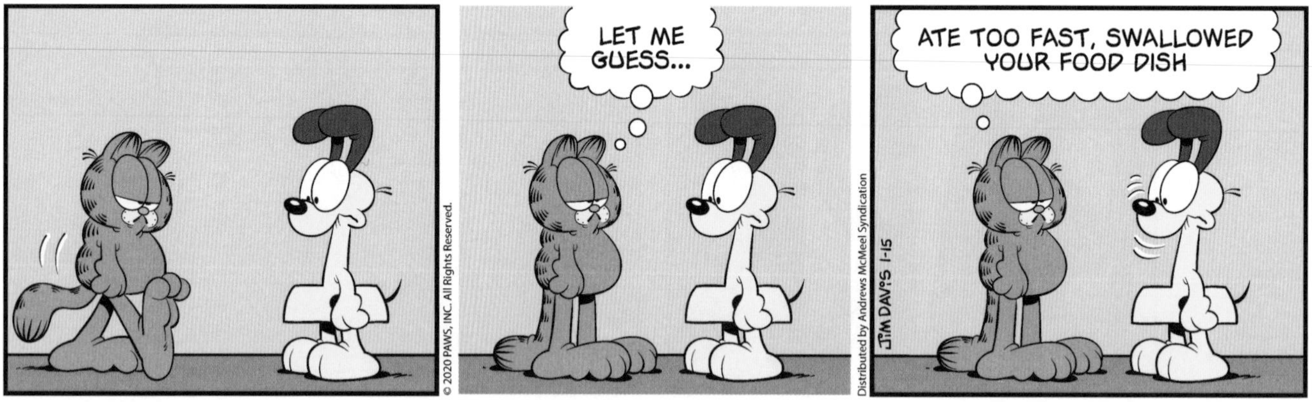
© 2020 PAWS, INC. All Rights Reserved.
LET ME GUESS...
Distributed by Andrews McMeel Syndication
JIM DAVIS 1-15
ATE TOO FAST, SWALLOWED YOUR FOOD DISH

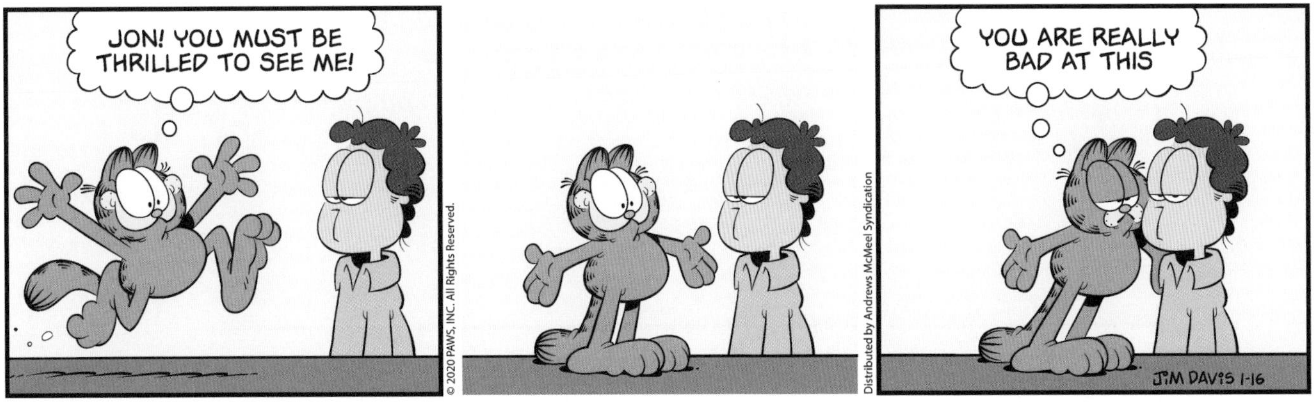
JON! YOU MUST BE THRILLED TO SEE ME!
© 2020 PAWS, INC. All Rights Reserved.
Distributed by Andrews McMeel Syndication
YOU ARE REALLY BAD AT THIS
JIM DAVIS 1-16

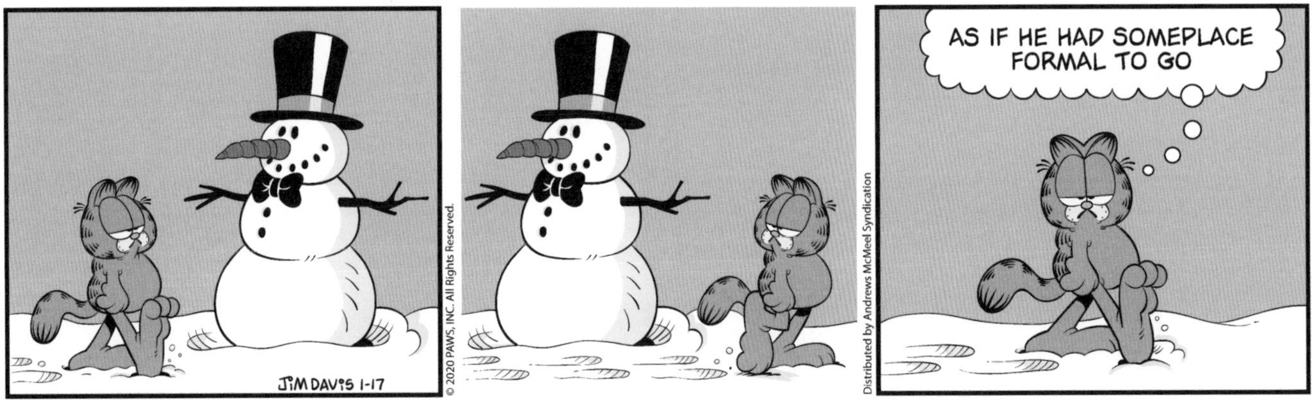
JIM DAVIS 1-17
© 2020 PAWS, INC. All Rights Reserved.
Distributed by Andrews McMeel Syndication
AS IF HE HAD SOMEPLACE FORMAL TO GO

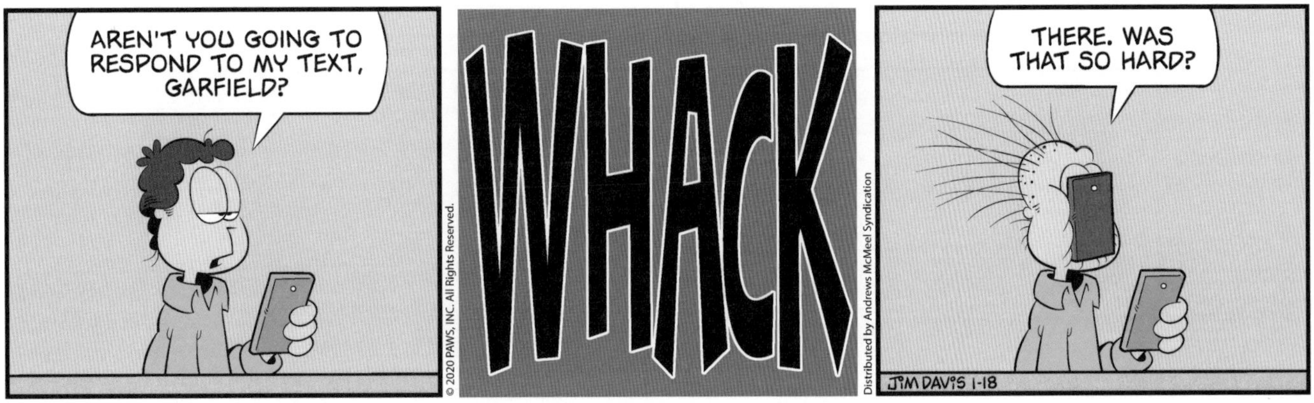
AREN'T YOU GOING TO RESPOND TO MY TEXT, GARFIELD?
© 2020 PAWS, INC. All Rights Reserved.
WHACK
Distributed by Andrews McMeel Syndication
THERE. WAS THAT SO HARD?
JIM DAVIS 1-18

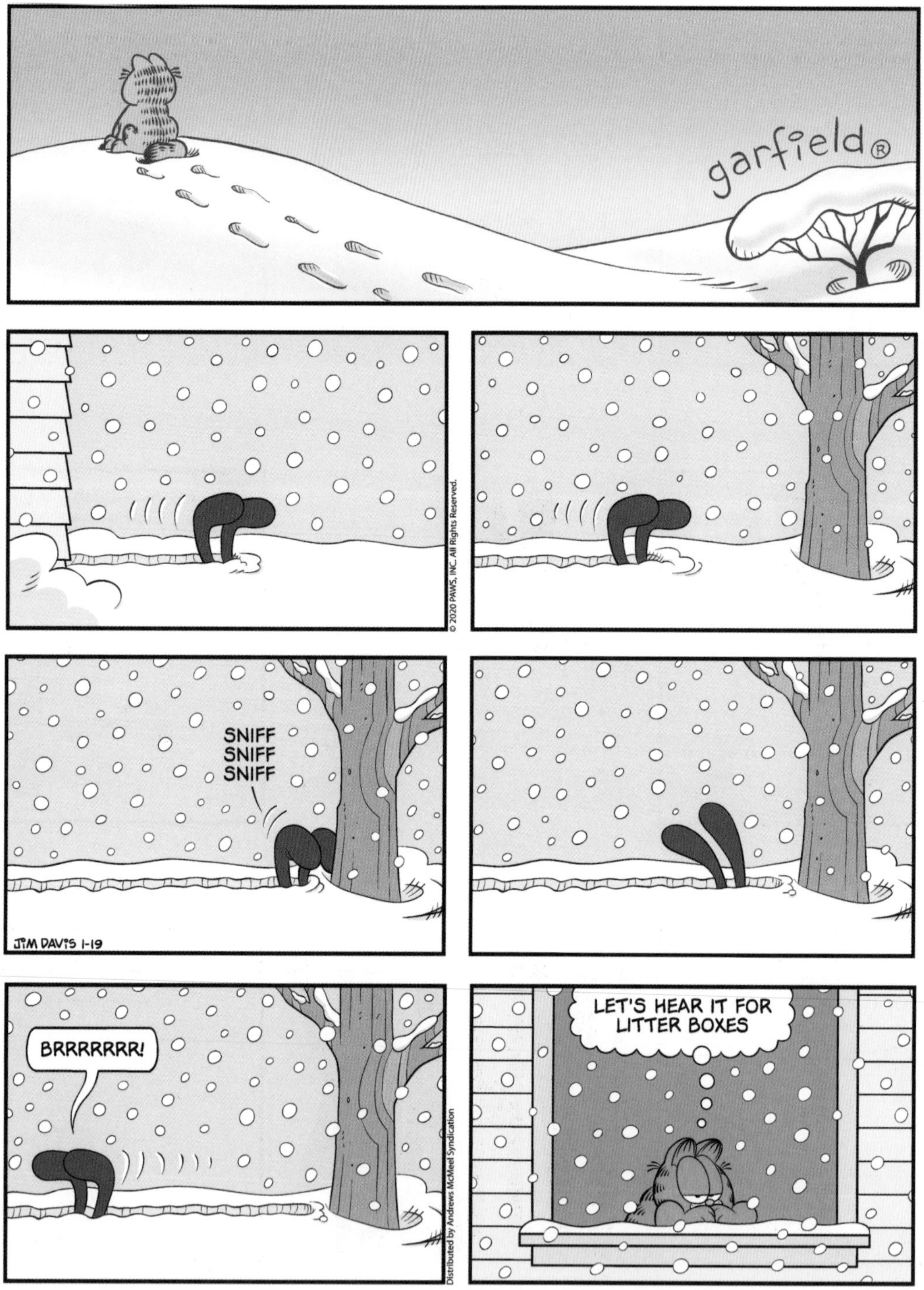
garfield®
© 2020 PAWS, INC. All Rights Reserved.
SNIFF
SNIFF
SNIFF
JIM DAVIS 1-19
BRRRRRRR!
Distributed by Andrews McMeel Syndication
LET'S HEAR IT FOR
LITTER BOXES

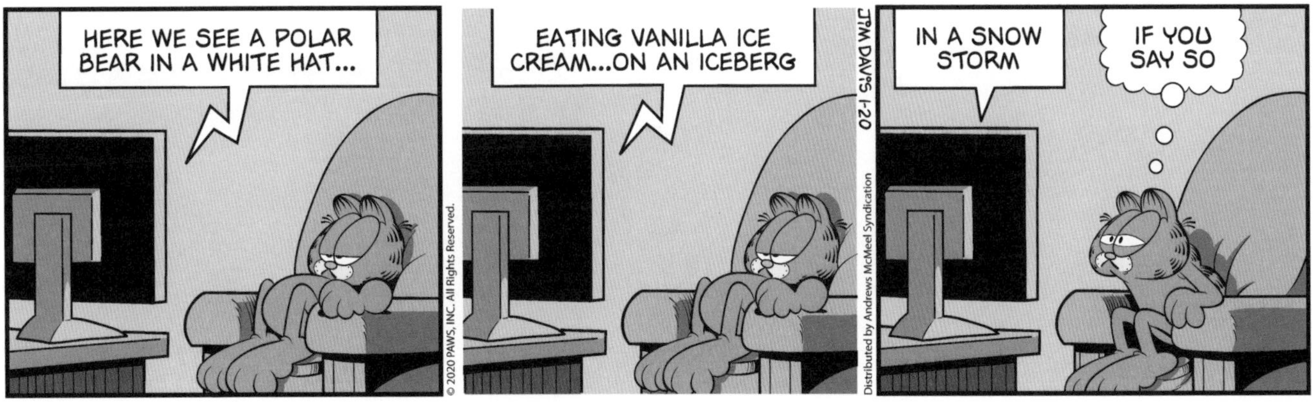
HERE WE SEE A POLAR BEAR IN A WHITE HAT...
© 2020 PAWS, INC. All Rights Reserved.
EATING VANILLA ICE CREAM...ON AN ICEBERG
JIM DAVIS 1-20
Distributed by Andrews McMeel Syndication
IN A SNOW STORM
IF YOU SAY SO

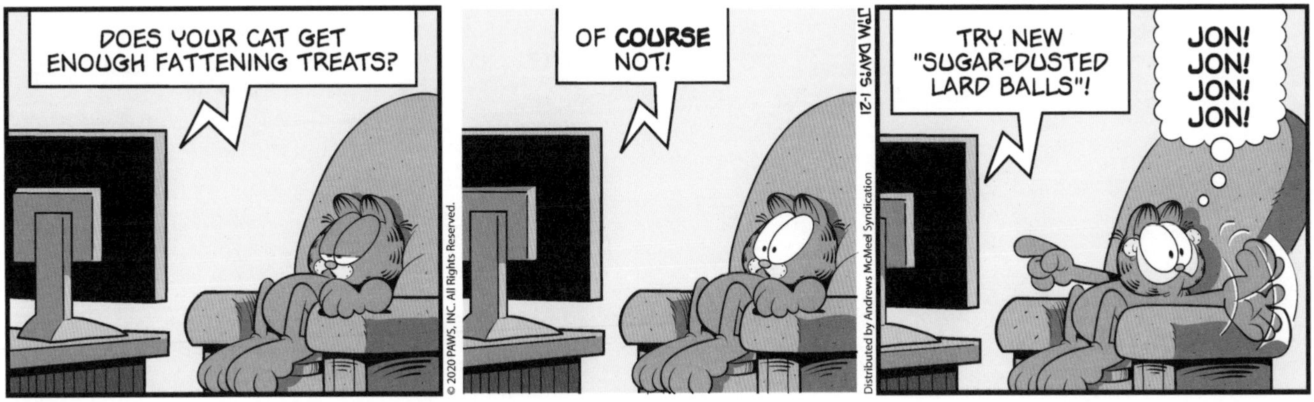
DOES YOUR CAT GET ENOUGH FATTENING TREATS?
© 2020 PAWS, INC. All Rights Reserved.
OF COURSE NOT!
JIM DAVIS 1-21
Distributed by Andrews McMeel Syndication
TRY NEW "SUGAR-DUSTED LARD BALLS"!
JON! JON! JON! JON!

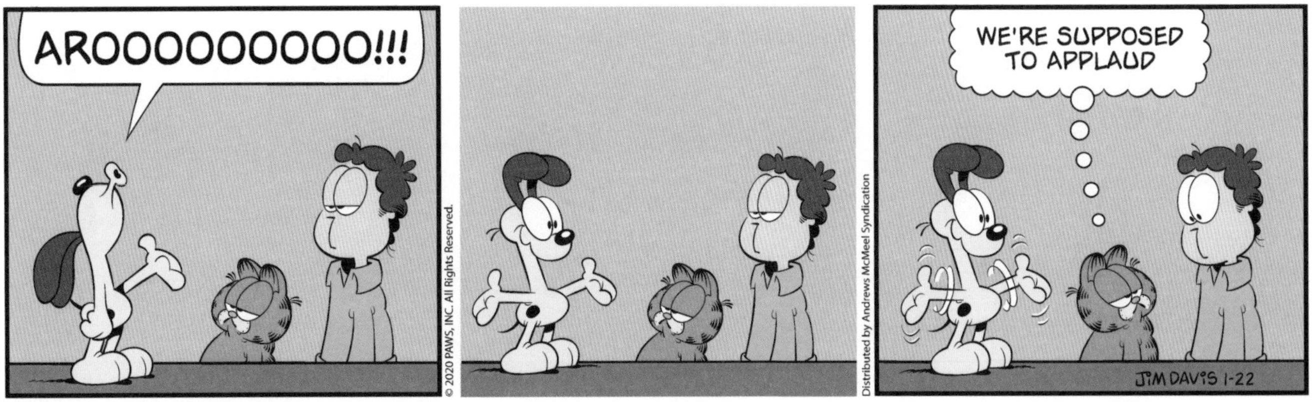
AROOOOOOOOO!!!
© 2020 PAWS, INC. All Rights Reserved.
Distributed by Andrews McMeel Syndication
WE'RE SUPPOSED TO APPLAUD
JIM DAVIS 1-22

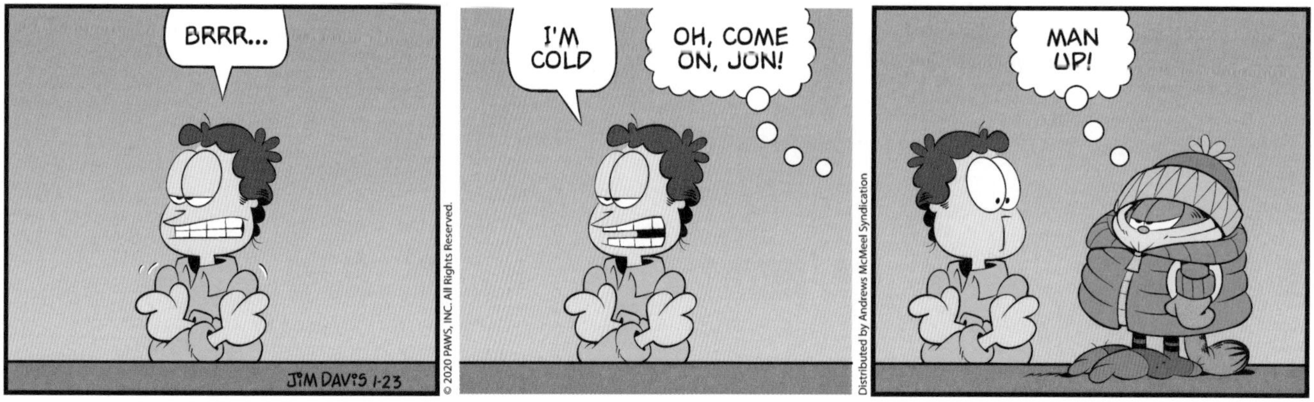
BRRR...
JIM DAVIS 1-23
I'M COLD
OH, COME ON, JON!
© 2020 PAWS, INC. All Rights Reserved.
MAN UP!
Distributed by Andrews McMeel Syndication

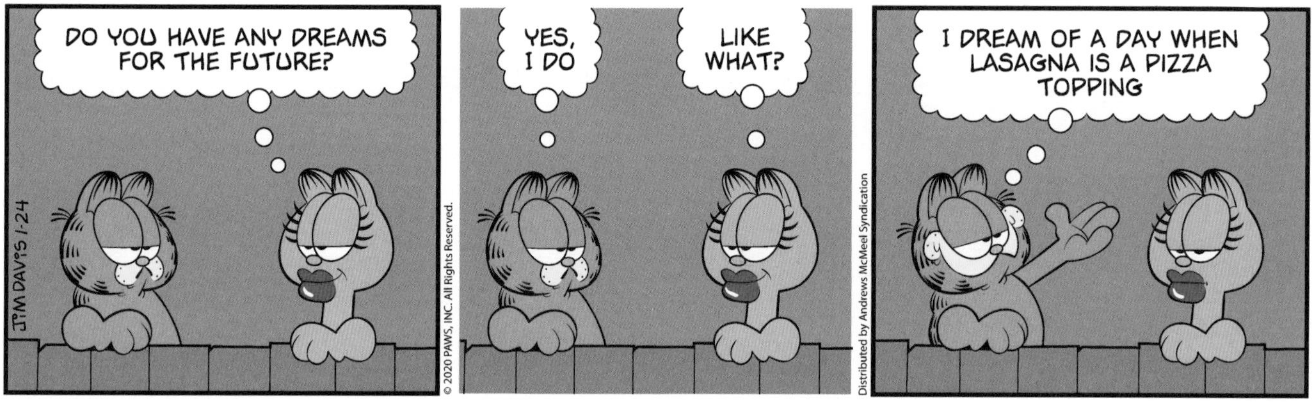
DO YOU HAVE ANY DREAMS FOR THE FUTURE?
JIM DAVIS 1-24
YES, I DO
LIKE WHAT?
© 2020 PAWS, INC. All Rights Reserved.
I DREAM OF A DAY WHEN LASAGNA IS A PIZZA TOPPING
Distributed by Andrews McMeel Syndication

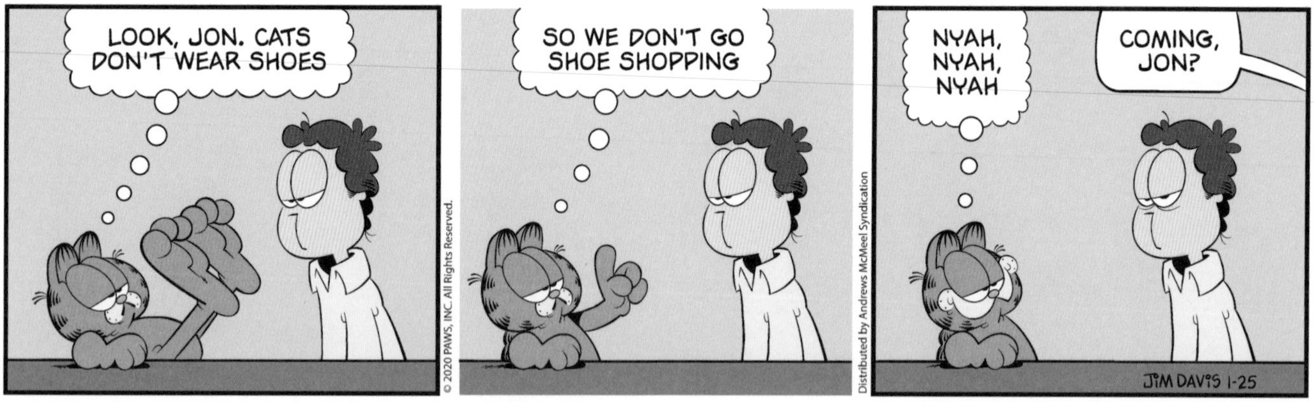
LOOK, JON. CATS DON'T WEAR SHOES
SO WE DON'T GO SHOE SHOPPING
© 2020 PAWS, INC. All Rights Reserved.
NYAH, NYAH, NYAH
COMING, JON?
Distributed by Andrews McMeel Syndication
JIM DAVIS 1-25

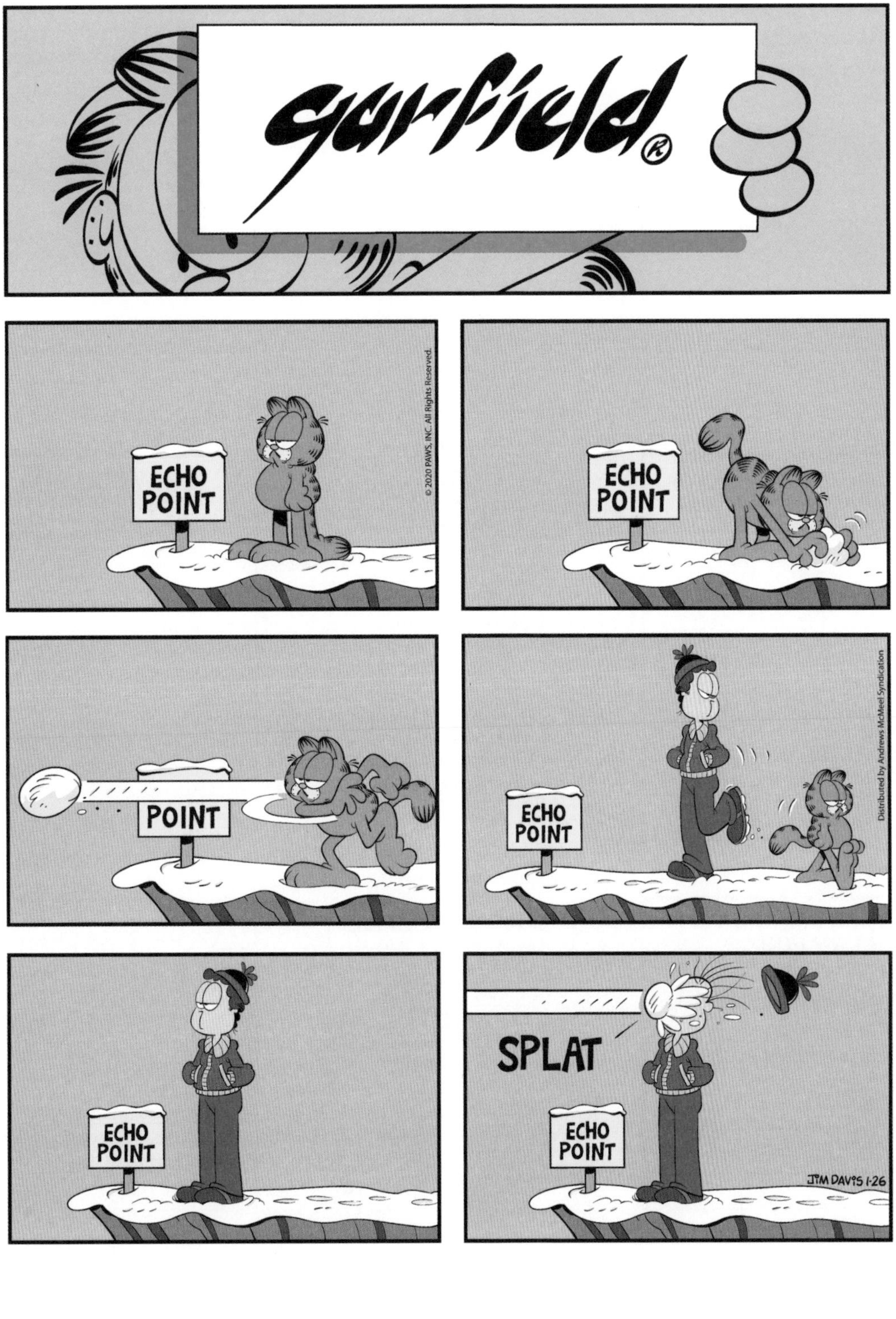
garfield®
ECHO POINT
© 2020 PAWS, INC. All Rights Reserved.
ECHO POINT
POINT
ECHO POINT
Distributed by Andrews McMeel Syndication
ECHO POINT
SPLAT
ECHO POINT
JIM DAVIS 1-26

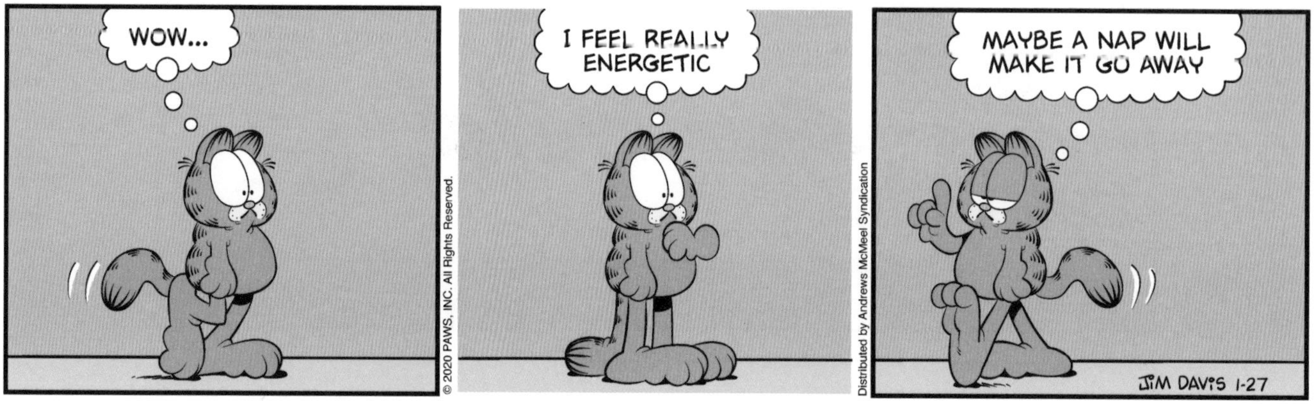
WOW...
I FEEL REALLY ENERGETIC
MAYBE A NAP WILL MAKE IT GO AWAY
© 2020 PAWS, INC. All Rights Reserved.
Distributed by Andrews McMeel Syndication
JIM DAVIS 1-27

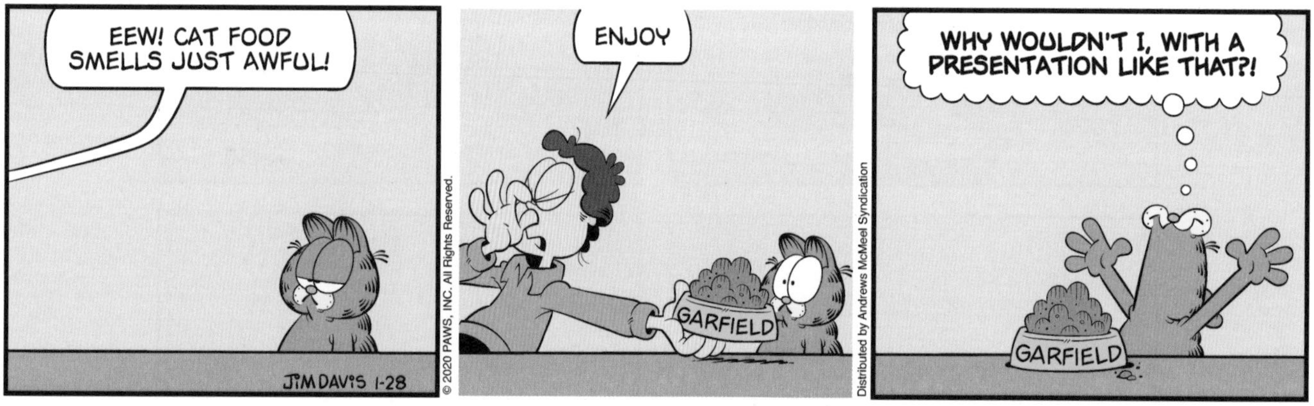
EEW! CAT FOOD SMELLS JUST AWFUL!
JIM DAVIS 1-28
ENJOY
GARFIELD
© 2020 PAWS, INC. All Rights Reserved.
Distributed by Andrews McMeel Syndication
WHY WOULDN'T I, WITH A PRESENTATION LIKE THAT?!
GARFIELD

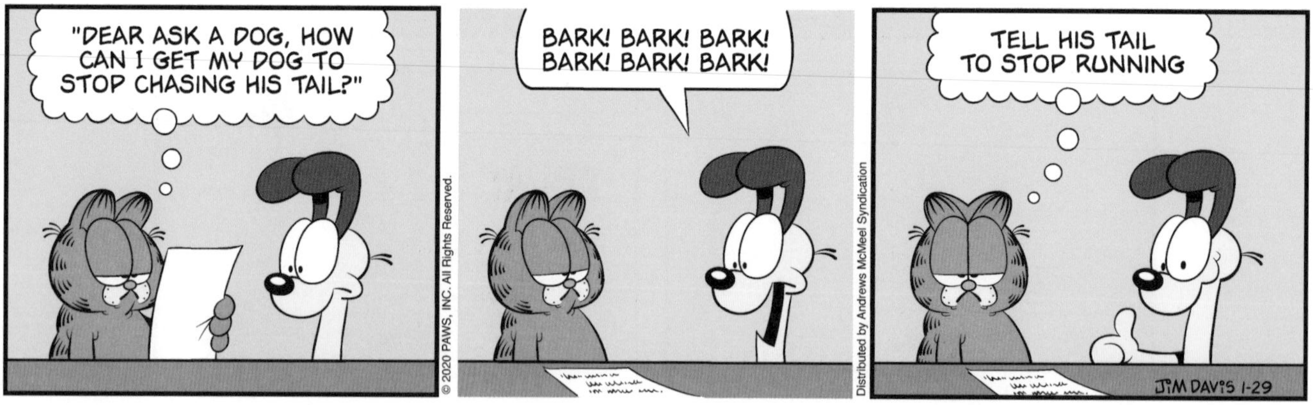
"DEAR ASK A DOG, HOW CAN I GET MY DOG TO STOP CHASING HIS TAIL?"
BARK! BARK! BARK! BARK! BARK! BARK!
© 2020 PAWS, INC. All Rights Reserved.
Distributed by Andrews McMeel Syndication
TELL HIS TAIL TO STOP RUNNING
JIM DAVIS 1-29

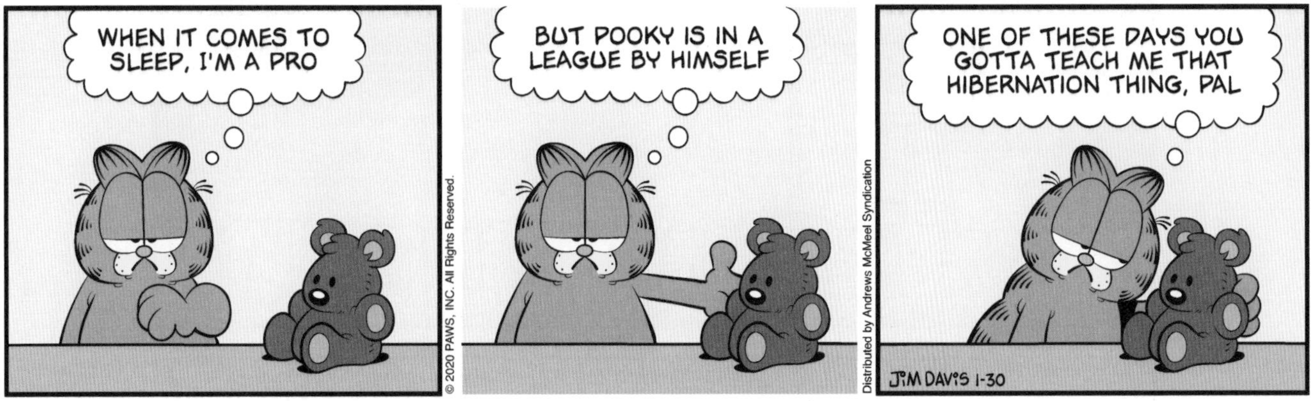
WHEN IT COMES TO SLEEP, I'M A PRO
BUT POOKY IS IN A LEAGUE BY HIMSELF
ONE OF THESE DAYS YOU GOTTA TEACH ME THAT HIBERNATION THING, PAL
JIM DAVIS 1-30

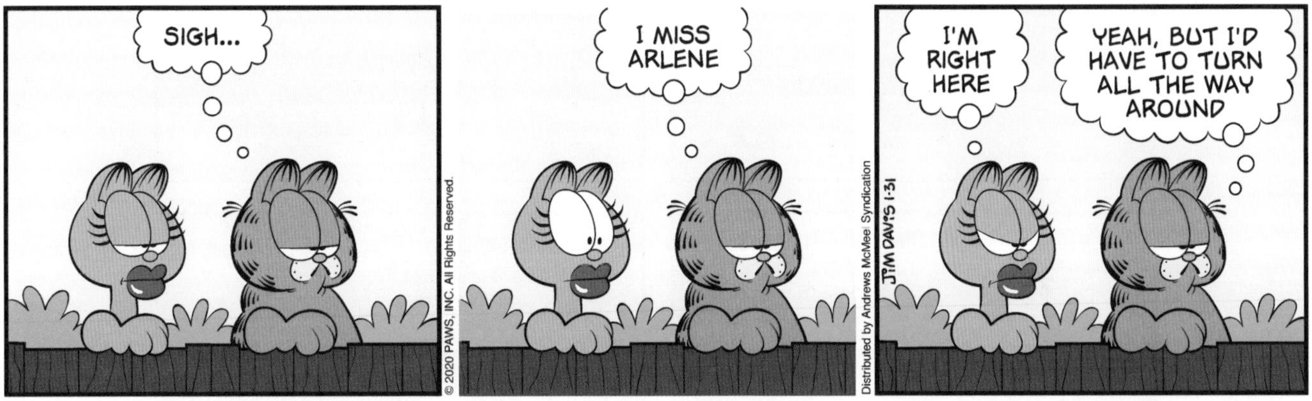
SIGH...
I MISS ARLENE
I'M RIGHT HERE
YEAH, BUT I'D HAVE TO TURN ALL THE WAY AROUND
JIM DAVIS 1-31

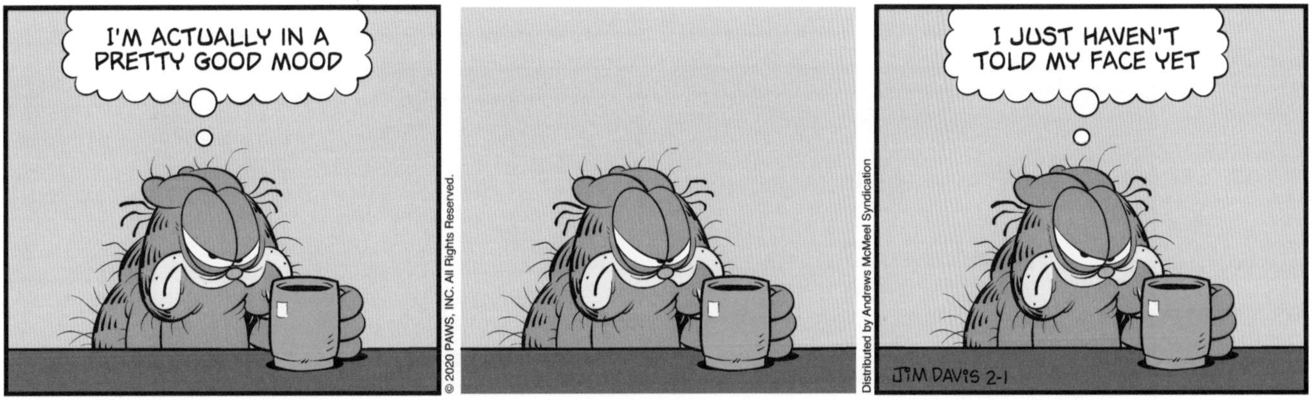
I'M ACTUALLY IN A PRETTY GOOD MOOD
I JUST HAVEN'T TOLD MY FACE YET
JIM DAVIS 2-1

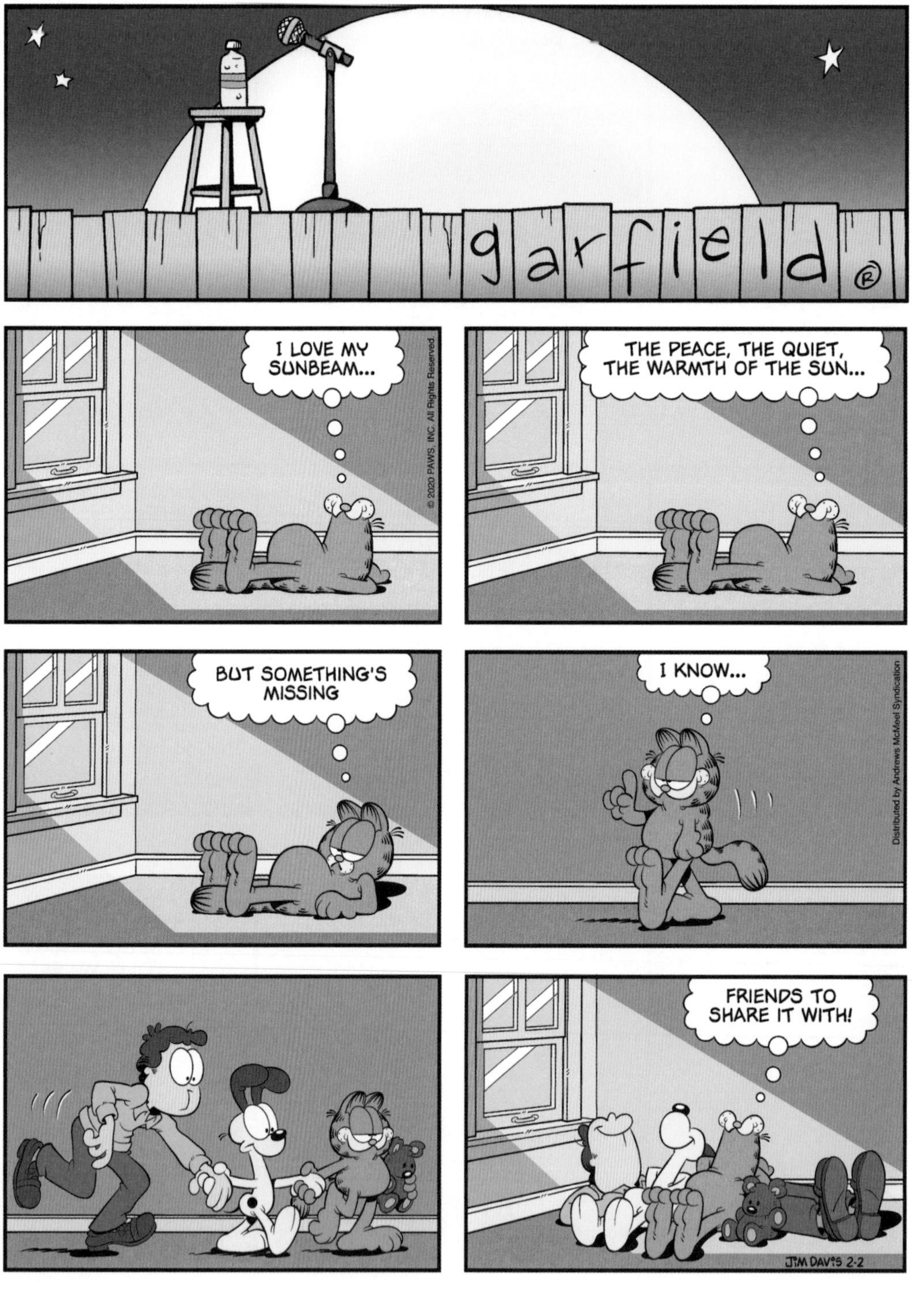
garfield
I LOVE MY SUNBEAM...
© 2020 PAWS, INC. All Rights Reserved.
THE PEACE, THE QUIET, THE WARMTH OF THE SUN...
BUT SOMETHING'S MISSING
I KNOW...
Distributed by Andrews McMeel Syndication
FRIENDS TO SHARE IT WITH!
JIM DAVIS 2-2

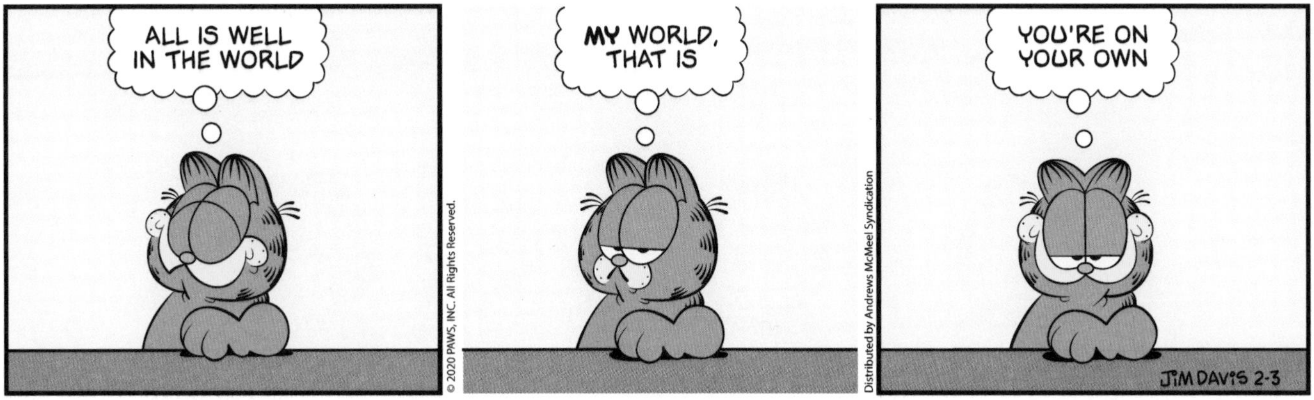
ALL IS WELL IN THE WORLD
MY WORLD, THAT IS
YOU'RE ON YOUR OWN
© 2020 PAWS, INC. All Rights Reserved.
Distributed by Andrews McMeel Syndication
JIM DAVIS 2-3

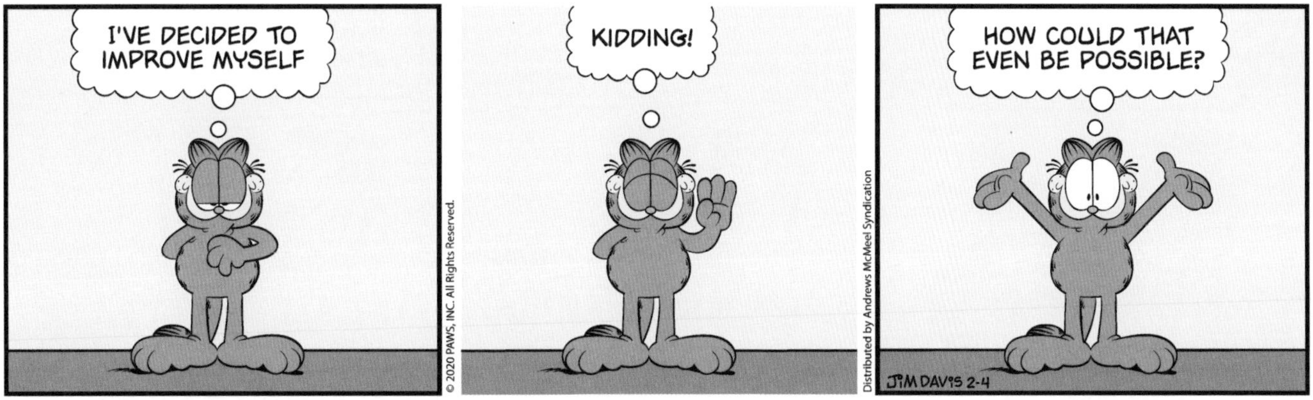
I'VE DECIDED TO IMPROVE MYSELF
KIDDING!
HOW COULD THAT EVEN BE POSSIBLE?
© 2020 PAWS, INC. All Rights Reserved.
Distributed by Andrews McMeel Syndication
JIM DAVIS 2-4

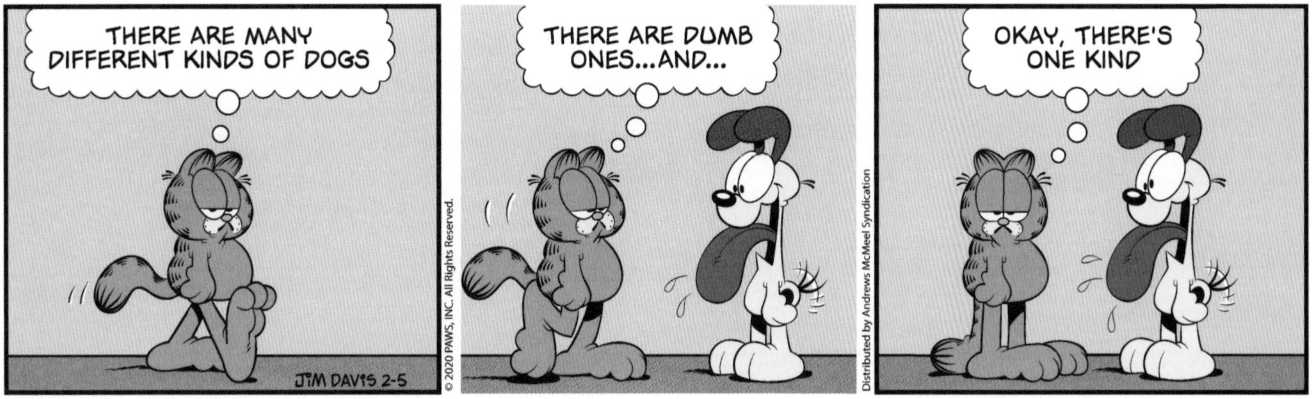
THERE ARE MANY DIFFERENT KINDS OF DOGS
THERE ARE DUMB ONES...AND...
OKAY, THERE'S ONE KIND
© 2020 PAWS, INC. All Rights Reserved.
Distributed by Andrews McMeel Syndication
JIM DAVIS 2-5

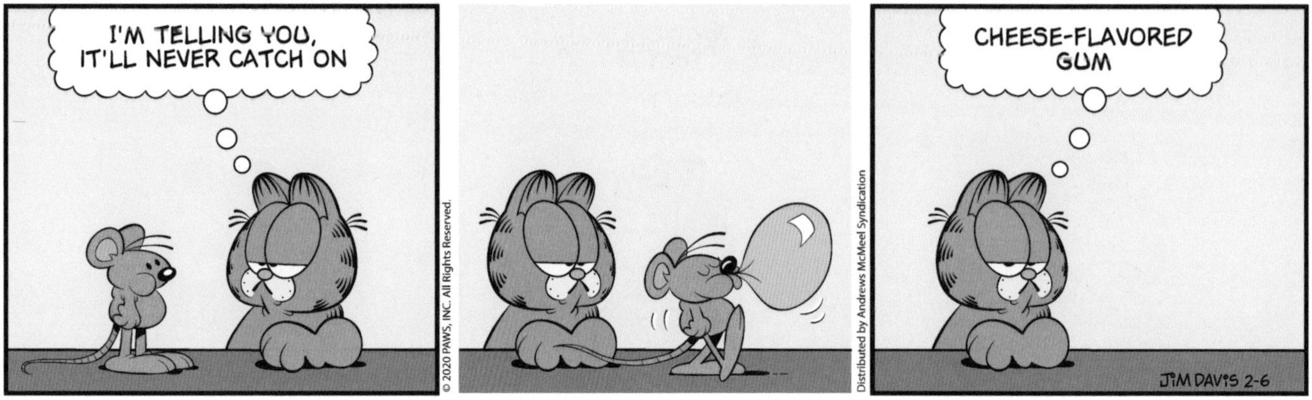
I'M TELLING YOU, IT'LL NEVER CATCH ON
© 2020 PAWS, INC. All Rights Reserved.
Distributed by Andrews McMeel Syndication
CHEESE-FLAVORED GUM
JIM DAVIS 2-6

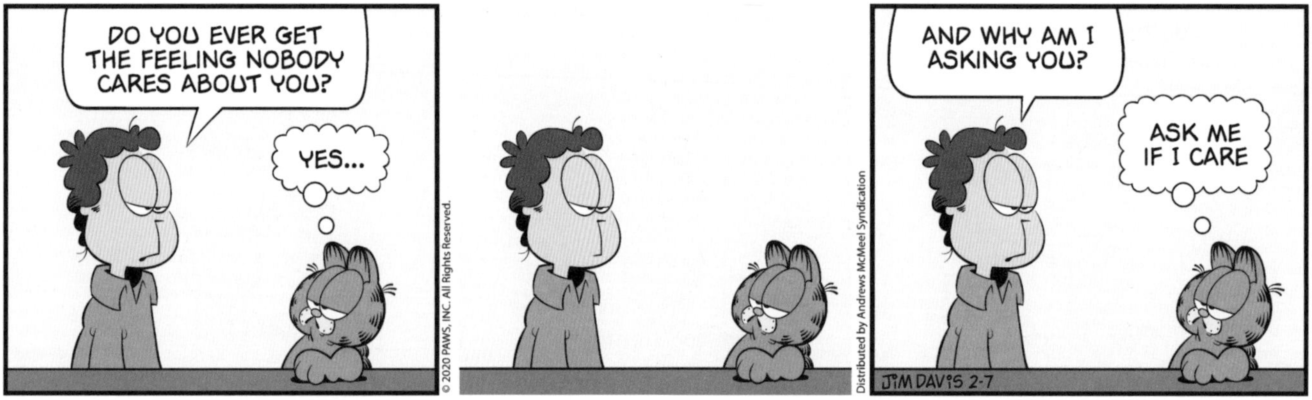
DO YOU EVER GET THE FEELING NOBODY CARES ABOUT YOU?
YES...
© 2020 PAWS, INC. All Rights Reserved.
Distributed by Andrews McMeel Syndication
AND WHY AM I ASKING YOU?
ASK ME IF I CARE
JIM DAVIS 2-7

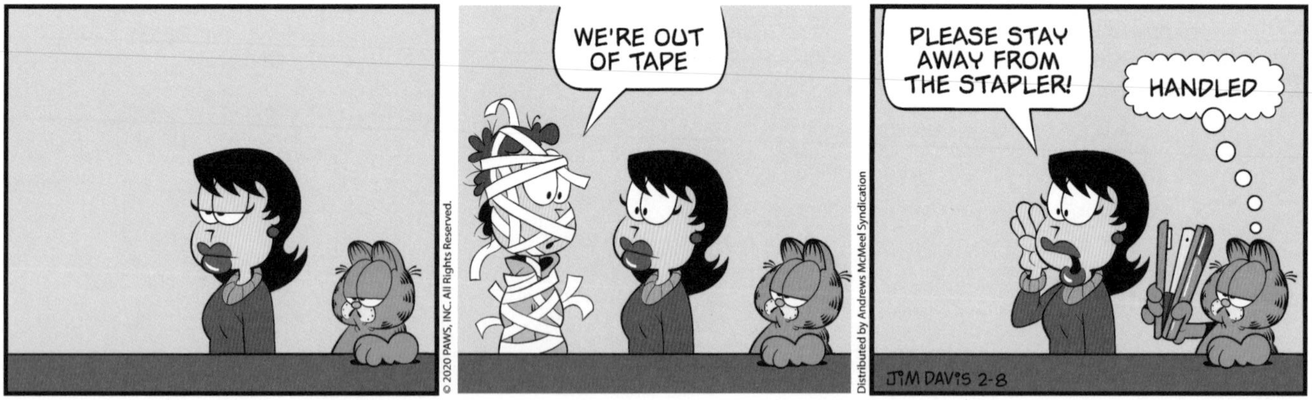
© 2020 PAWS, INC. All Rights Reserved.
WE'RE OUT OF TAPE
Distributed by Andrews McMeel Syndication
PLEASE STAY AWAY FROM THE STAPLER!
HANDLED
JIM DAVIS 2-8

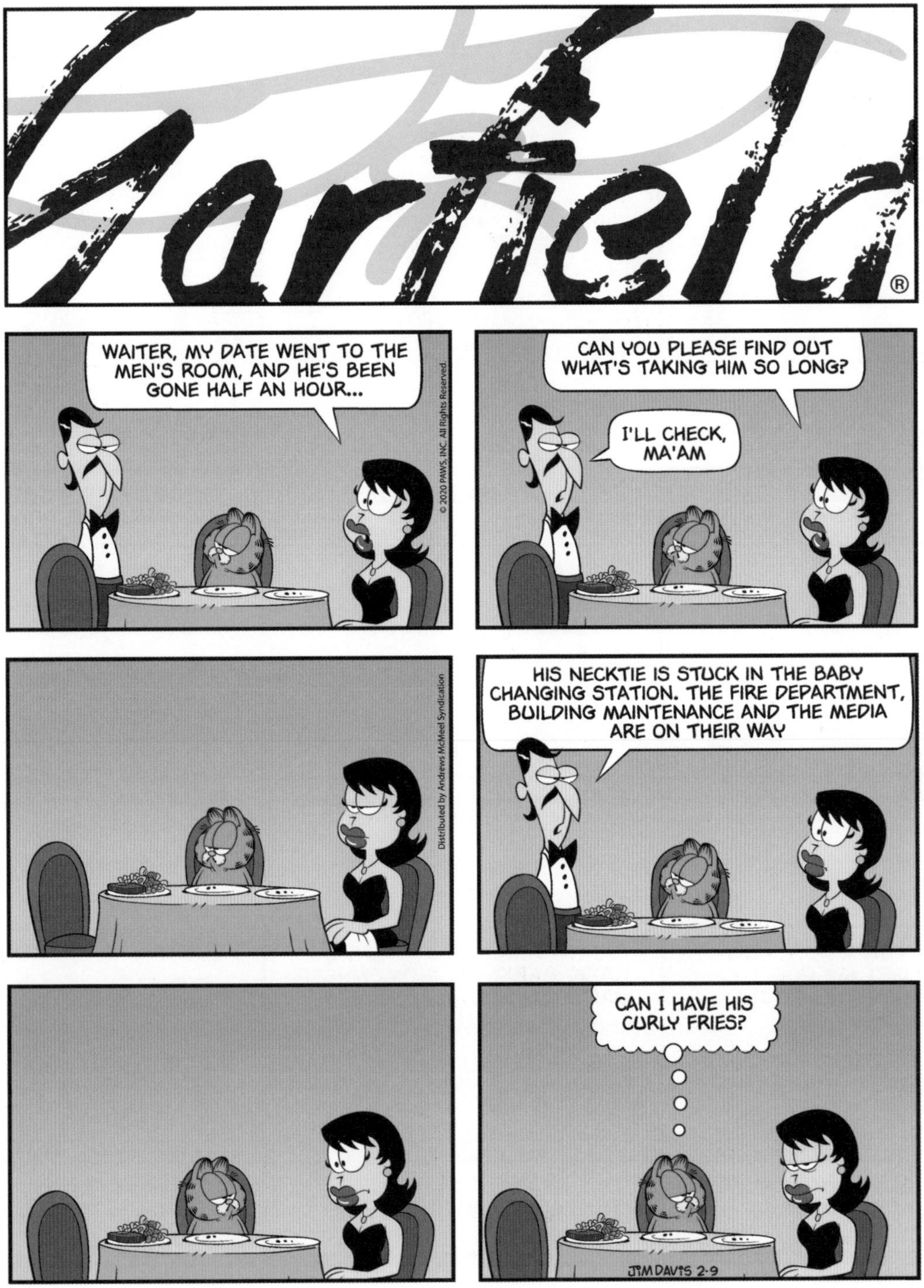
Garfield®
WAITER, MY DATE WENT TO THE MEN'S ROOM, AND HE'S BEEN GONE HALF AN HOUR...
CAN YOU PLEASE FIND OUT WHAT'S TAKING HIM SO LONG?
I'LL CHECK, MA'AM
HIS NECKTIE IS STUCK IN THE BABY CHANGING STATION. THE FIRE DEPARTMENT, BUILDING MAINTENANCE AND THE MEDIA ARE ON THEIR WAY
CAN I HAVE HIS CURLY FRIES?
JIM DAVIS 2-9

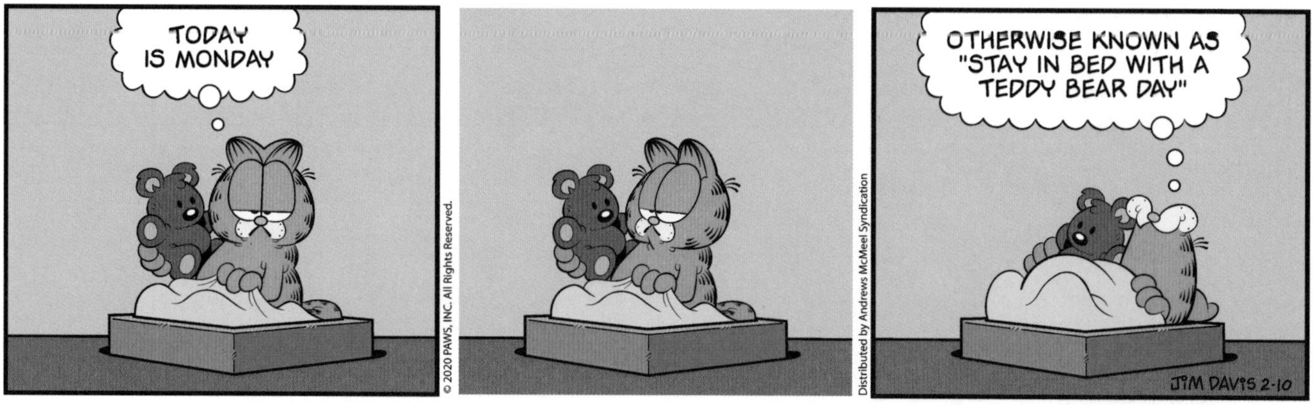
TODAY IS MONDAY
OTHERWISE KNOWN AS "STAY IN BED WITH A TEDDY BEAR DAY"
© 2020 PAWS, INC. All Rights Reserved.
Distributed by Andrews McMeel Syndication
JIM DAVIS 2-10

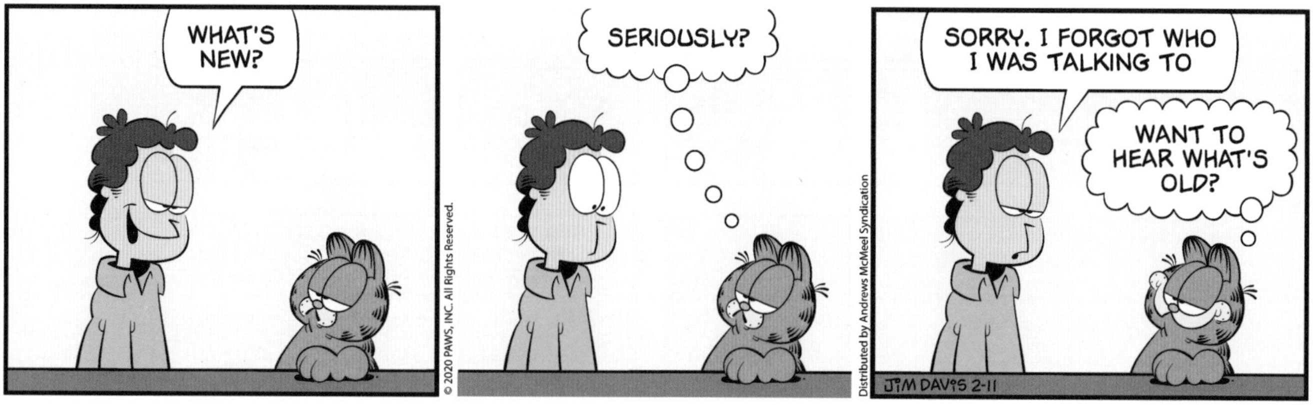
WHAT'S NEW?
SERIOUSLY?
SORRY. I FORGOT WHO I WAS TALKING TO
WANT TO HEAR WHAT'S OLD?
© 2020 PAWS, INC. All Rights Reserved.
Distributed by Andrews McMeel Syndication
JIM DAVIS 2-11

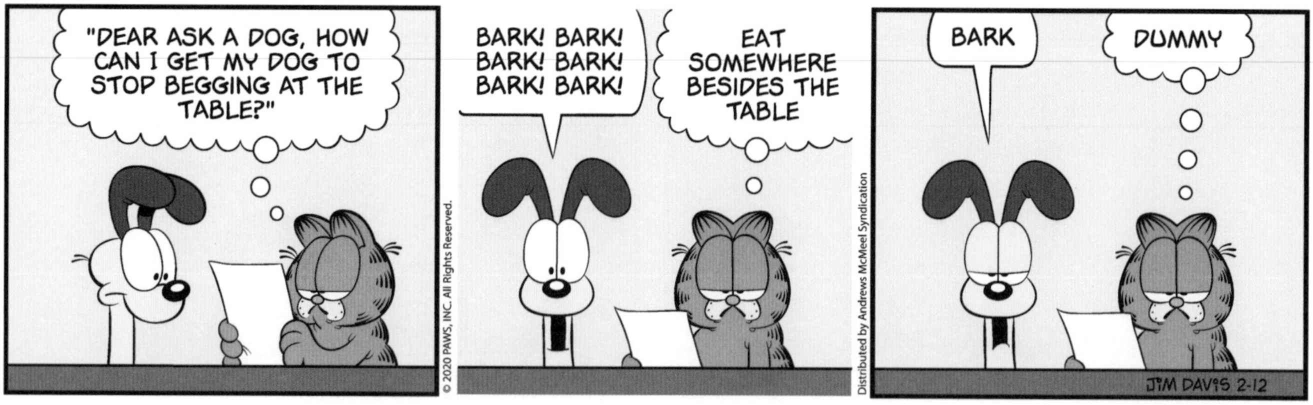
"DEAR ASK A DOG, HOW CAN I GET MY DOG TO STOP BEGGING AT THE TABLE?"
BARK! BARK! BARK! BARK! BARK! BARK!
EAT SOMEWHERE BESIDES THE TABLE
BARK
DUMMY
© 2020 PAWS, INC. All Rights Reserved.
Distributed by Andrews McMeel Syndication
JIM DAVIS 2-12

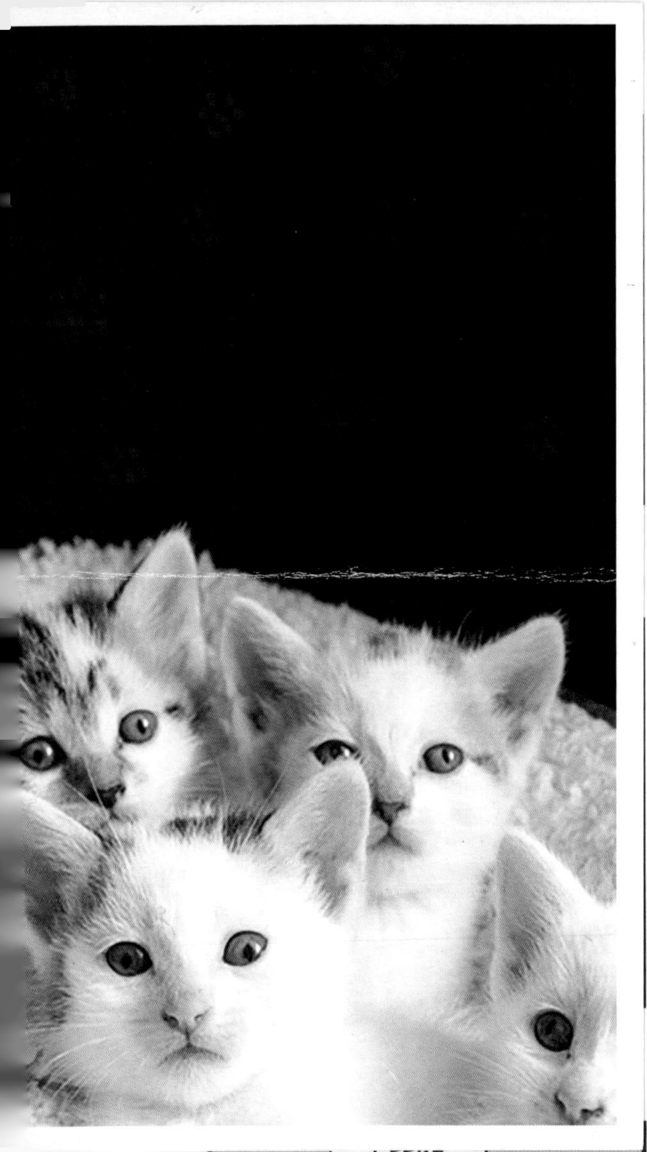

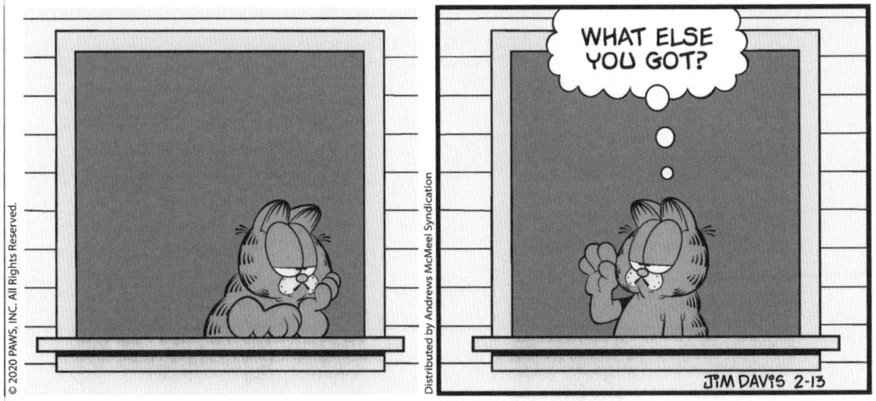
© 2020 PAWS, INC. All Rights Reserved.
Distributed by Andrews McMeel Syndication
WHAT ELSE YOU GOT?
JIM DAVIS 2-13

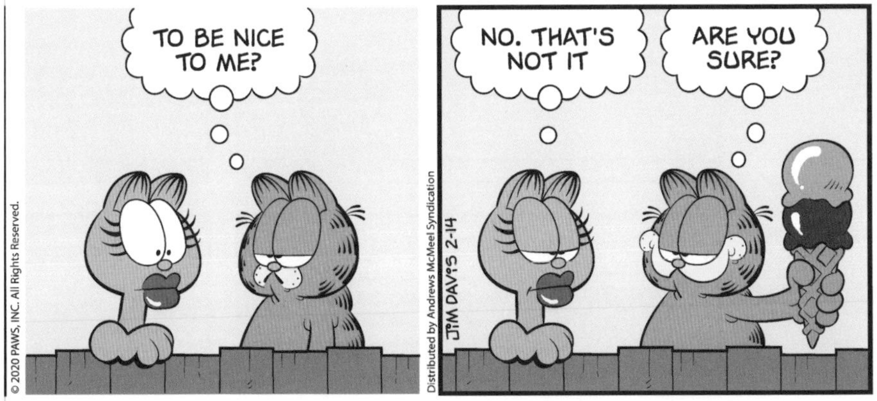
© 2020 PAWS, INC. All Rights Reserved.
TO BE NICE TO ME?
Distributed by Andrews McMeel Syndication
JIM DAVIS 2-14
NO. THAT'S NOT IT
ARE YOU SURE?

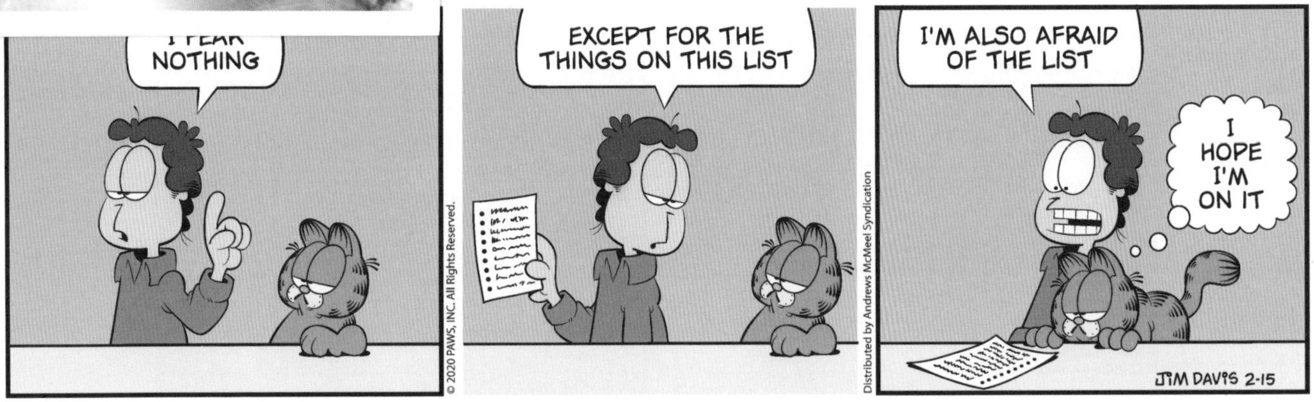
NOTHING
© 2020 PAWS, INC. All Rights Reserved.
EXCEPT FOR THE THINGS ON THIS LIST
Distributed by Andrews McMeel Syndication
I'M ALSO AFRAID OF THE LIST
I HOPE I'M ON IT
JIM DAVIS 2-15

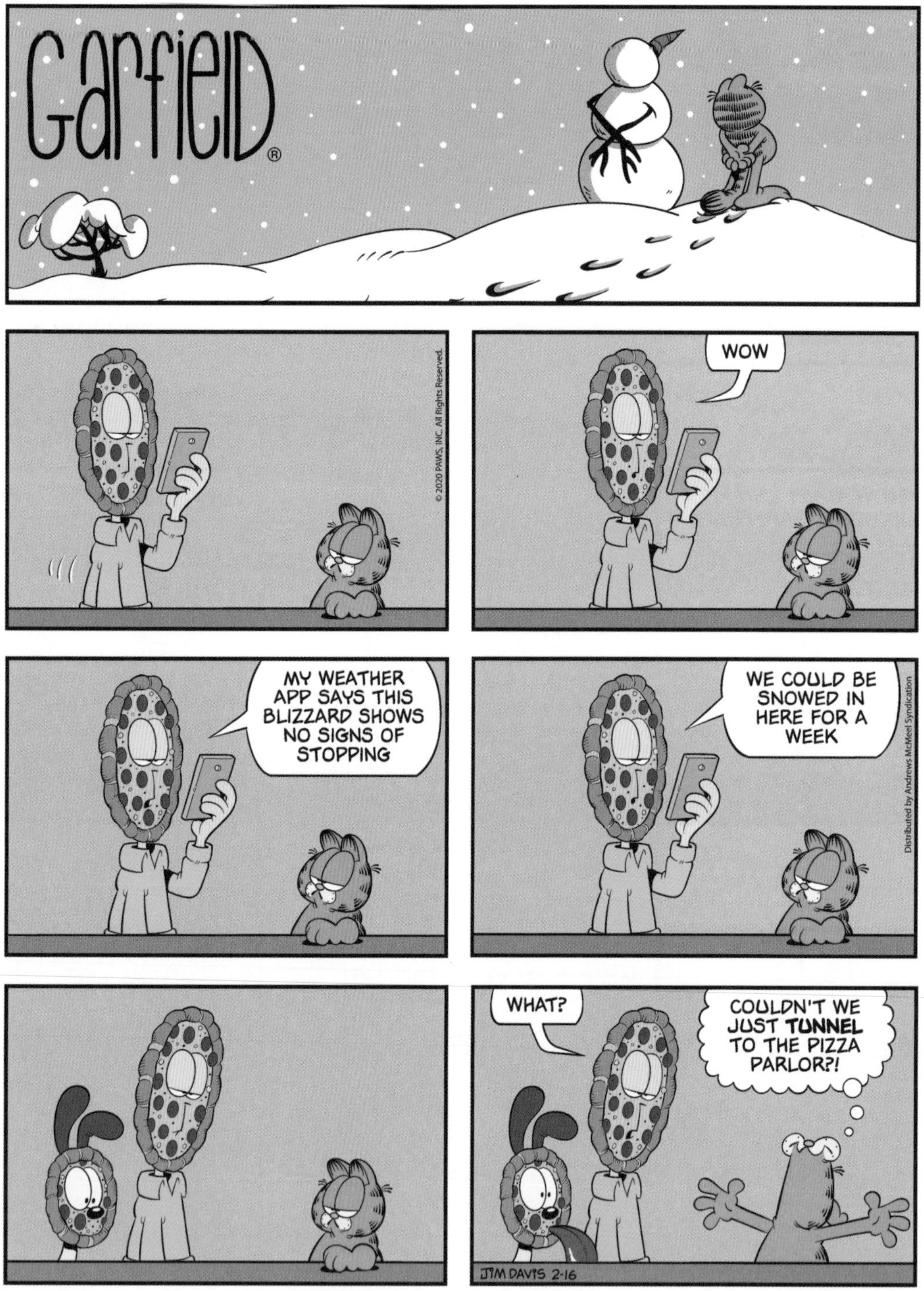
GARFIELD®
© 2020 PAWS, INC. All Rights Reserved.
WOW
MY WEATHER APP SAYS THIS BLIZZARD SHOWS NO SIGNS OF STOPPING
WE COULD BE SNOWED IN HERE FOR A WEEK
Distributed by Andrews McMeel Syndication
WHAT?
COULDN'T WE JUST **TUNNEL** TO THE PIZZA PARLOR?!
JIM DAVIS 2-16

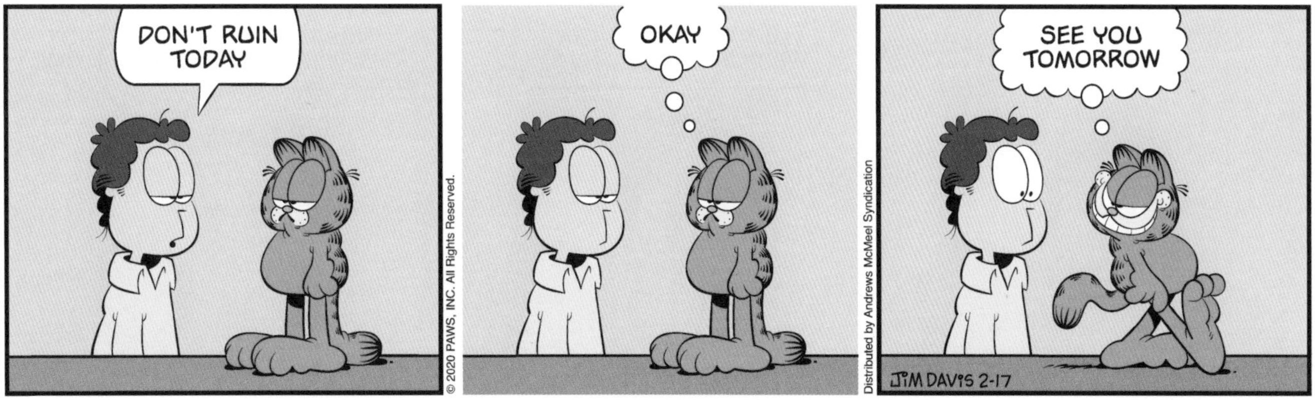
DON'T RUIN TODAY
OKAY
SEE YOU TOMORROW
© 2020 PAWS, INC. All Rights Reserved.
Distributed by Andrews McMeel Syndication
JIM DAVIS 2-17

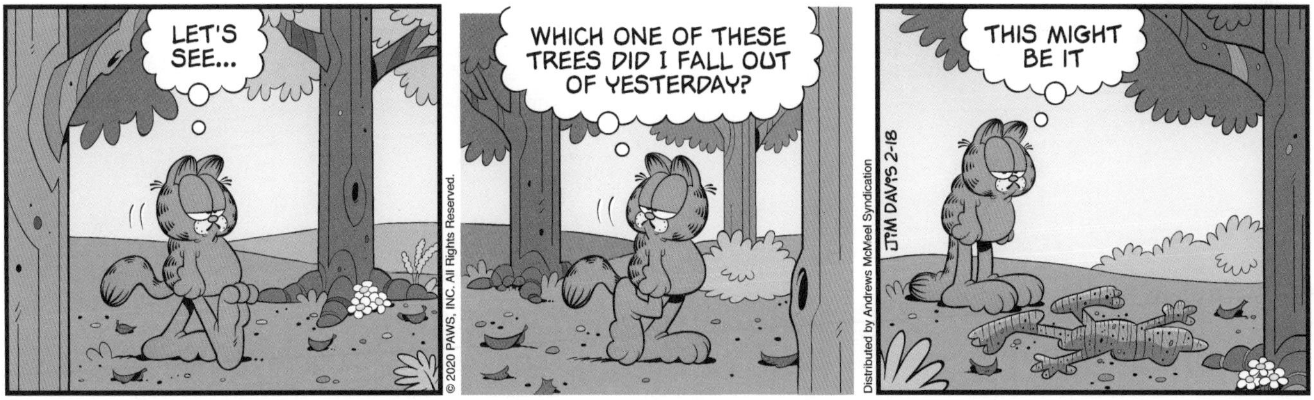
LET'S SEE...
WHICH ONE OF THESE TREES DID I FALL OUT OF YESTERDAY?
THIS MIGHT BE IT
© 2020 PAWS, INC. All Rights Reserved.
Distributed by Andrews McMeel Syndication
JIM DAVIS 2-18

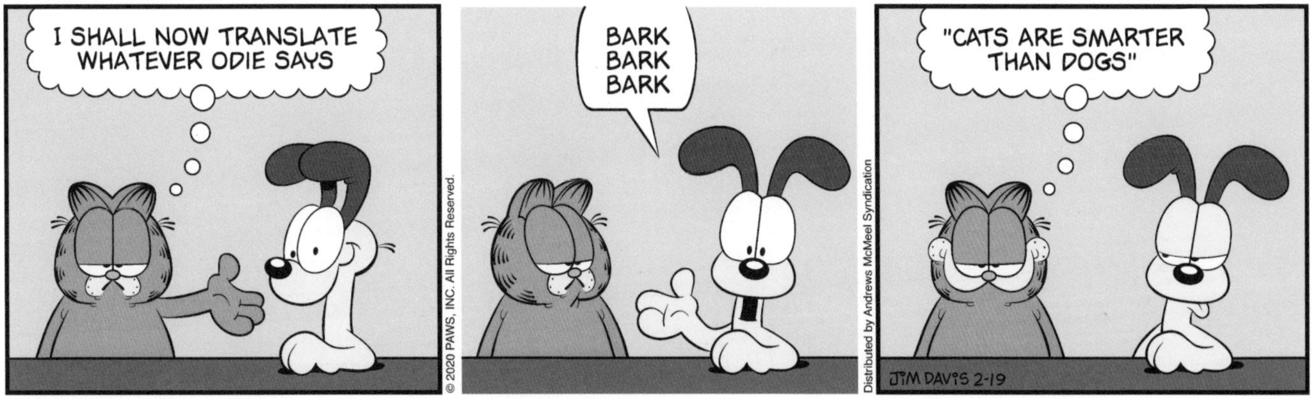
I SHALL NOW TRANSLATE WHATEVER ODIE SAYS
BARK
BARK
BARK
"CATS ARE SMARTER THAN DOGS"
© 2020 PAWS, INC. All Rights Reserved.
Distributed by Andrews McMeel Syndication
JIM DAVIS 2-19

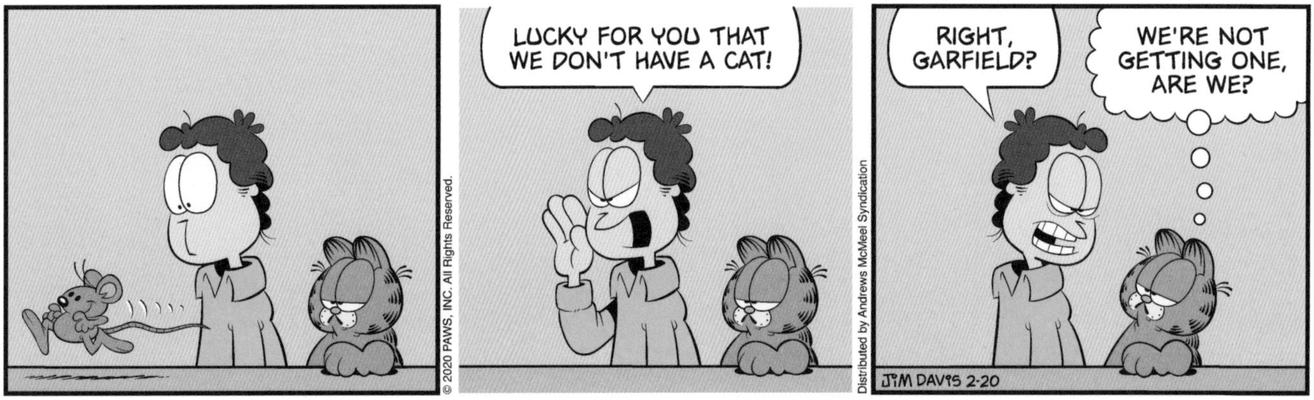
LUCKY FOR YOU THAT WE DON'T HAVE A CAT!
© 2020 PAWS, INC. All Rights Reserved.
RIGHT, GARFIELD?
WE'RE NOT GETTING ONE, ARE WE?
Distributed by Andrews McMeel Syndication
JIM DAVIS 2-20

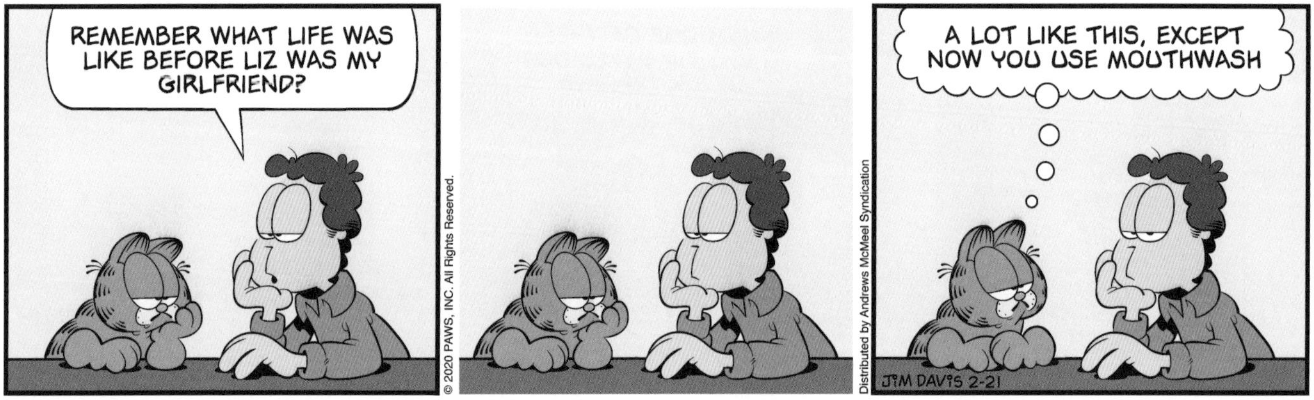
REMEMBER WHAT LIFE WAS LIKE BEFORE LIZ WAS MY GIRLFRIEND?
© 2020 PAWS, INC. All Rights Reserved.
A LOT LIKE THIS, EXCEPT NOW YOU USE MOUTHWASH
Distributed by Andrews McMeel Syndication
JIM DAVIS 2-21

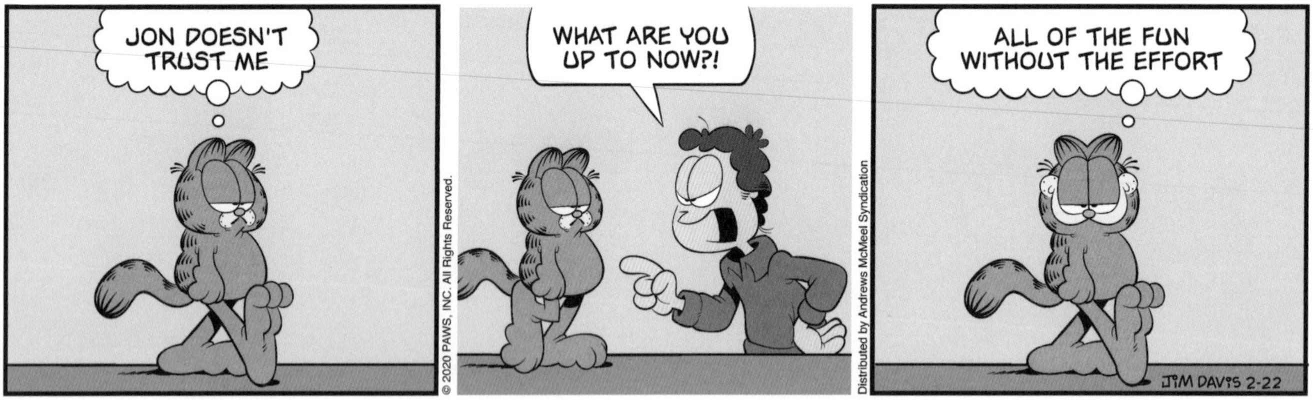
JON DOESN'T TRUST ME
© 2020 PAWS, INC. All Rights Reserved.
WHAT ARE YOU UP TO NOW?!
Distributed by Andrews McMeel Syndication
ALL OF THE FUN WITHOUT THE EFFORT
JIM DAVIS 2-22

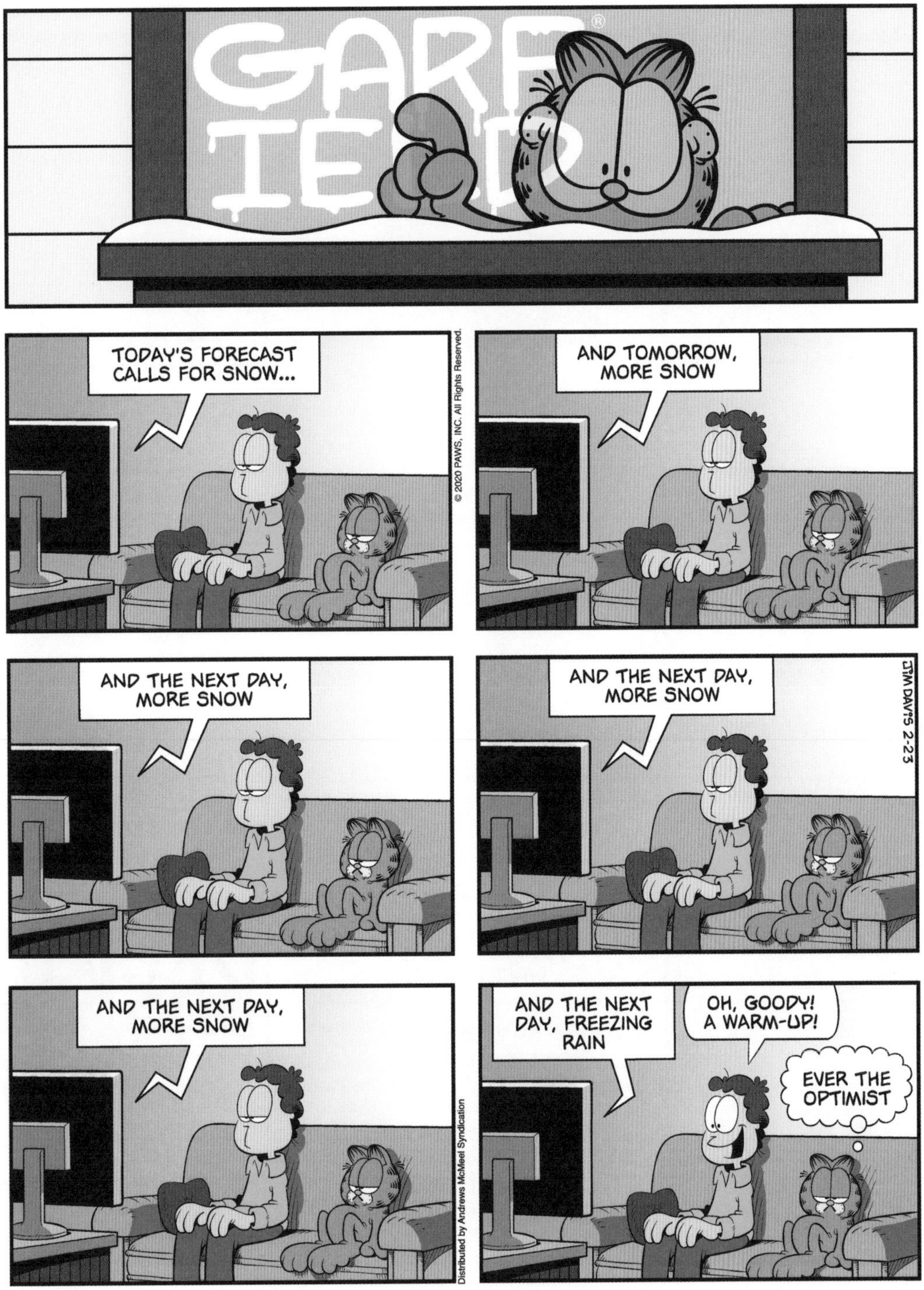

TODAY'S FORECAST CALLS FOR SNOW...
© 2020 PAWS, INC. All Rights Reserved.
AND TOMORROW, MORE SNOW
AND THE NEXT DAY, MORE SNOW
AND THE NEXT DAY, MORE SNOW
JIM DAVIS 2-23
AND THE NEXT DAY, MORE SNOW
Distributed by Andrews McMeel Syndication
AND THE NEXT DAY, FREEZING RAIN
OH, GOODY! A WARM-UP!
EVER THE OPTIMIST

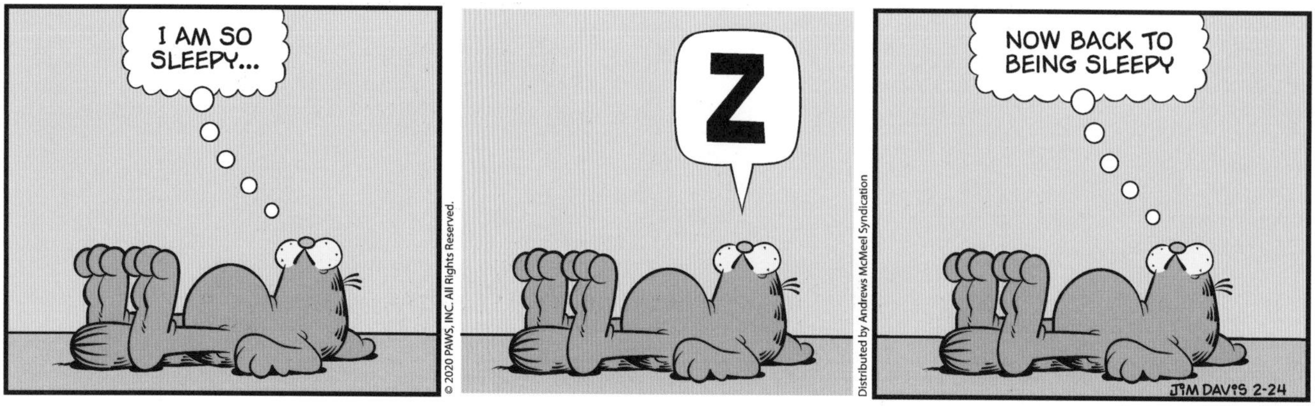
I AM SO SLEEPY...
Z
NOW BACK TO BEING SLEEPY
JIM DAVIS 2-24
© 2020 PAWS, INC. All Rights Reserved.
Distributed by Andrews McMeel Syndication

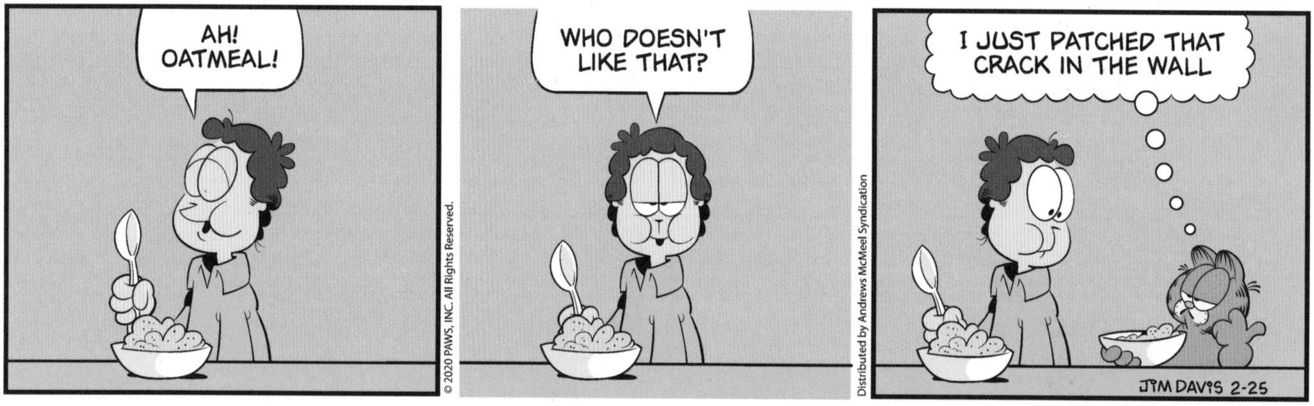
AH! OATMEAL!
WHO DOESN'T LIKE THAT?
I JUST PATCHED THAT CRACK IN THE WALL
JIM DAVIS 2-25
© 2020 PAWS, INC. All Rights Reserved.
Distributed by Andrews McMeel Syndication

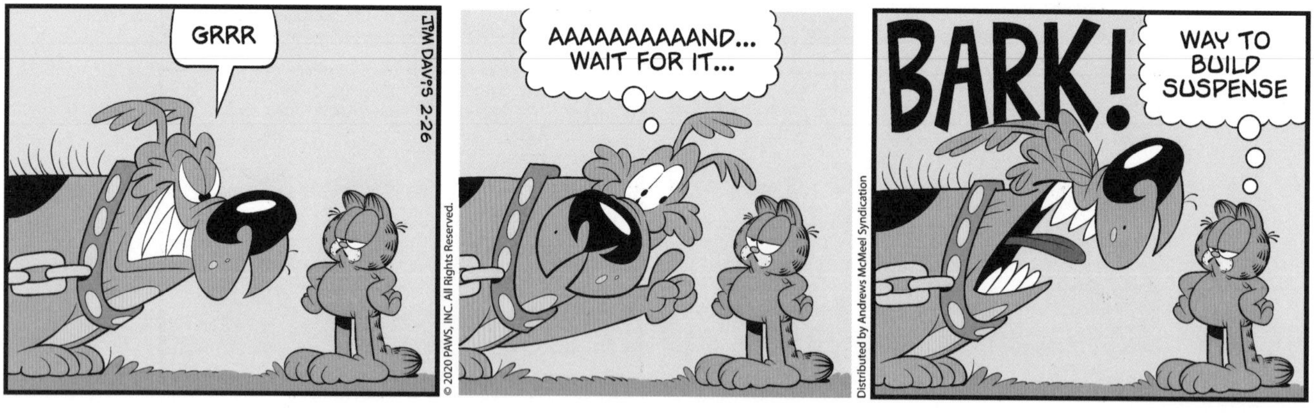
GRRR
JIM DAVIS 2-26
AAAAAAAAAAND... WAIT FOR IT...
BARK!
WAY TO BUILD SUSPENSE
© 2020 PAWS, INC. All Rights Reserved.
Distributed by Andrews McMeel Syndication

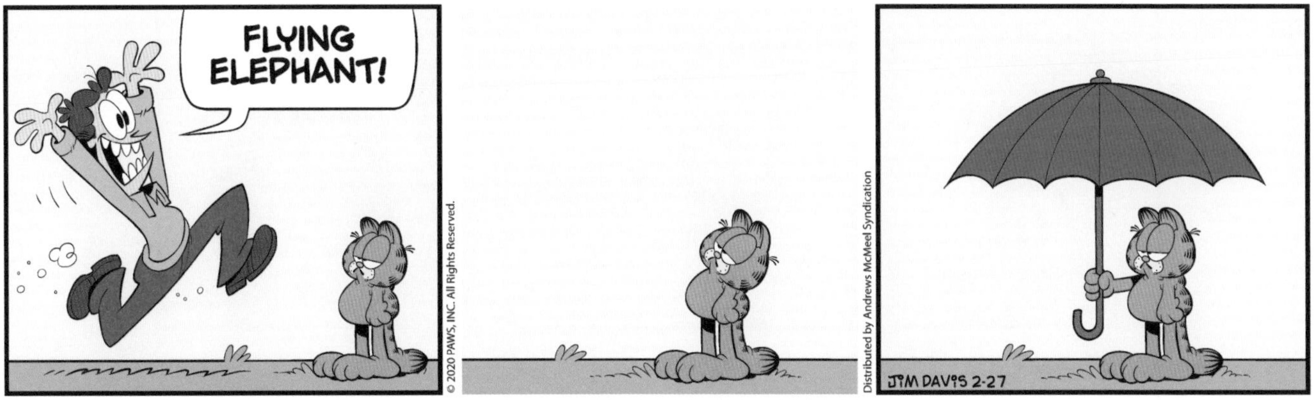
FLYING ELEPHANT!
© 2020 PAWS, INC. All Rights Reserved.
Distributed by Andrews McMeel Syndication
JIM DAVIS 2-27

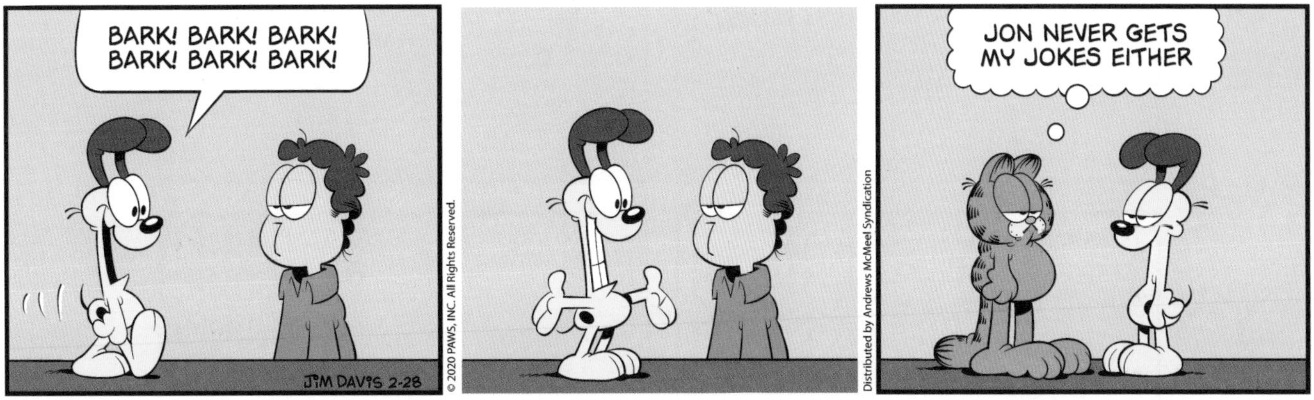
BARK! BARK! BARK! BARK! BARK! BARK!
JIM DAVIS 2-28
© 2020 PAWS, INC. All Rights Reserved.
Distributed by Andrews McMeel Syndication
JON NEVER GETS MY JOKES EITHER

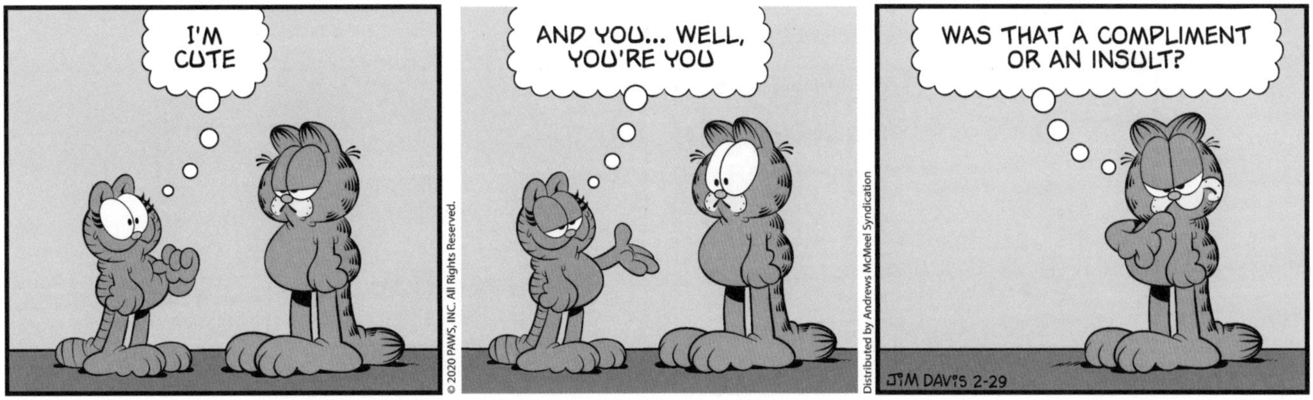
I'M CUTE
© 2020 PAWS, INC. All Rights Reserved.
AND YOU... WELL, YOU'RE YOU
Distributed by Andrews McMeel Syndication
WAS THAT A COMPLIMENT OR AN INSULT?
JIM DAVIS 2-29

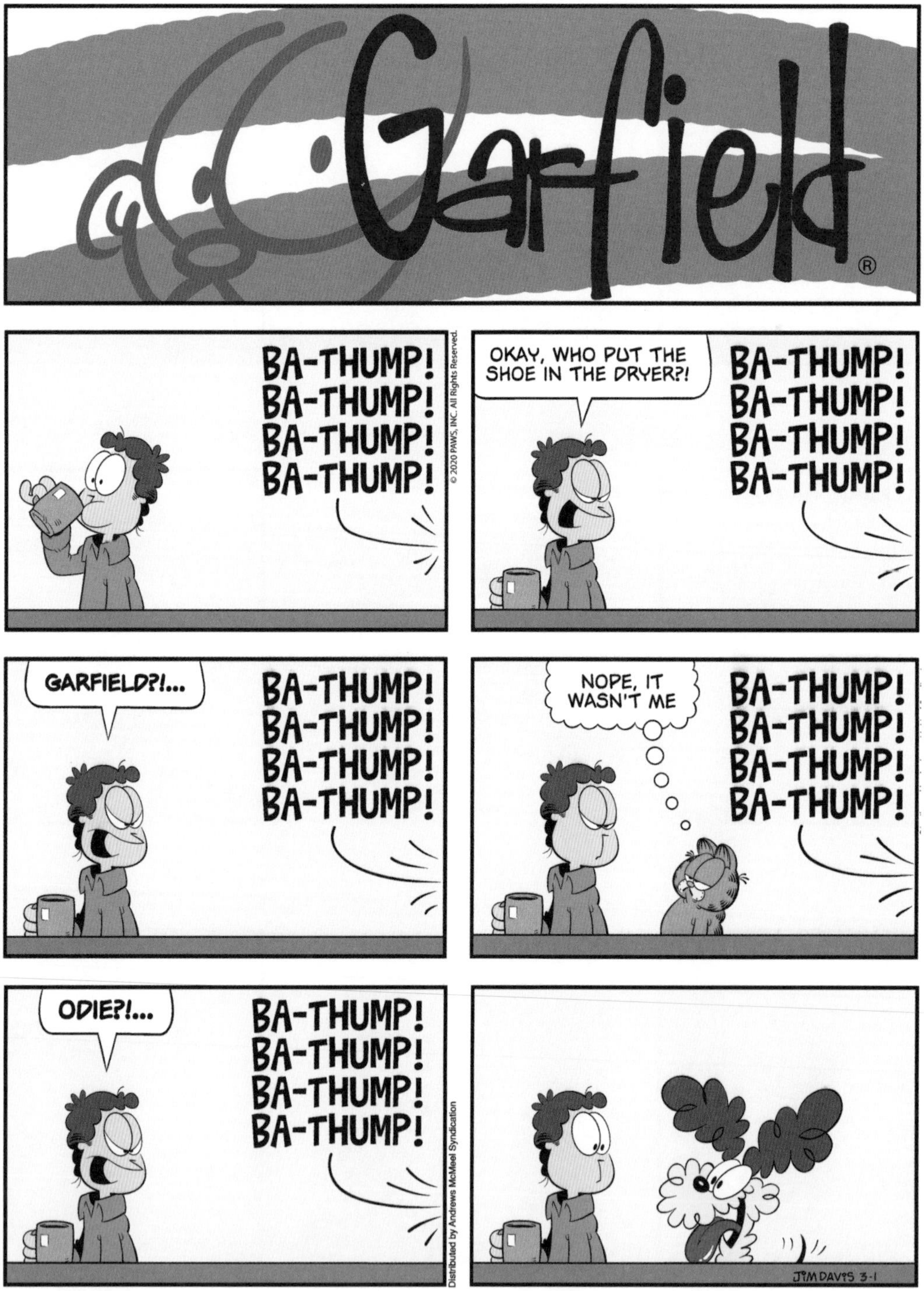
Garfield®
© 2020 PAWS, INC. All Rights Reserved.
BA-THUMP! BA-THUMP! BA-THUMP! BA-THUMP!
OKAY, WHO PUT THE SHOE IN THE DRYER?!
BA-THUMP! BA-THUMP! BA-THUMP! BA-THUMP!
GARFIELD?!...
BA-THUMP! BA-THUMP! BA-THUMP! BA-THUMP!
NOPE, IT WASN'T ME
BA-THUMP! BA-THUMP! BA-THUMP! BA-THUMP!
ODIE?!...
BA-THUMP! BA-THUMP! BA-THUMP! BA-THUMP!
Distributed by Andrews McMeel Syndication
JIM DAVIS 3-1

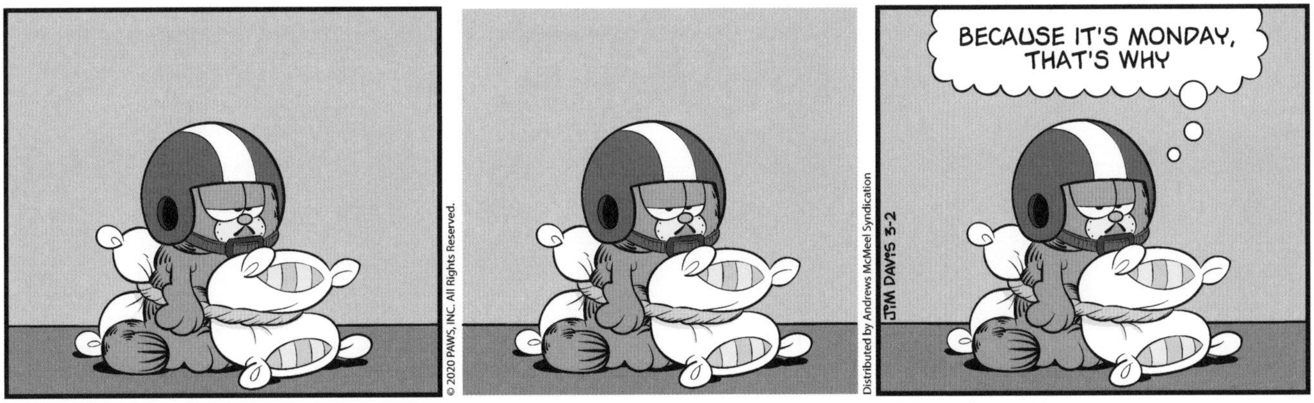
© 2020 PAWS, INC. All Rights Reserved.
Distributed by Andrews McMeel Syndication
JIM DAVIS 3-2
BECAUSE IT'S MONDAY, THAT'S WHY

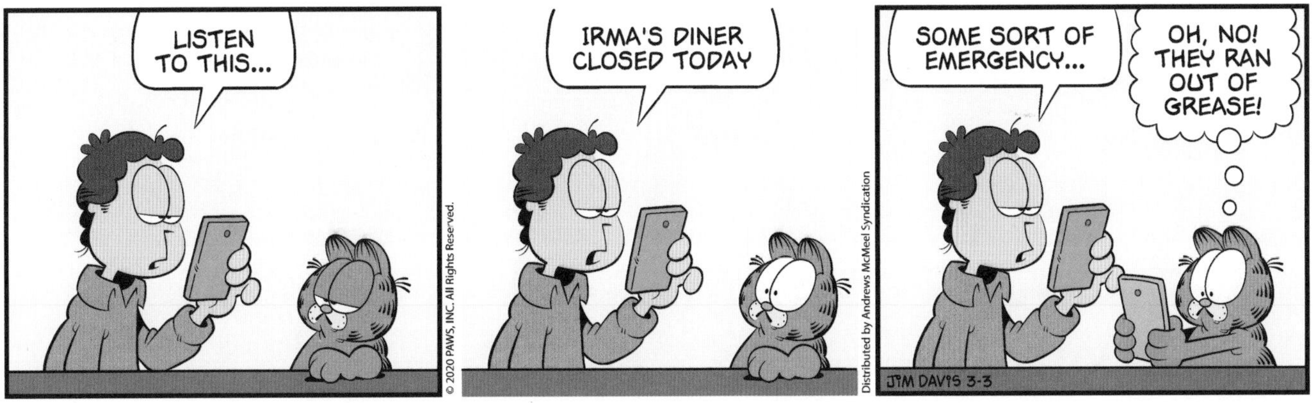
LISTEN TO THIS...
© 2020 PAWS, INC. All Rights Reserved.
IRMA'S DINER CLOSED TODAY
Distributed by Andrews McMeel Syndication
SOME SORT OF EMERGENCY...
OH, NO! THEY RAN OUT OF GREASE!
JIM DAVIS 3-3

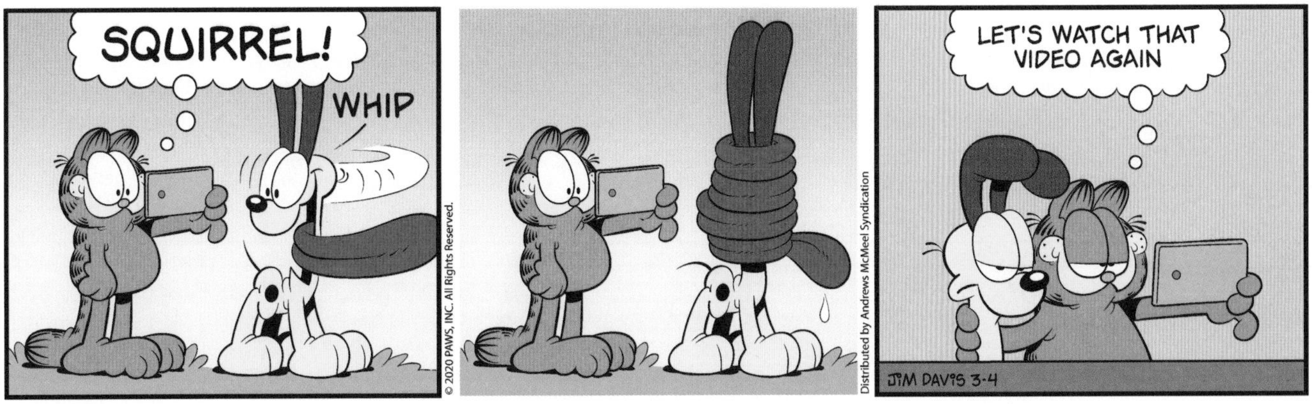
SQUIRREL!
WHIP
© 2020 PAWS, INC. All Rights Reserved.
Distributed by Andrews McMeel Syndication
LET'S WATCH THAT VIDEO AGAIN
JIM DAVIS 3-4

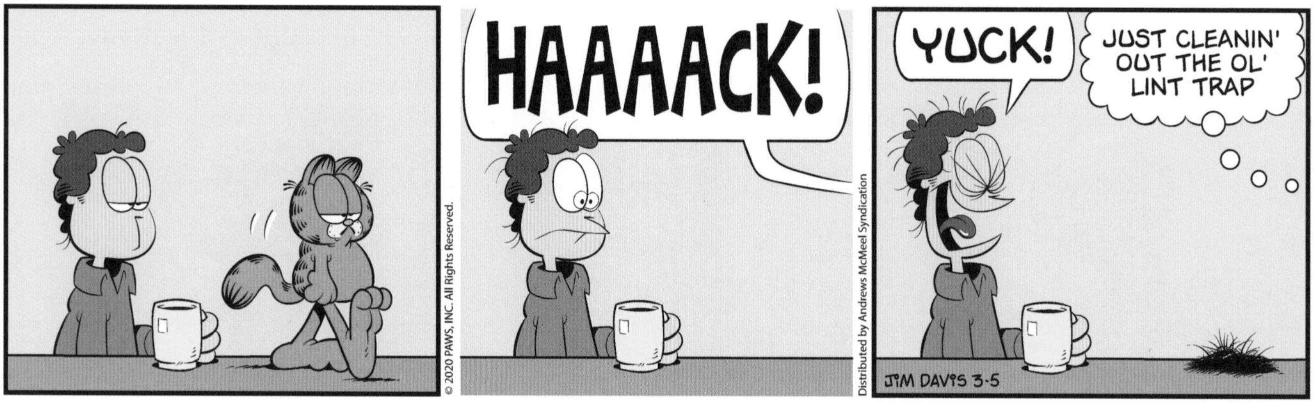
HAAAACK!
YUCK!
JUST CLEANIN' OUT THE OL' LINT TRAP
© 2020 PAWS, INC. All Rights Reserved.
Distributed by Andrews McMeel Syndication
JIM DAVIS 3-5

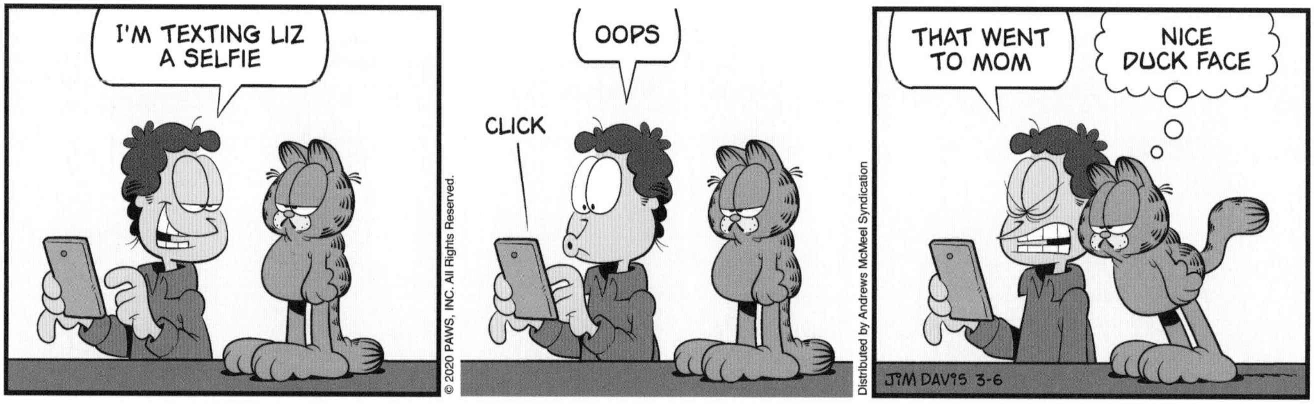
I'M TEXTING LIZ A SELFIE
CLICK
OOPS
THAT WENT TO MOM
NICE DUCK FACE
© 2020 PAWS, INC. All Rights Reserved.
Distributed by Andrews McMeel Syndication
JIM DAVIS 3-6

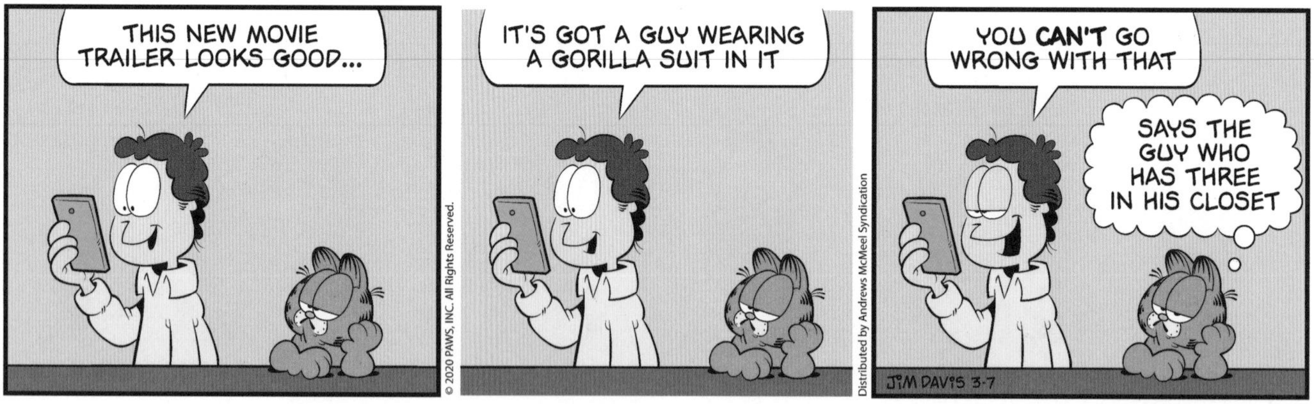
THIS NEW MOVIE TRAILER LOOKS GOOD...
IT'S GOT A GUY WEARING A GORILLA SUIT IN IT
YOU CAN'T GO WRONG WITH THAT
SAYS THE GUY WHO HAS THREE IN HIS CLOSET
© 2020 PAWS, INC. All Rights Reserved.
Distributed by Andrews McMeel Syndication
JIM DAVIS 3-7

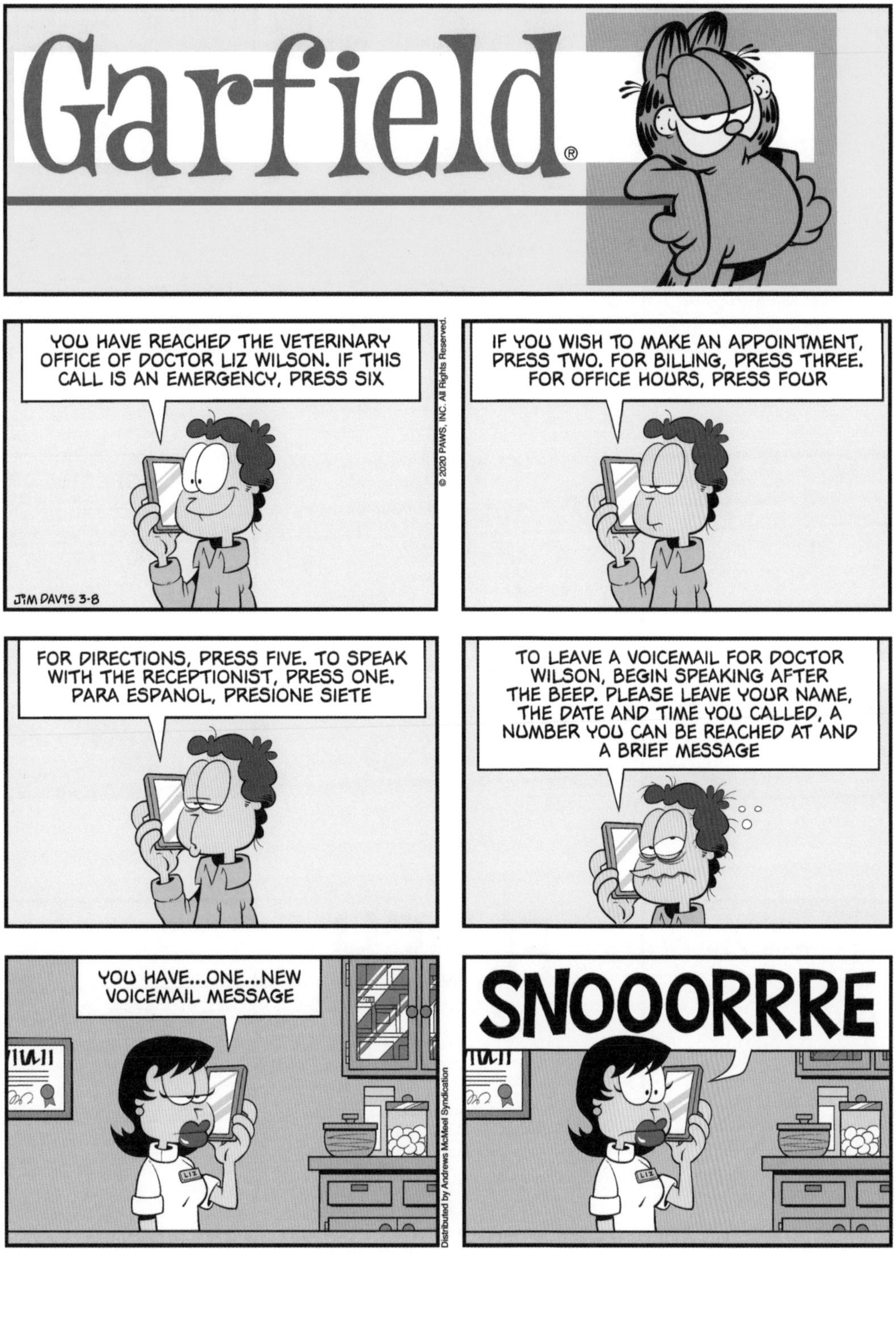
Garfield®
YOU HAVE REACHED THE VETERINARY OFFICE OF DOCTOR LIZ WILSON. IF THIS CALL IS AN EMERGENCY, PRESS SIX
JIM DAVIS 3-8
© 2020 PAWS, INC. All Rights Reserved.
IF YOU WISH TO MAKE AN APPOINTMENT, PRESS TWO. FOR BILLING, PRESS THREE. FOR OFFICE HOURS, PRESS FOUR
FOR DIRECTIONS, PRESS FIVE. TO SPEAK WITH THE RECEPTIONIST, PRESS ONE. PARA ESPANOL, PRESIONE SIETE
TO LEAVE A VOICEMAIL FOR DOCTOR WILSON, BEGIN SPEAKING AFTER THE BEEP. PLEASE LEAVE YOUR NAME, THE DATE AND TIME YOU CALLED, A NUMBER YOU CAN BE REACHED AT AND A BRIEF MESSAGE
YOU HAVE...ONE...NEW VOICEMAIL MESSAGE
Distributed by Andrews McMeel Syndication
LIZ
SNOOORRRE

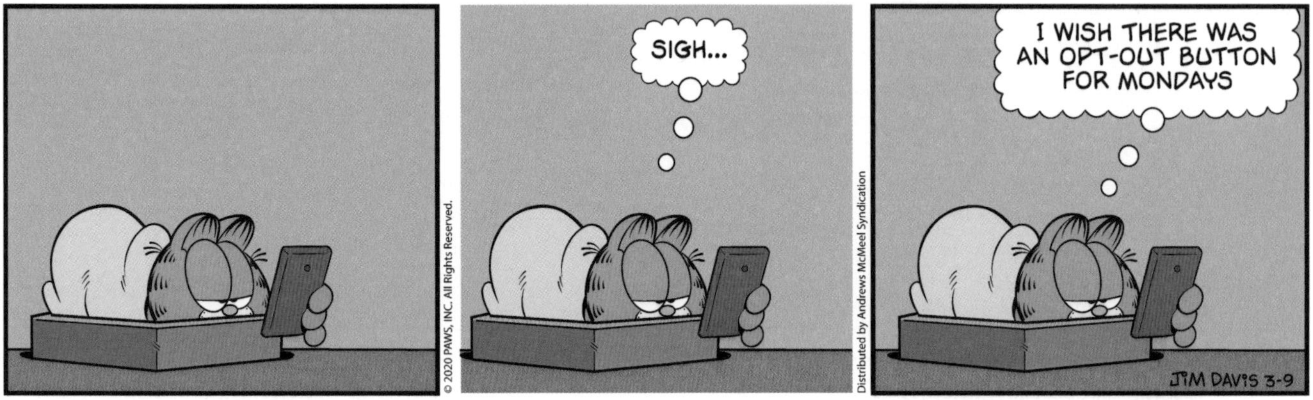
SIGH...
I WISH THERE WAS AN OPT-OUT BUTTON FOR MONDAYS
© 2020 PAWS, INC. All Rights Reserved.
Distributed by Andrews McMeel Syndication
JIM DAVIS 3-9

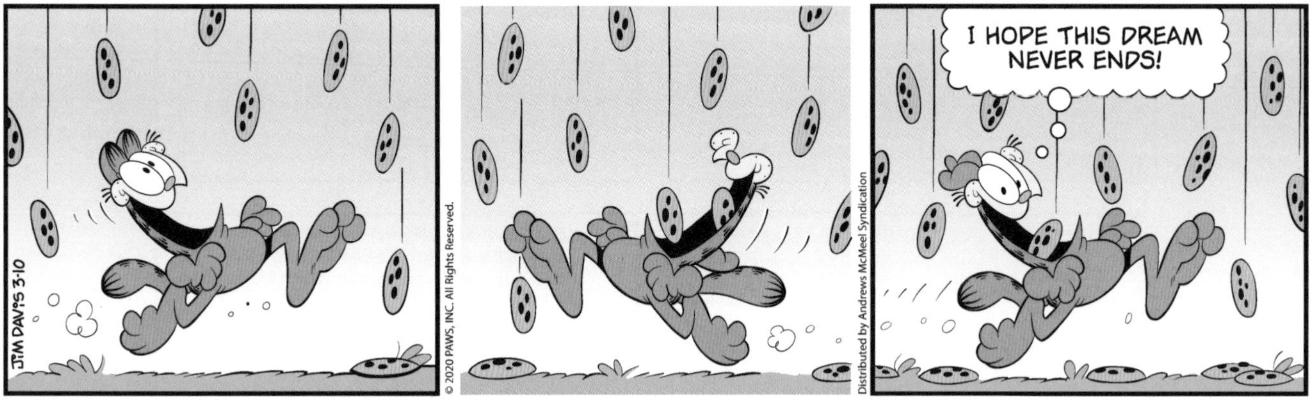
JIM DAVIS 3-10
I HOPE THIS DREAM NEVER ENDS!
© 2020 PAWS, INC. All Rights Reserved.
Distributed by Andrews McMeel Syndication

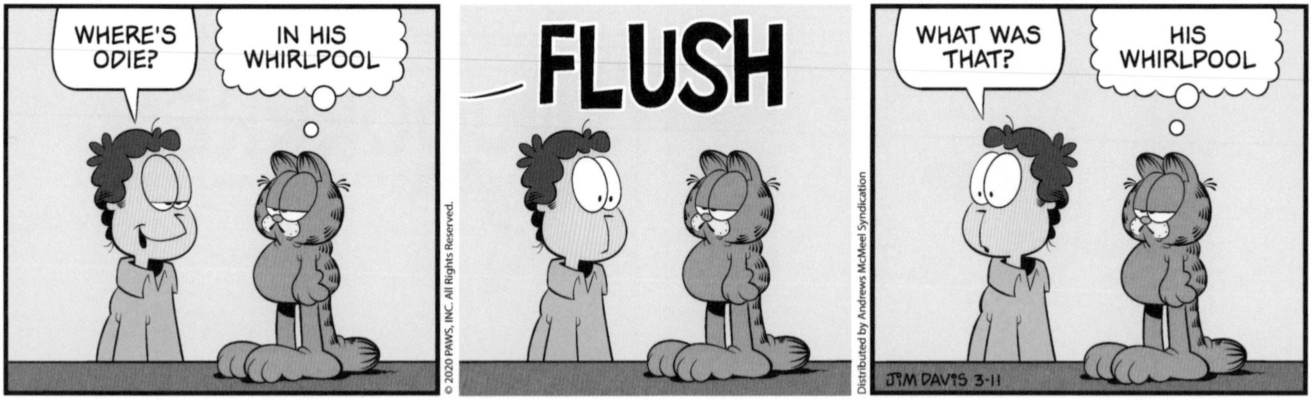
WHERE'S ODIE?
IN HIS WHIRLPOOL
FLUSH
WHAT WAS THAT?
HIS WHIRLPOOL
© 2020 PAWS, INC. All Rights Reserved.
Distributed by Andrews McMeel Syndication
JIM DAVIS 3-11

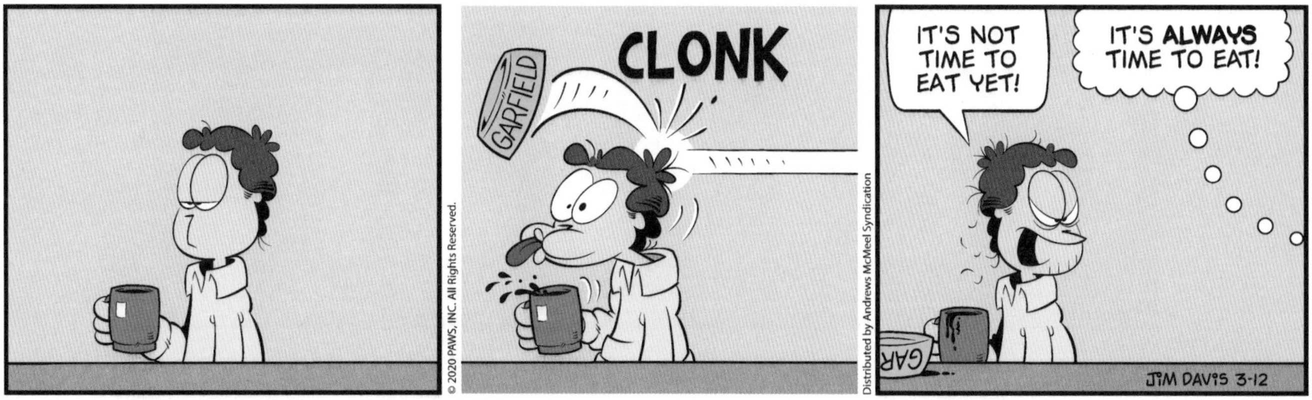
GARFIELD
CLONK
© 2020 PAWS, INC. All Rights Reserved.
IT'S NOT TIME TO EAT YET!
IT'S **ALWAYS** TIME TO EAT!
GAR
Distributed by Andrews McMeel Syndication
JIM DAVIS 3-12

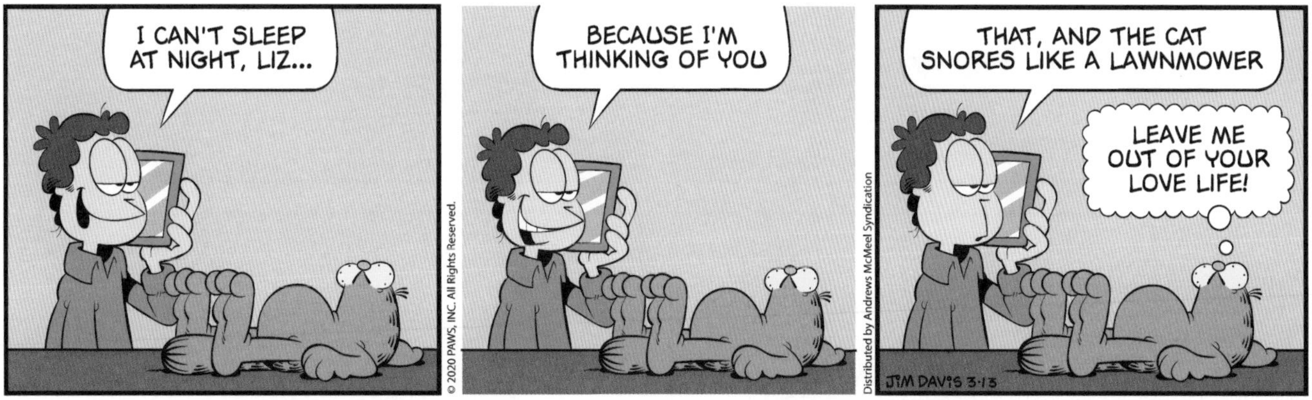
I CAN'T SLEEP AT NIGHT, LIZ...
© 2020 PAWS, INC. All Rights Reserved.
BECAUSE I'M THINKING OF YOU
THAT, AND THE CAT SNORES LIKE A LAWNMOWER
LEAVE ME OUT OF YOUR LOVE LIFE!
Distributed by Andrews McMeel Syndication
JIM DAVIS 3-13

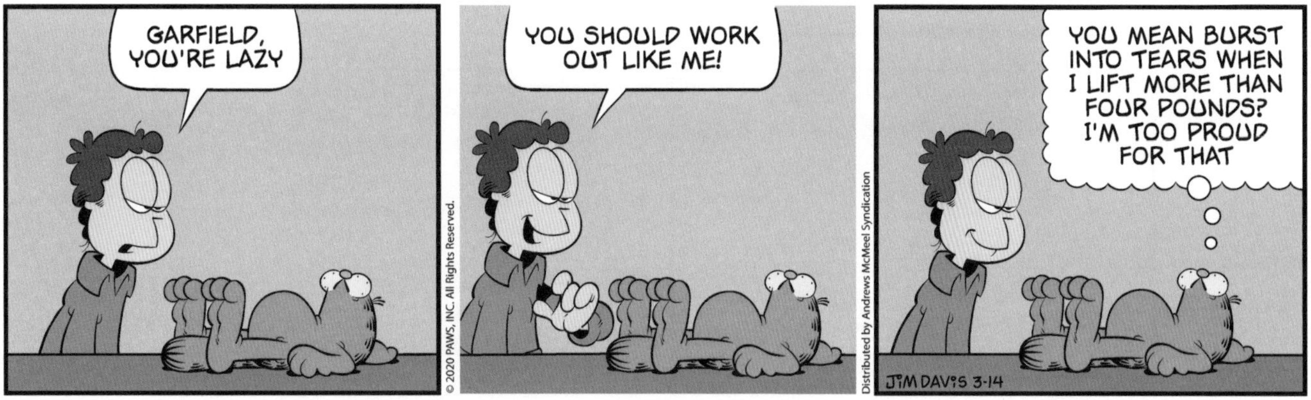
GARFIELD, YOU'RE LAZY
© 2020 PAWS, INC. All Rights Reserved.
YOU SHOULD WORK OUT LIKE ME!
YOU MEAN BURST INTO TEARS WHEN I LIFT MORE THAN FOUR POUNDS? I'M TOO PROUD FOR THAT
Distributed by Andrews McMeel Syndication
JIM DAVIS 3-14

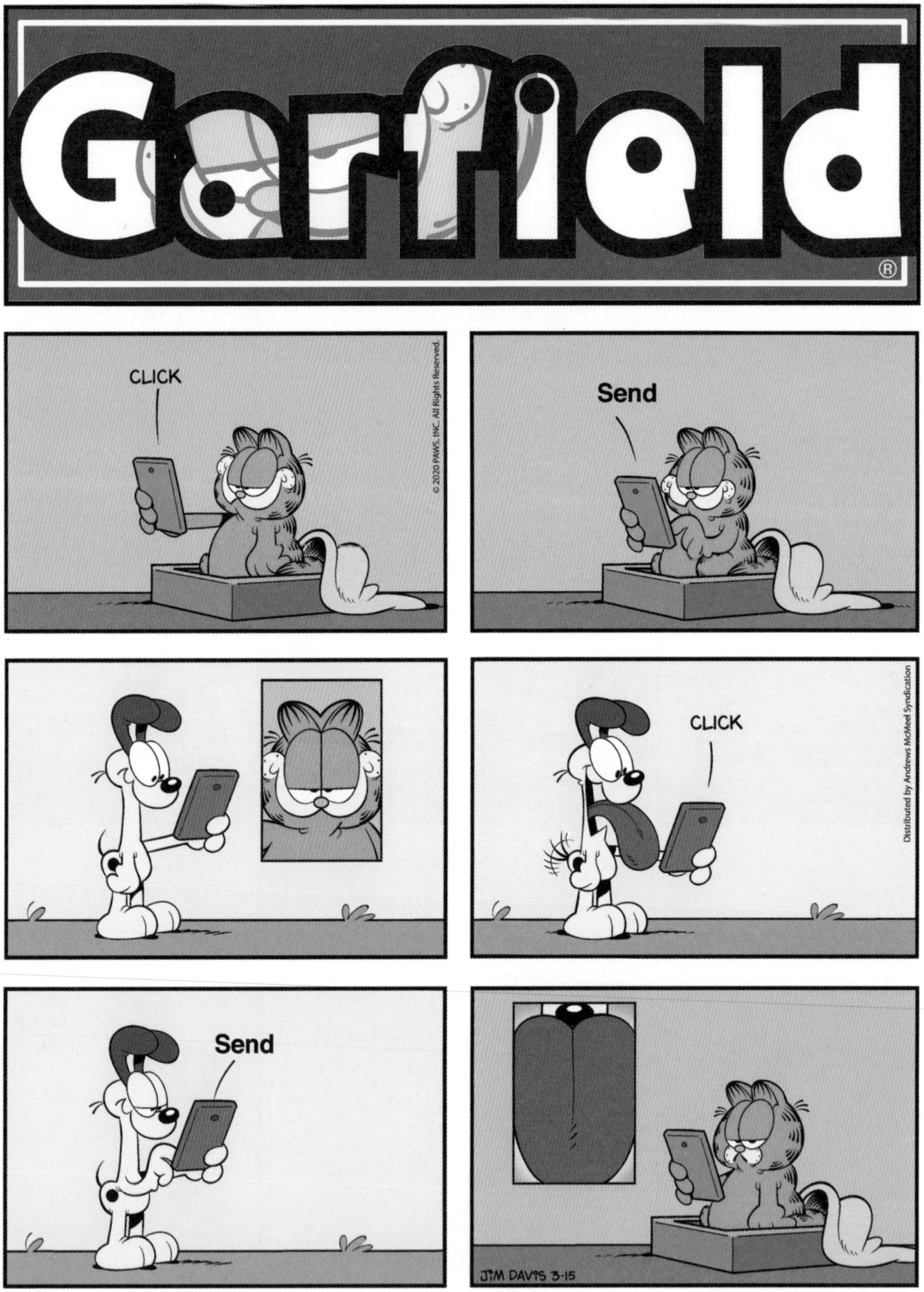
Garfield
CLICK
Send
CLICK
Send
JIM DAVIS 3-15

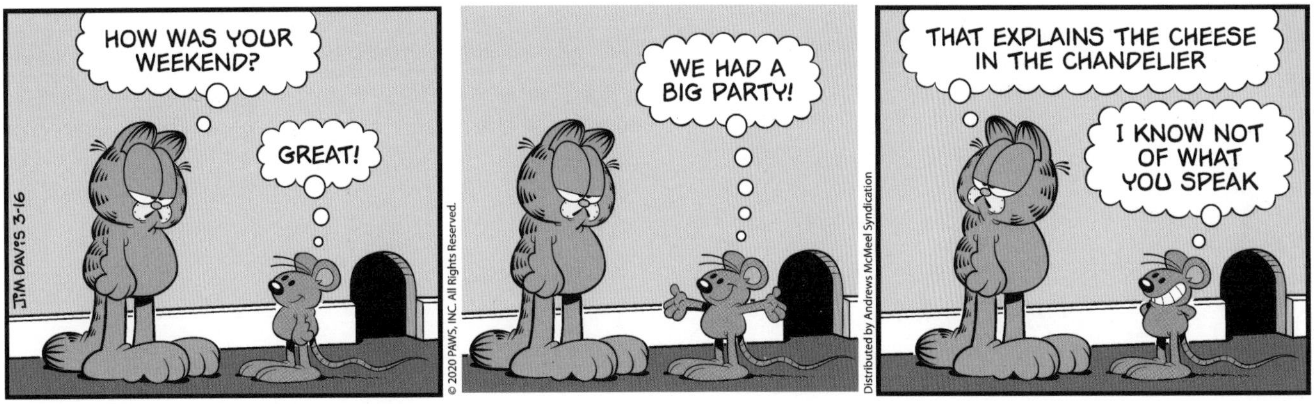
HOW WAS YOUR WEEKEND?
GREAT!
JIM DAVIS 3-16
© 2020 PAWS, INC. All Rights Reserved.
WE HAD A BIG PARTY!
Distributed by Andrews McMeel Syndication
THAT EXPLAINS THE CHEESE IN THE CHANDELIER
I KNOW NOT OF WHAT YOU SPEAK

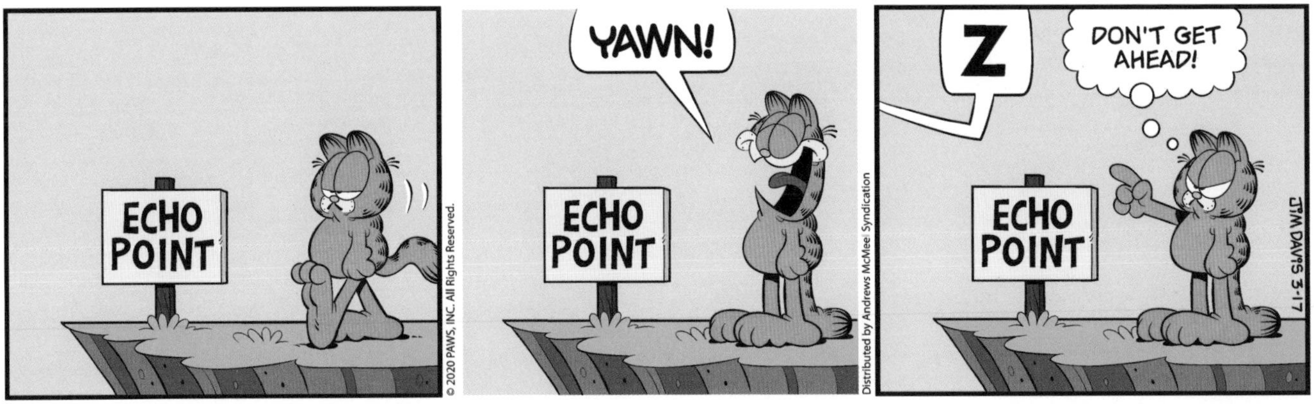
ECHO POINT
© 2020 PAWS, INC. All Rights Reserved.
YAWN!
ECHO POINT
Distributed by Andrews McMeel Syndication
Z
DON'T GET AHEAD!
ECHO POINT
JIM DAVIS 3-17

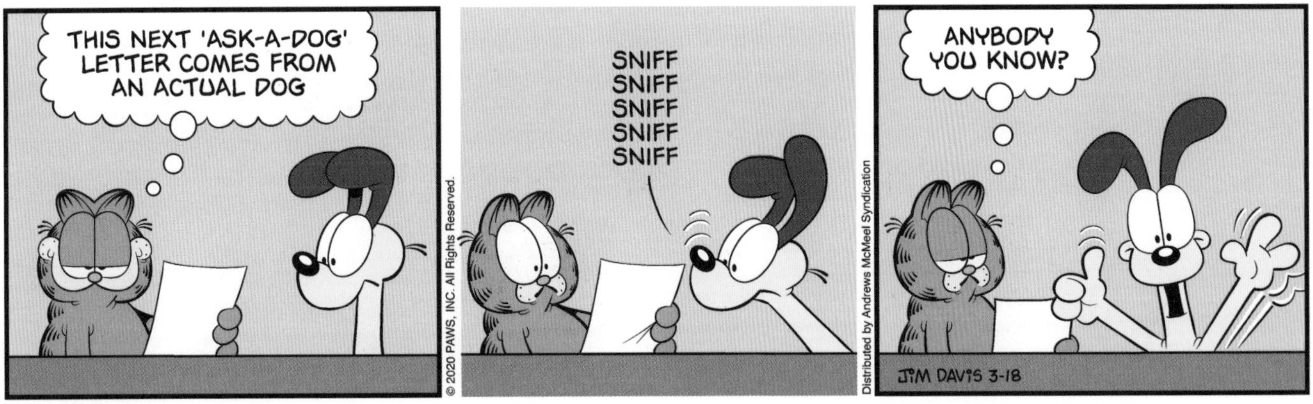
THIS NEXT 'ASK-A-DOG' LETTER COMES FROM AN ACTUAL DOG
© 2020 PAWS, INC. All Rights Reserved.
SNIFF SNIFF SNIFF SNIFF SNIFF
Distributed by Andrews McMeel Syndication
ANYBODY YOU KNOW?
JIM DAVIS 3-18

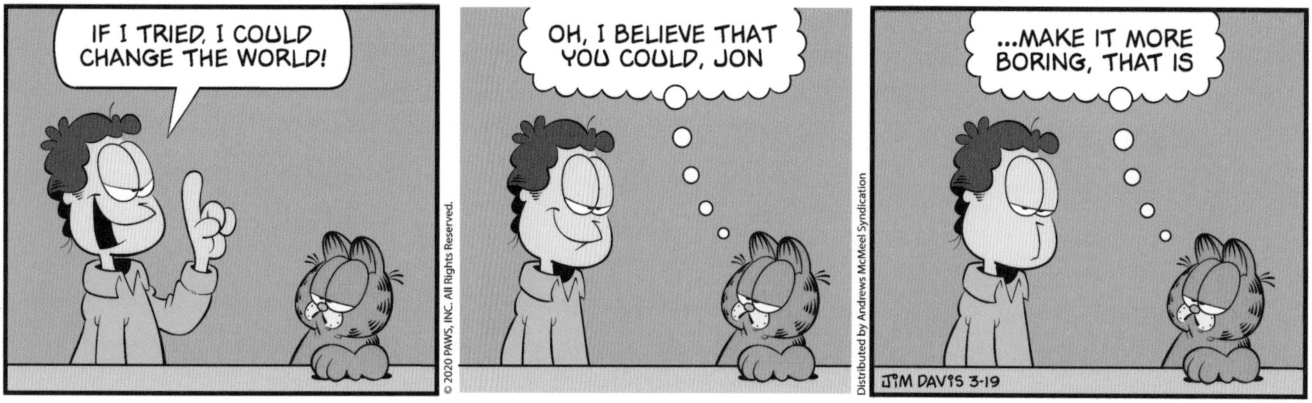
IF I TRIED, I COULD CHANGE THE WORLD!
OH, I BELIEVE THAT YOU COULD, JON
...MAKE IT MORE BORING, THAT IS
JIM DAVIS 3-19
© 2020 PAWS, INC. All Rights Reserved.
Distributed by Andrews McMeel Syndication

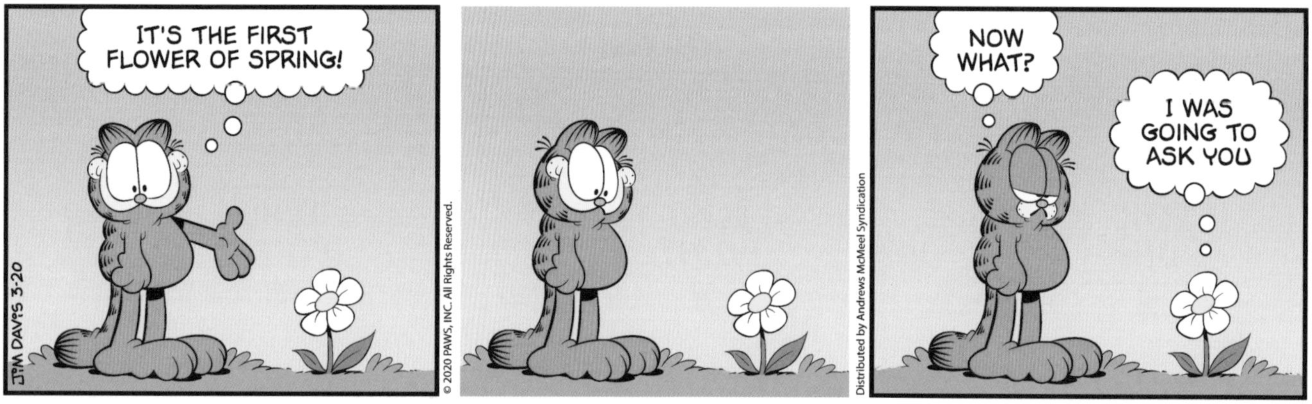
IT'S THE FIRST FLOWER OF SPRING!
NOW WHAT?
I WAS GOING TO ASK YOU
JIM DAVIS 3-20
© 2020 PAWS, INC. All Rights Reserved.
Distributed by Andrews McMeel Syndication

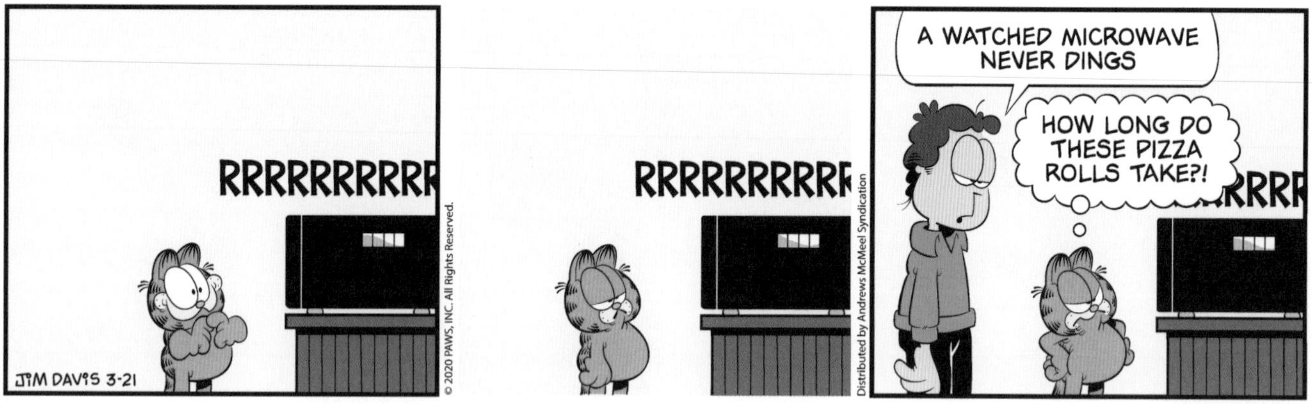
RRRRRRRRRR
RRRRRRRRRR
A WATCHED MICROWAVE NEVER DINGS
HOW LONG DO THESE PIZZA ROLLS TAKE?!
JIM DAVIS 3-21
© 2020 PAWS, INC. All Rights Reserved.
Distributed by Andrews McMeel Syndication

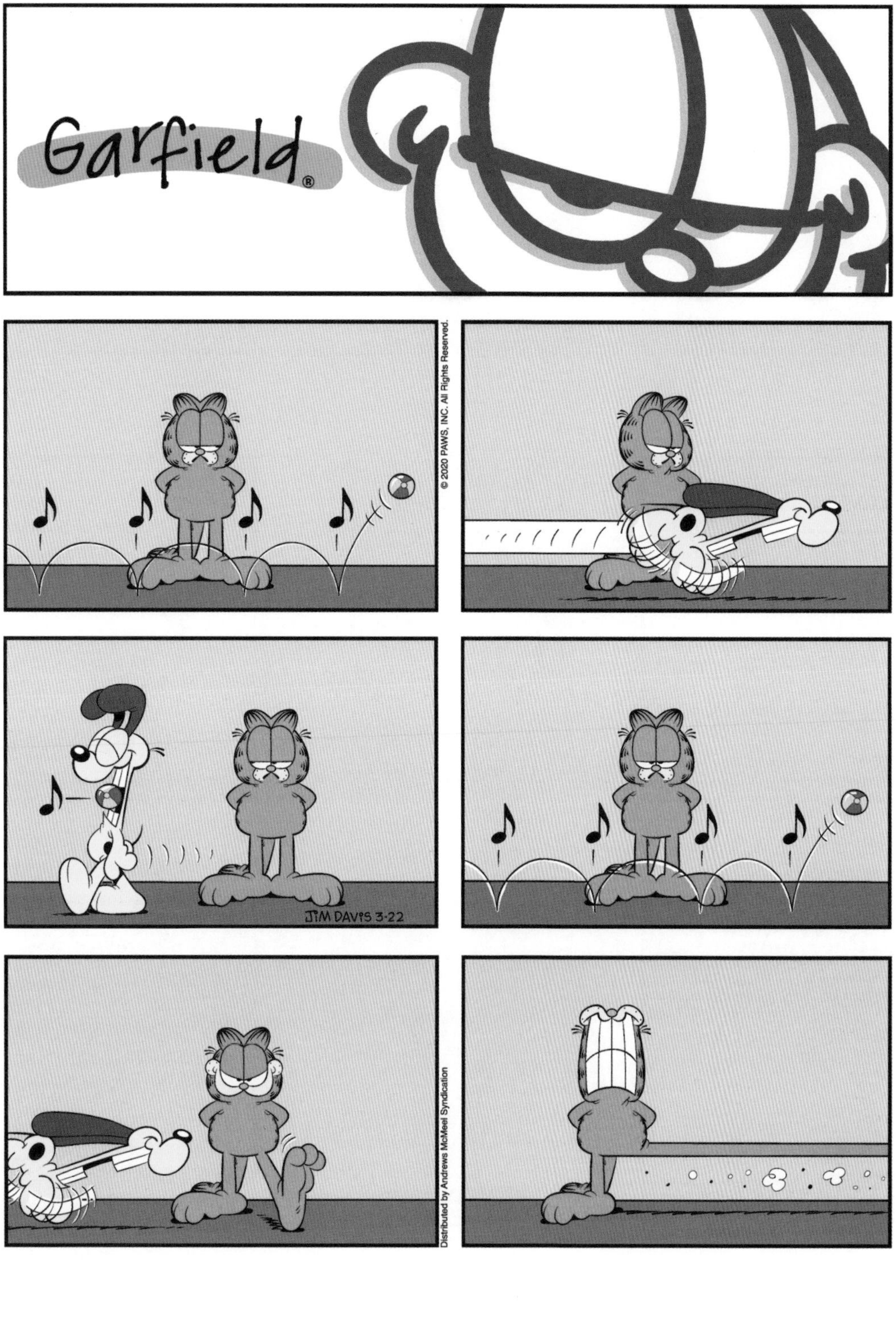
Garfield®
© 2020 PAWS, INC. All Rights Reserved.
JIM DAVIS 3-22
Distributed by Andrews McMeel Syndication

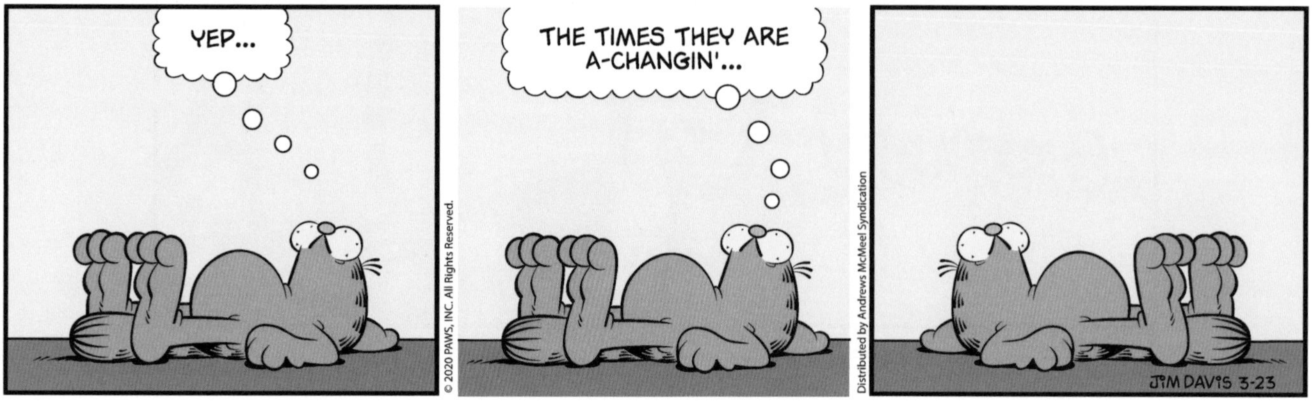
YEP...
THE TIMES THEY ARE A-CHANGIN'...
JIM DAVIS 3-23
© 2020 PAWS, INC. All Rights Reserved.
Distributed by Andrews McMeel Syndication

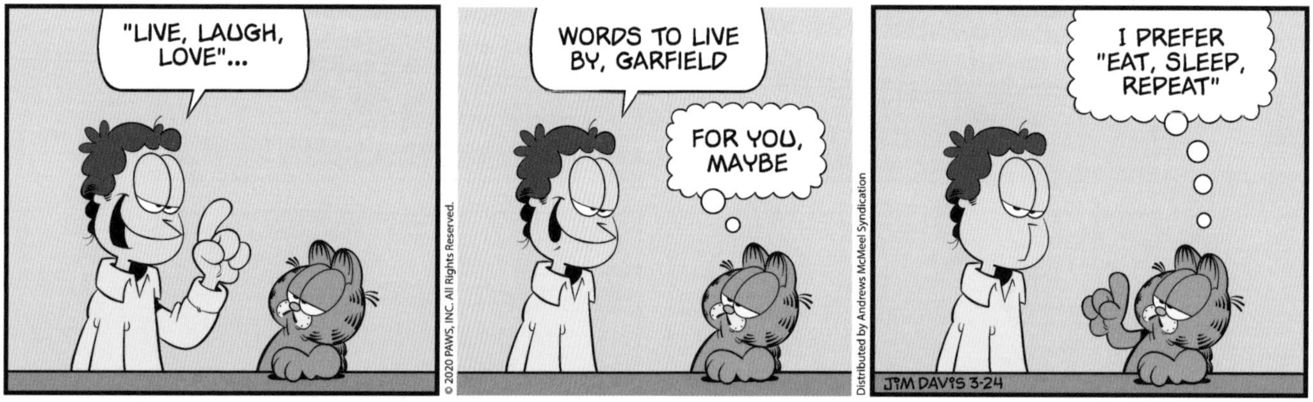
"LIVE, LAUGH, LOVE"...
WORDS TO LIVE BY, GARFIELD
FOR YOU, MAYBE
I PREFER "EAT, SLEEP, REPEAT"
JIM DAVIS 3-24
© 2020 PAWS, INC. All Rights Reserved.
Distributed by Andrews McMeel Syndication

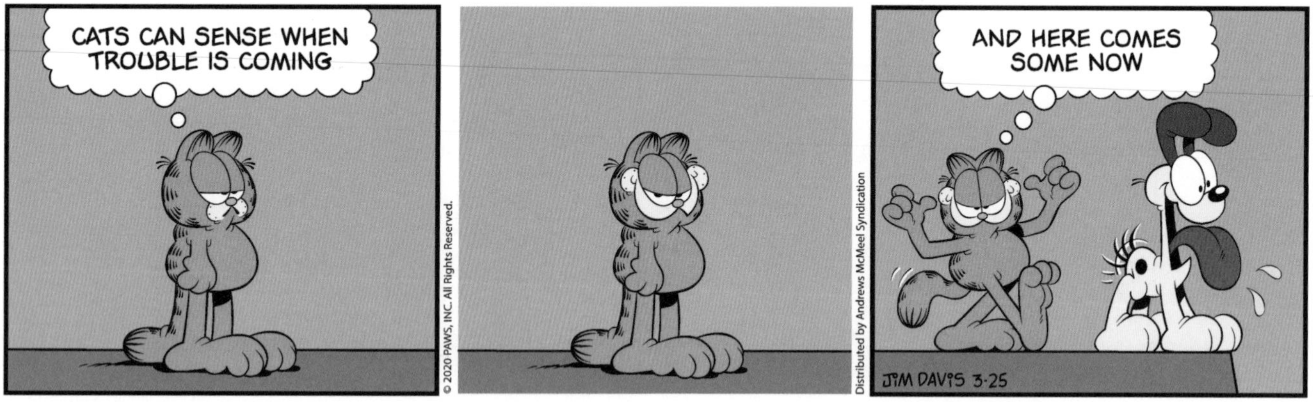
CATS CAN SENSE WHEN TROUBLE IS COMING
AND HERE COMES SOME NOW
JIM DAVIS 3-25
© 2020 PAWS, INC. All Rights Reserved.
Distributed by Andrews McMeel Syndication

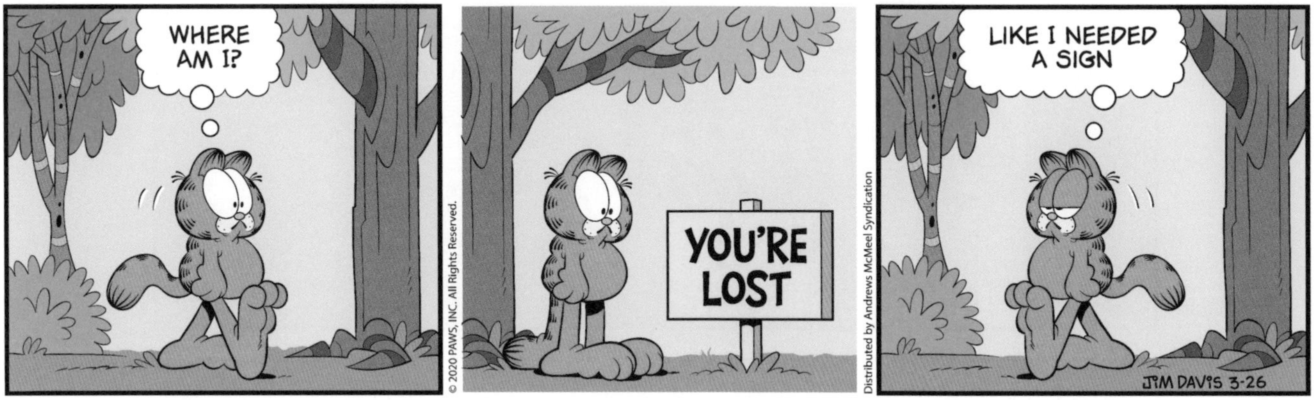
WHERE AM I?
YOU'RE LOST
LIKE I NEEDED A SIGN
JIM DAVIS 3-26
© 2020 PAWS, INC. All Rights Reserved.
Distributed by Andrews McMeel Syndication

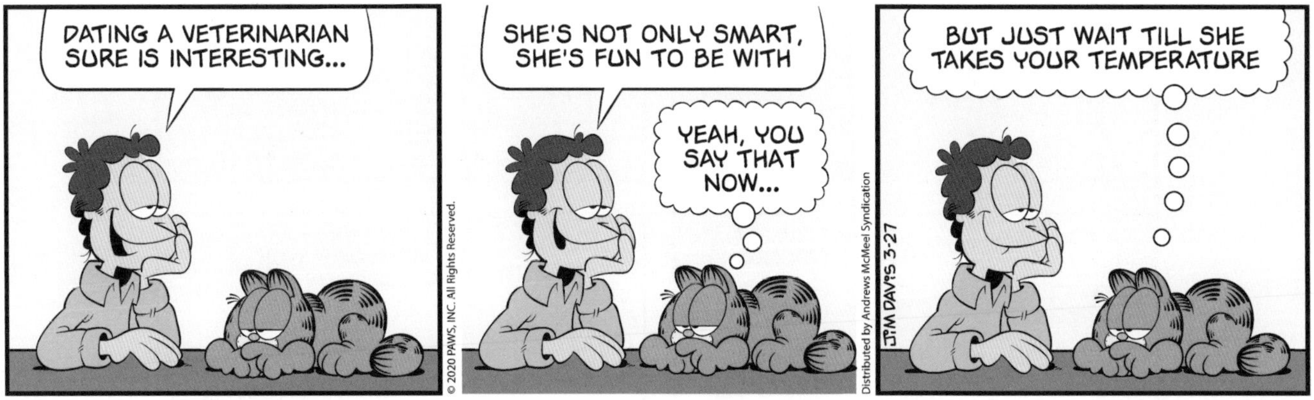
DATING A VETERINARIAN SURE IS INTERESTING...
SHE'S NOT ONLY SMART, SHE'S FUN TO BE WITH
YEAH, YOU SAY THAT NOW...
BUT JUST WAIT TILL SHE TAKES YOUR TEMPERATURE
JIM DAVIS 3-27
© 2020 PAWS, INC. All Rights Reserved.
Distributed by Andrews McMeel Syndication

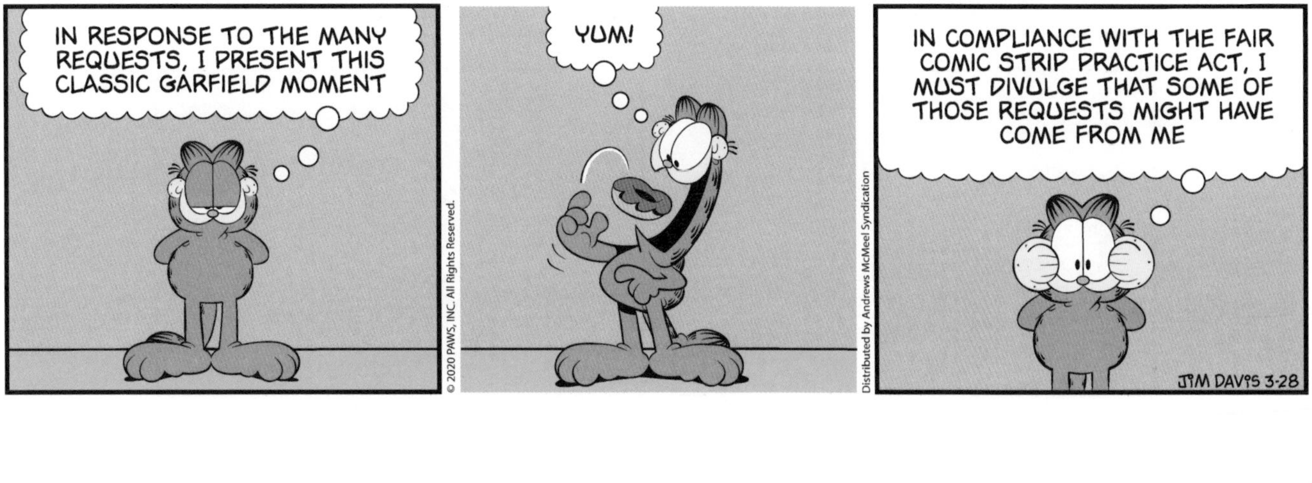
IN RESPONSE TO THE MANY REQUESTS, I PRESENT THIS CLASSIC GARFIELD MOMENT
YUM!
IN COMPLIANCE WITH THE FAIR COMIC STRIP PRACTICE ACT, I MUST DIVULGE THAT SOME OF THOSE REQUESTS MIGHT HAVE COME FROM ME
JIM DAVIS 3-28
© 2020 PAWS, INC. All Rights Reserved.
Distributed by Andrews McMeel Syndication

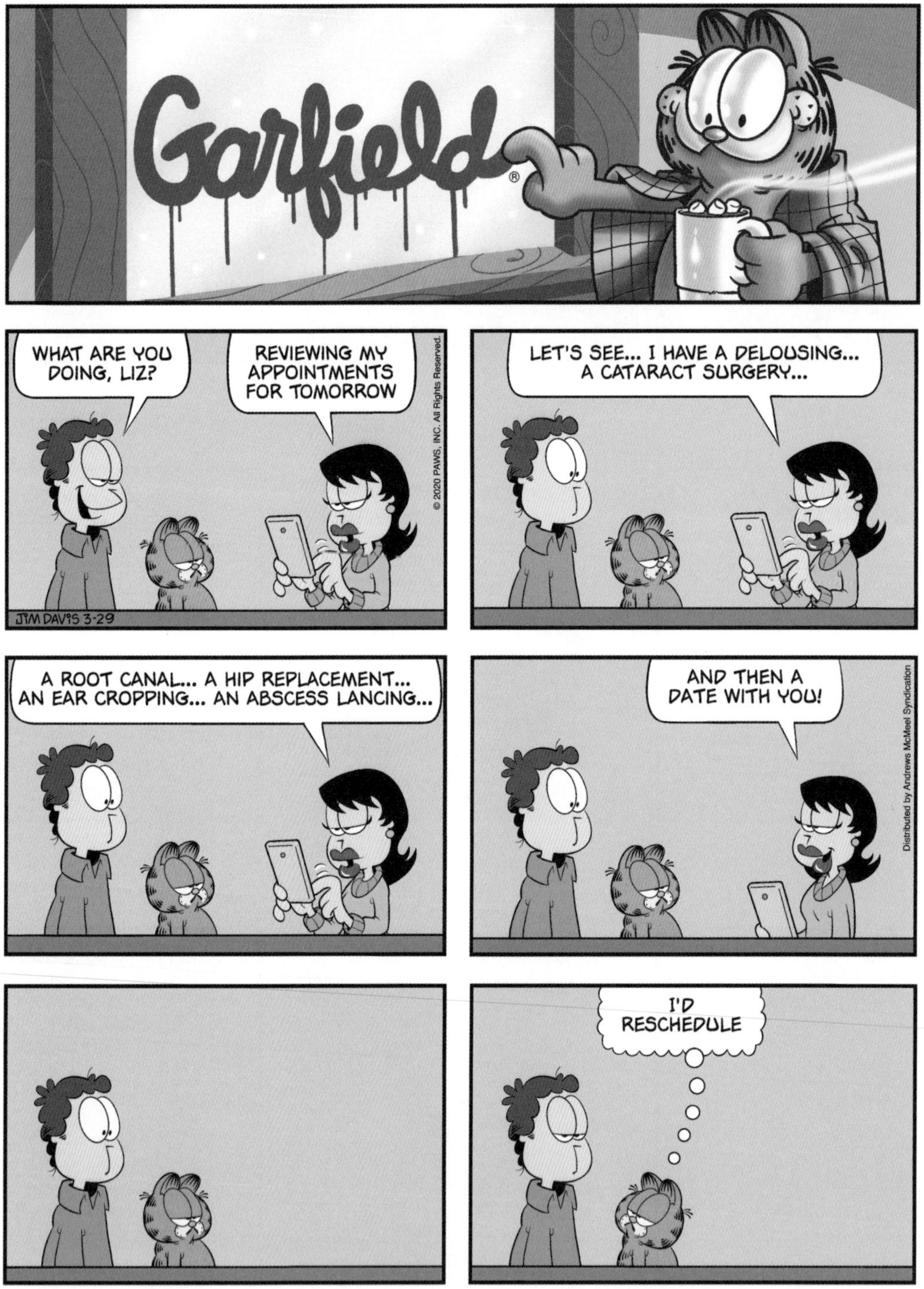
Garfield®
WHAT ARE YOU DOING, LIZ?
REVIEWING MY APPOINTMENTS FOR TOMORROW
© 2020 PAWS, INC. All Rights Reserved.
JIM DAVIS 3-29
LET'S SEE... I HAVE A DELOUSING... A CATARACT SURGERY...
A ROOT CANAL... A HIP REPLACEMENT... AN EAR CROPPING... AN ABSCESS LANCING...
AND THEN A DATE WITH YOU!
Distributed by Andrews McMeel Syndication
I'D RESCHEDULE

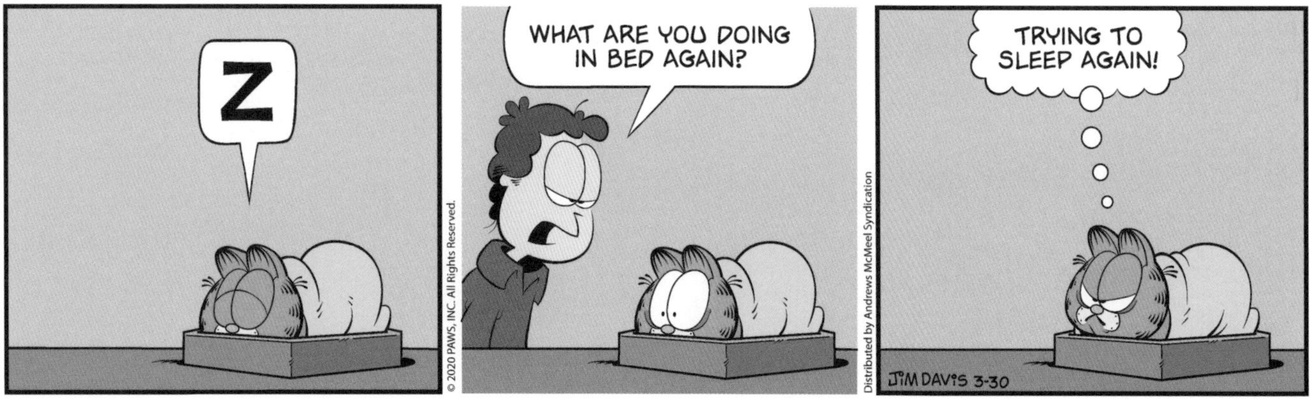
Z
WHAT ARE YOU DOING IN BED AGAIN?
TRYING TO SLEEP AGAIN!
JIM DAVIS 3-30
© 2020 PAWS, INC. All Rights Reserved.
Distributed by Andrews McMeel Syndication

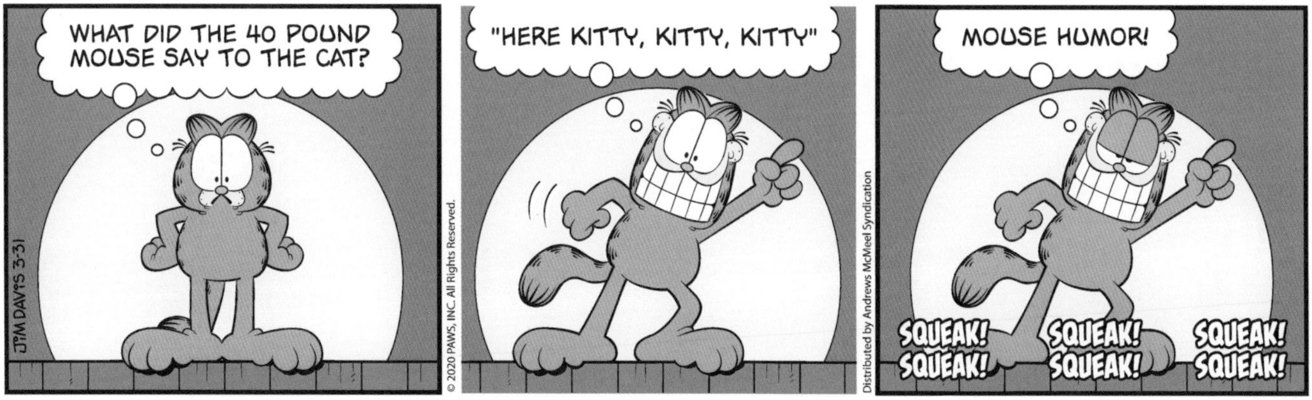
WHAT DID THE 40 POUND MOUSE SAY TO THE CAT?
"HERE KITTY, KITTY, KITTY"
MOUSE HUMOR!
SQUEAK! SQUEAK!
SQUEAK! SQUEAK!
SQUEAK! SQUEAK!
JIM DAVIS 3-31
© 2020 PAWS, INC. All Rights Reserved.
Distributed by Andrews McMeel Syndication

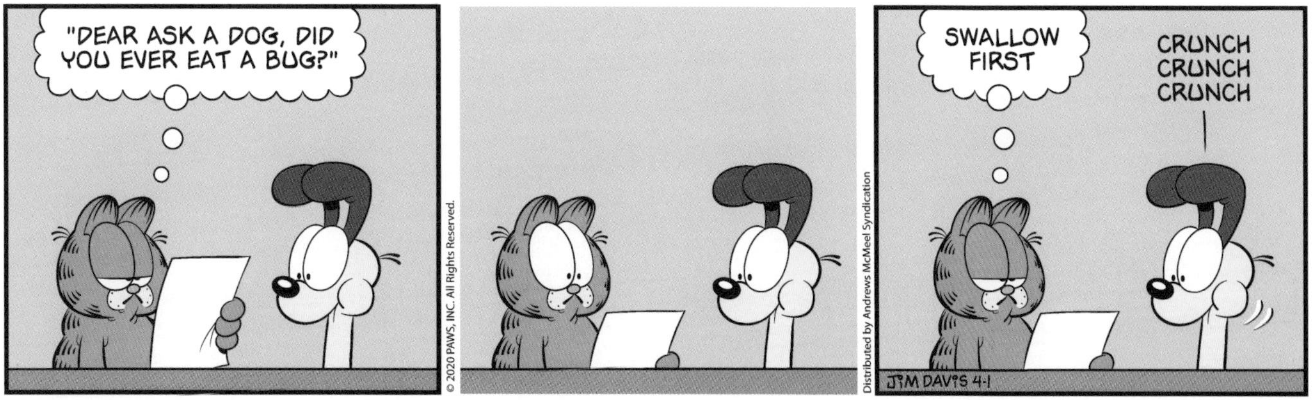
"DEAR ASK A DOG, DID YOU EVER EAT A BUG?"
SWALLOW FIRST
CRUNCH CRUNCH CRUNCH
JIM DAVIS 4-1
© 2020 PAWS, INC. All Rights Reserved.
Distributed by Andrews McMeel Syndication

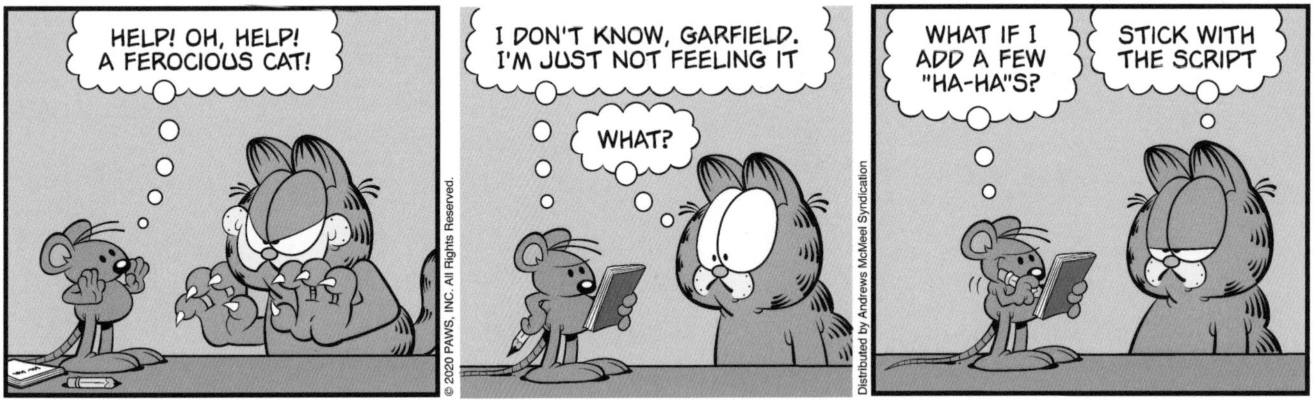
HELP! OH, HELP! A FEROCIOUS CAT!
© 2020 PAWS, INC. All Rights Reserved.
I DON'T KNOW, GARFIELD. I'M JUST NOT FEELING IT
WHAT?
Distributed by Andrews McMeel Syndication
WHAT IF I ADD A FEW "HA-HA"S?
STICK WITH THE SCRIPT

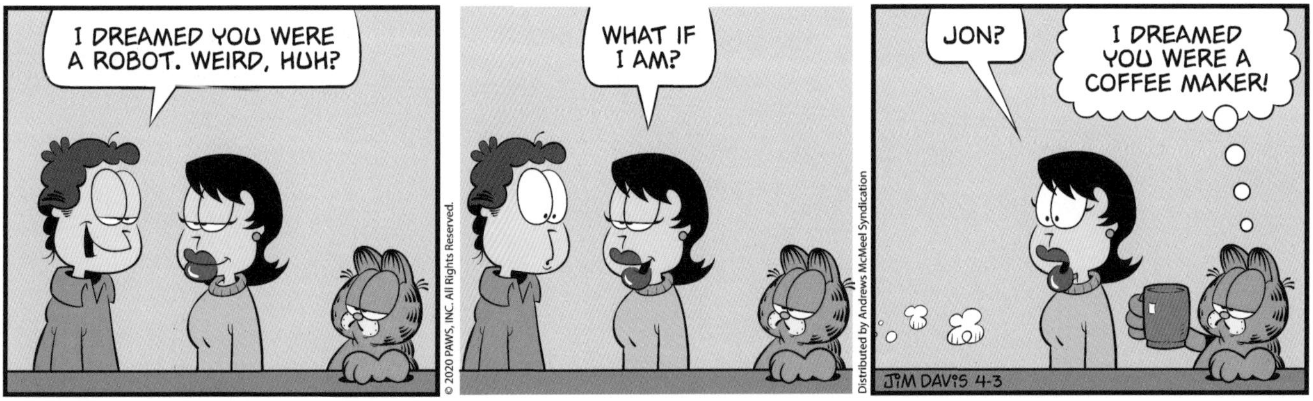
I DREAMED YOU WERE A ROBOT. WEIRD, HUH?
© 2020 PAWS, INC. All Rights Reserved.
WHAT IF I AM?
Distributed by Andrews McMeel Syndication
JON?
I DREAMED YOU WERE A COFFEE MAKER!
JIM DAVIS 4-3

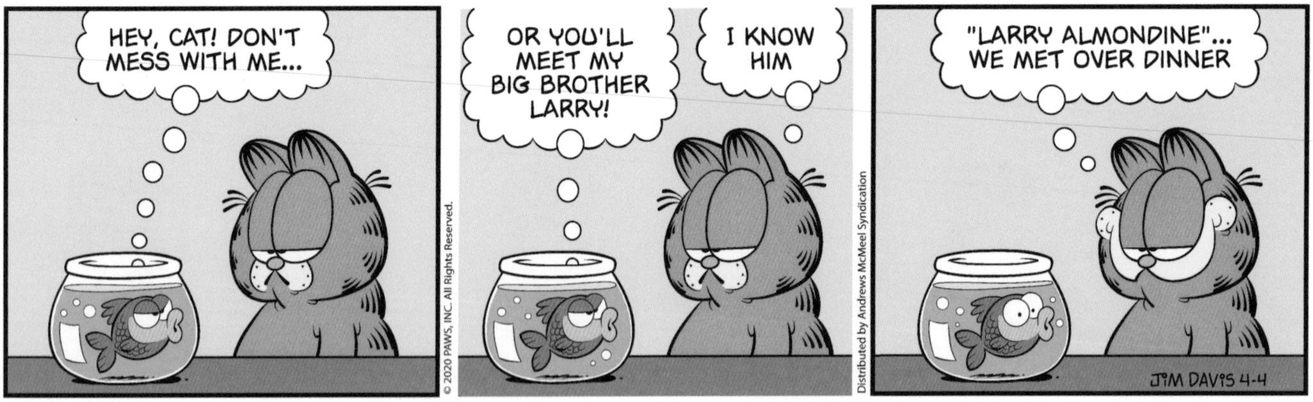
HEY, CAT! DON'T MESS WITH ME...
© 2020 PAWS, INC. All Rights Reserved.
OR YOU'LL MEET MY BIG BROTHER LARRY!
I KNOW HIM
Distributed by Andrews McMeel Syndication
"LARRY ALMONDINE"... WE MET OVER DINNER
JIM DAVIS 4-4

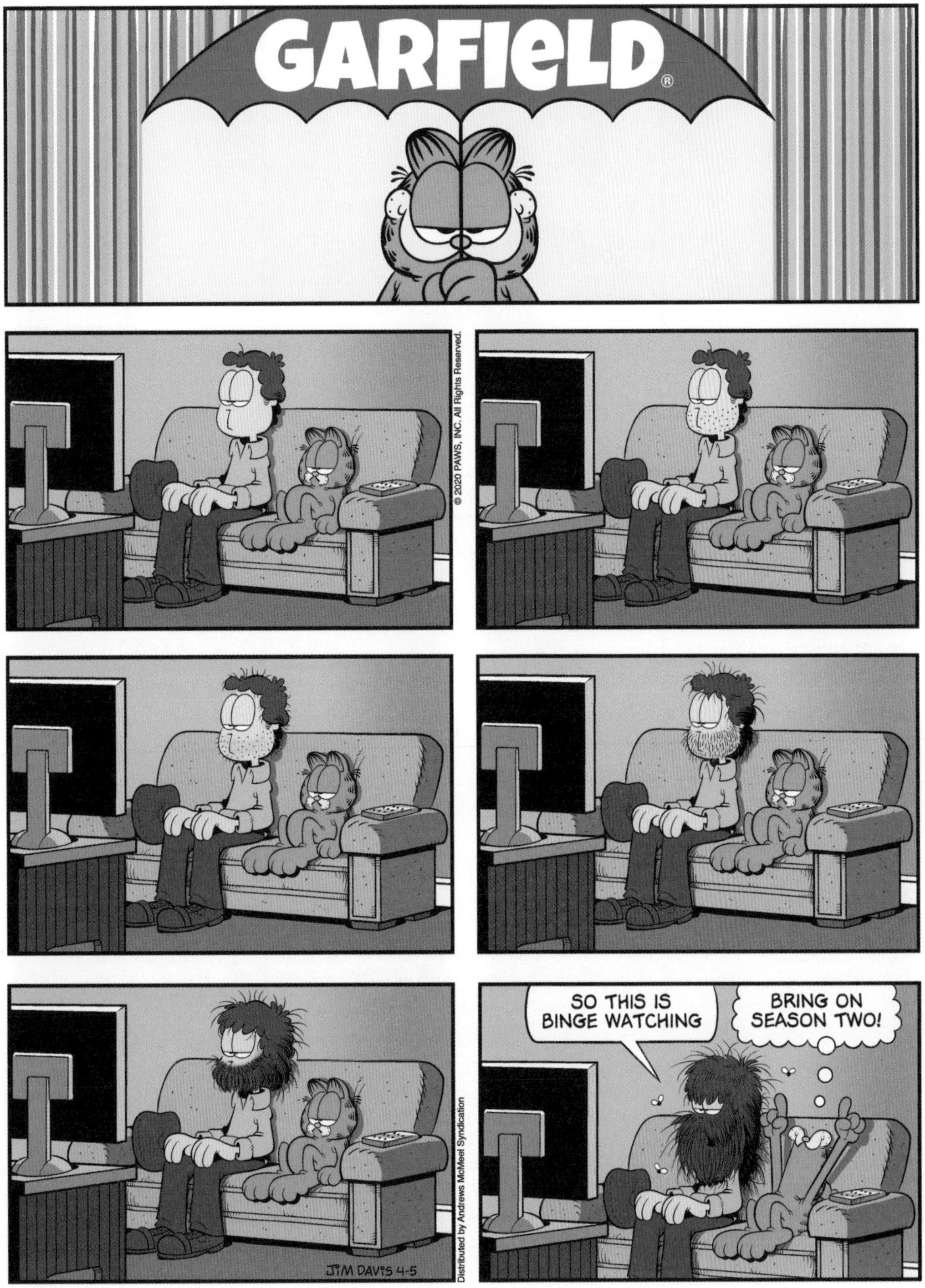
GARFIELD®
© 2020 PAWS, INC. All Rights Reserved.
Distributed by Andrews McMeel Syndication
JIM DAVIS 4-5
SO THIS IS BINGE WATCHING
BRING ON SEASON TWO!

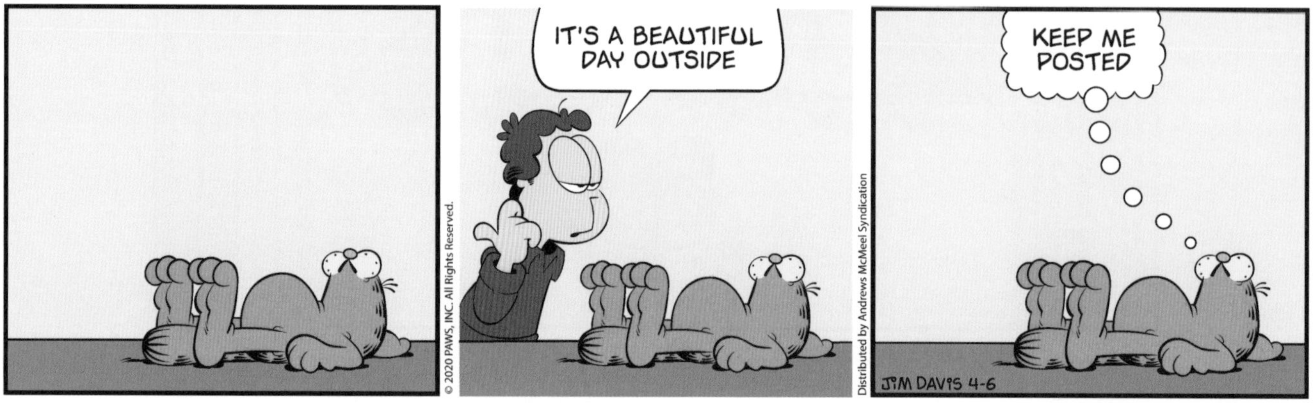
IT'S A BEAUTIFUL DAY OUTSIDE
KEEP ME POSTED
JIM DAVIS 4-6
© 2020 PAWS, INC. All Rights Reserved.
Distributed by Andrews McMeel Syndication

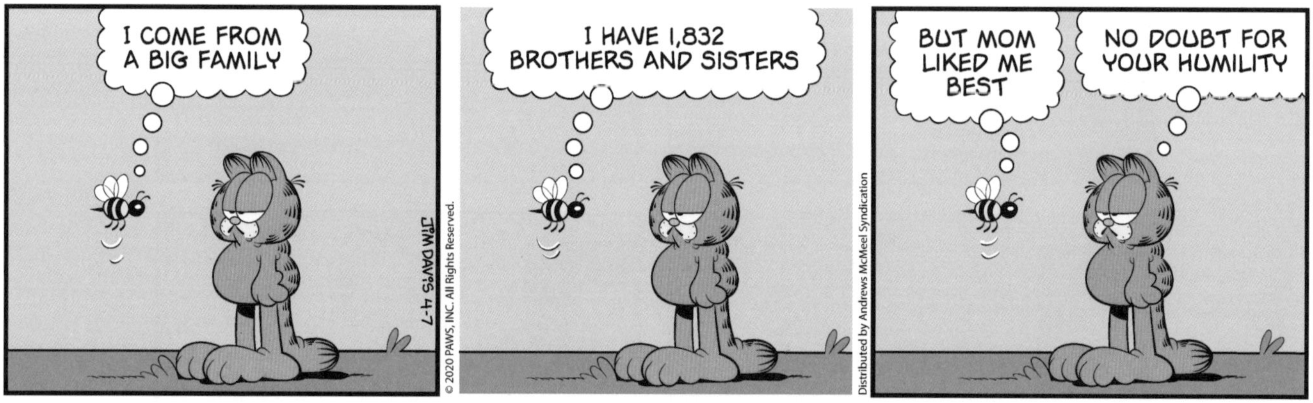
I COME FROM A BIG FAMILY
I HAVE 1,832 BROTHERS AND SISTERS
BUT MOM LIKED ME BEST
NO DOUBT FOR YOUR HUMILITY
JIM DAVIS 4-7
© 2020 PAWS, INC. All Rights Reserved.
Distributed by Andrews McMeel Syndication

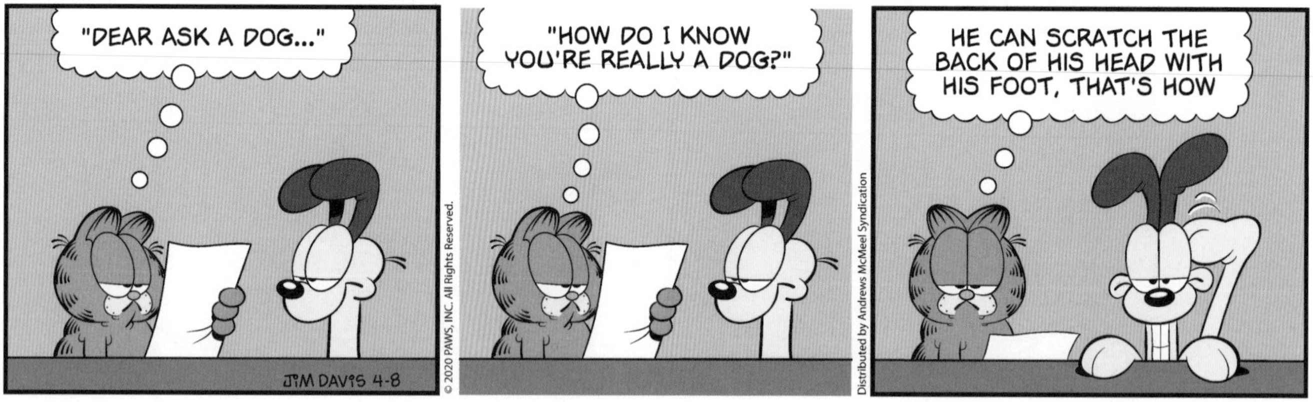
"DEAR ASK A DOG..."
"HOW DO I KNOW YOU'RE REALLY A DOG?"
HE CAN SCRATCH THE BACK OF HIS HEAD WITH HIS FOOT, THAT'S HOW
JIM DAVIS 4-8
© 2020 PAWS, INC. All Rights Reserved.
Distributed by Andrews McMeel Syndication

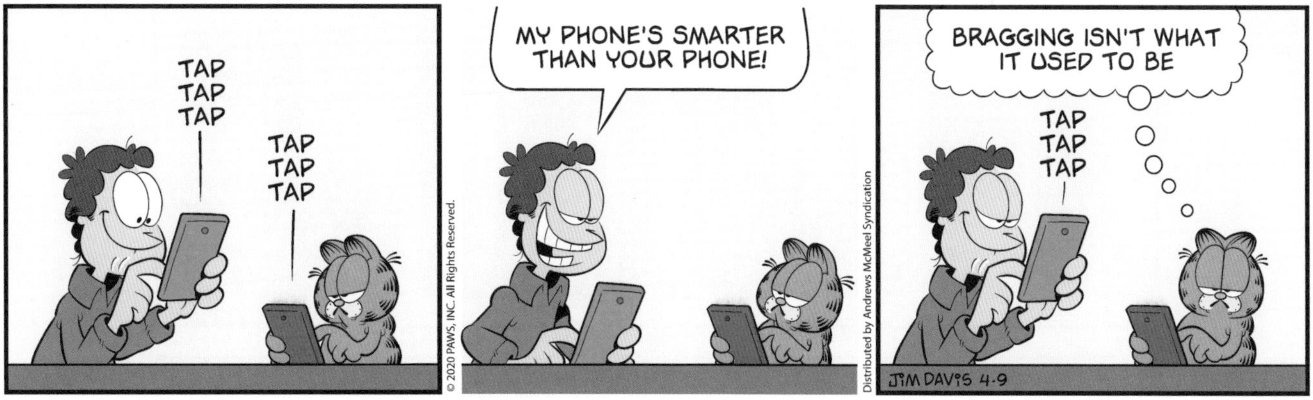
TAP
TAP
TAP
TAP
TAP
TAP
MY PHONE'S SMARTER THAN YOUR PHONE!
BRAGGING ISN'T WHAT IT USED TO BE
TAP
TAP
TAP
JIM DAVIS 4-9
© 2020 PAWS, INC. All Rights Reserved.
Distributed by Andrews McMeel Syndication

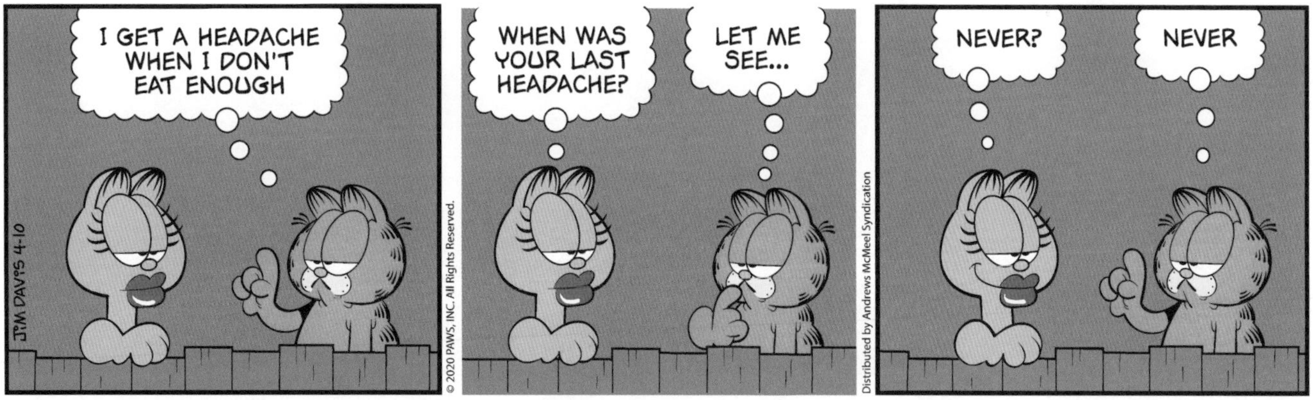
I GET A HEADACHE WHEN I DON'T EAT ENOUGH
JIM DAVIS 4-10
WHEN WAS YOUR LAST HEADACHE?
LET ME SEE...
NEVER?
NEVER
© 2020 PAWS, INC. All Rights Reserved.
Distributed by Andrews McMeel Syndication

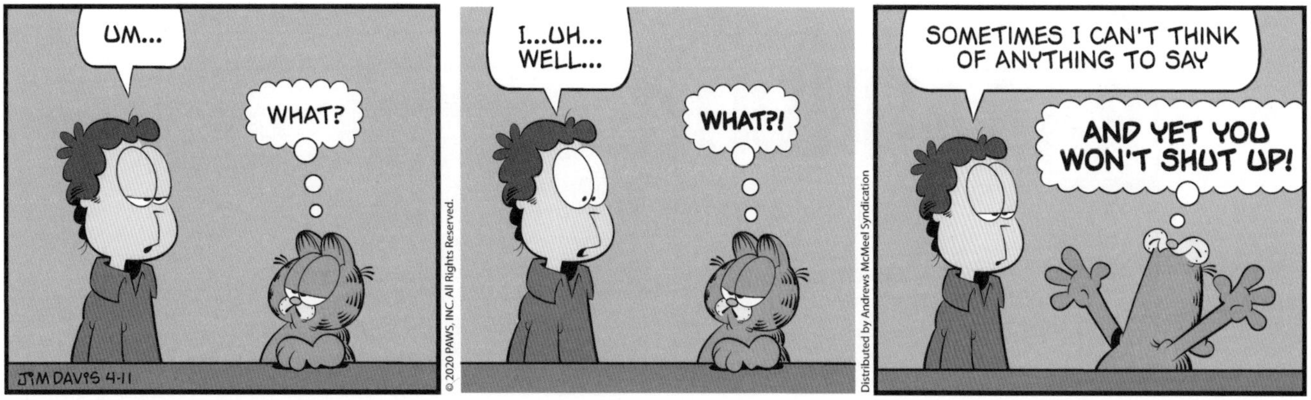
UM...
WHAT?
JIM DAVIS 4-11
I...UH... WELL...
WHAT?!
SOMETIMES I CAN'T THINK OF ANYTHING TO SAY
AND YET YOU WON'T SHUT UP!
© 2020 PAWS, INC. All Rights Reserved.
Distributed by Andrews McMeel Syndication

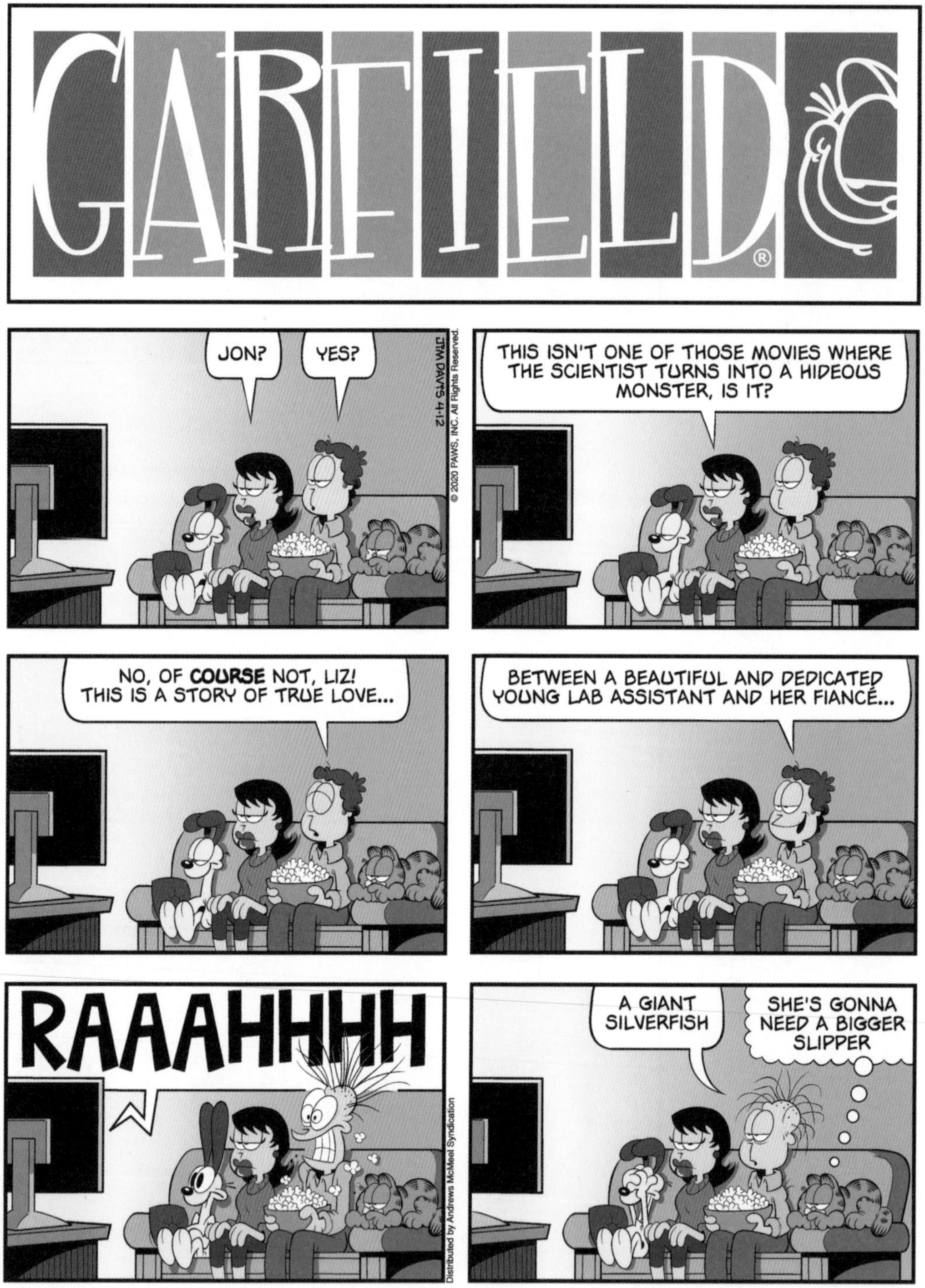
GARFIELD®
JON?
YES?
© 2020 PAWS, INC. All Rights Reserved.
JIM DAVIS 4-12
THIS ISN'T ONE OF THOSE MOVIES WHERE THE SCIENTIST TURNS INTO A HIDEOUS MONSTER, IS IT?
NO, OF **COURSE** NOT, LIZ! THIS IS A STORY OF TRUE LOVE...
BETWEEN A BEAUTIFUL AND DEDICATED YOUNG LAB ASSISTANT AND HER FIANCÉ...
RAAAHHHH
Distributed by Andrews McMeel Syndication
A GIANT SILVERFISH
SHE'S GONNA NEED A BIGGER SLIPPER

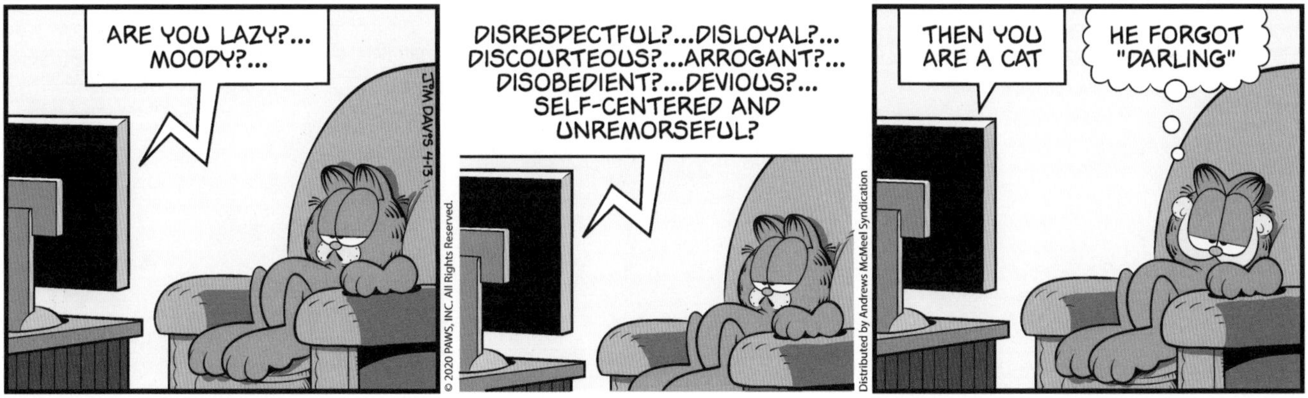
ARE YOU LAZY?... MOODY?...
JIM DAVIS 4-13
© 2020 PAWS, INC. All Rights Reserved.
DISRESPECTFUL?...DISLOYAL?... DISCOURTEOUS?...ARROGANT?... DISOBEDIENT?...DEVIOUS?... SELF-CENTERED AND UNREMORSEFUL?
Distributed by Andrews McMeel Syndication
THEN YOU ARE A CAT
HE FORGOT "DARLING"

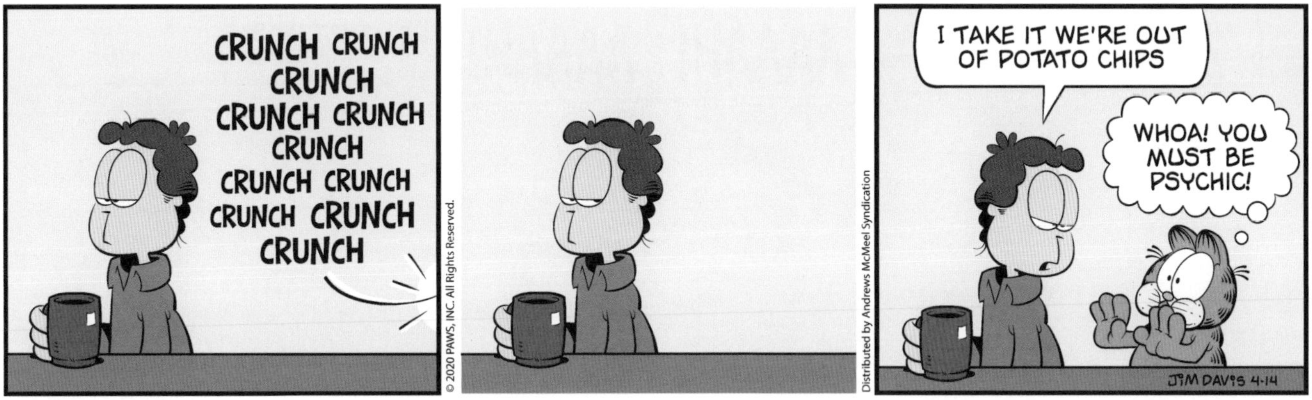
CRUNCH CRUNCH CRUNCH CRUNCH CRUNCH CRUNCH CRUNCH CRUNCH CRUNCH CRUNCH CRUNCH
© 2020 PAWS, INC. All Rights Reserved.
Distributed by Andrews McMeel Syndication
I TAKE IT WE'RE OUT OF POTATO CHIPS
WHOA! YOU MUST BE PSYCHIC!
JIM DAVIS 4-14

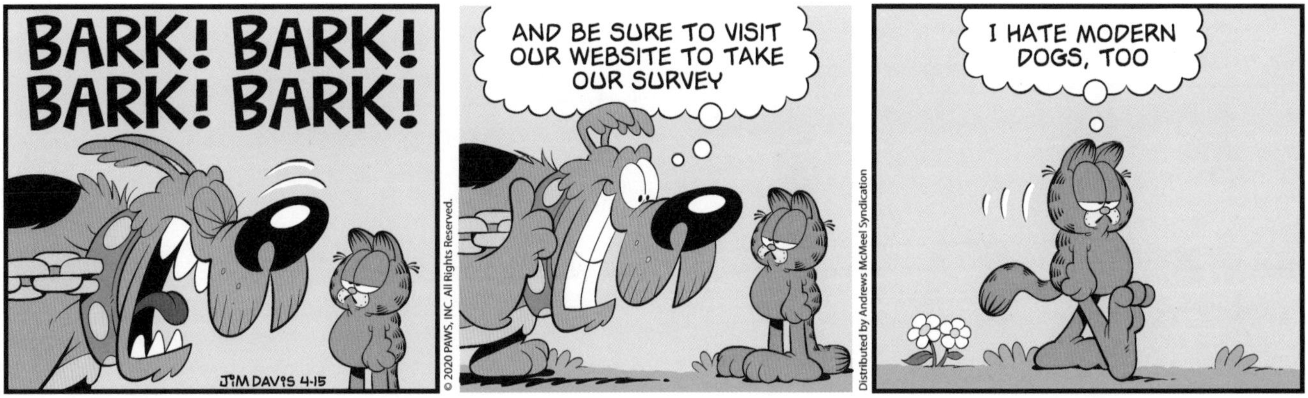
BARK! BARK! BARK! BARK!
JIM DAVIS 4-15
© 2020 PAWS, INC. All Rights Reserved.
AND BE SURE TO VISIT OUR WEBSITE TO TAKE OUR SURVEY
Distributed by Andrews McMeel Syndication
I HATE MODERN DOGS, TOO

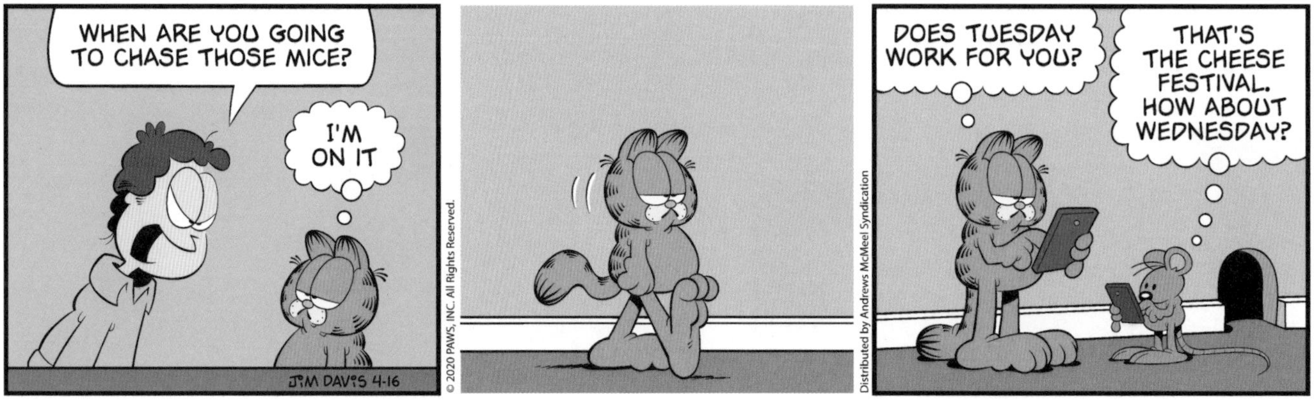
WHEN ARE YOU GOING TO CHASE THOSE MICE?
I'M ON IT
JIM DAVIS 4-16
© 2020 PAWS, INC. All Rights Reserved.
Distributed by Andrews McMeel Syndication
DOES TUESDAY WORK FOR YOU?
THAT'S THE CHEESE FESTIVAL. HOW ABOUT WEDNESDAY?

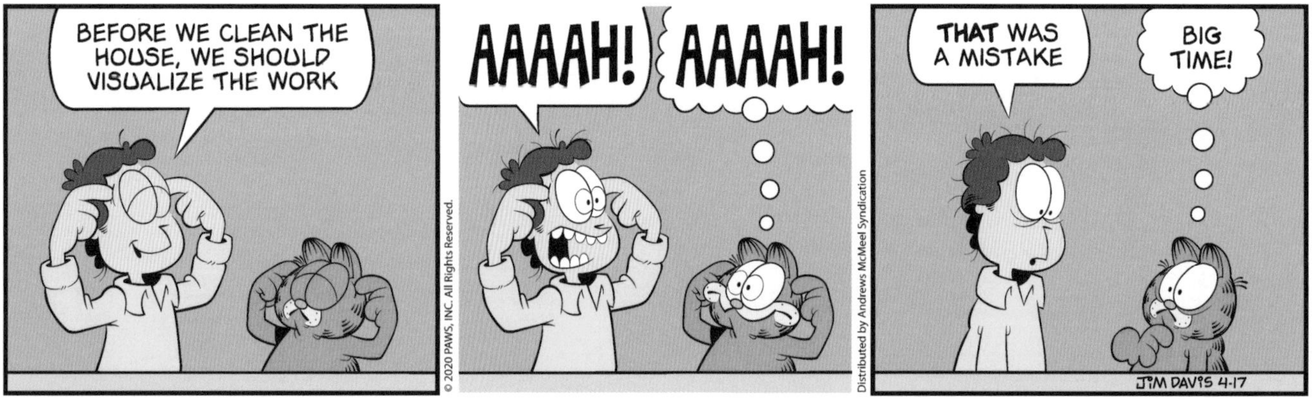
BEFORE WE CLEAN THE HOUSE, WE SHOULD VISUALIZE THE WORK
© 2020 PAWS, INC. All Rights Reserved.
AAAAH!
AAAAH!
Distributed by Andrews McMeel Syndication
THAT WAS A MISTAKE
BIG TIME!
JIM DAVIS 4-17

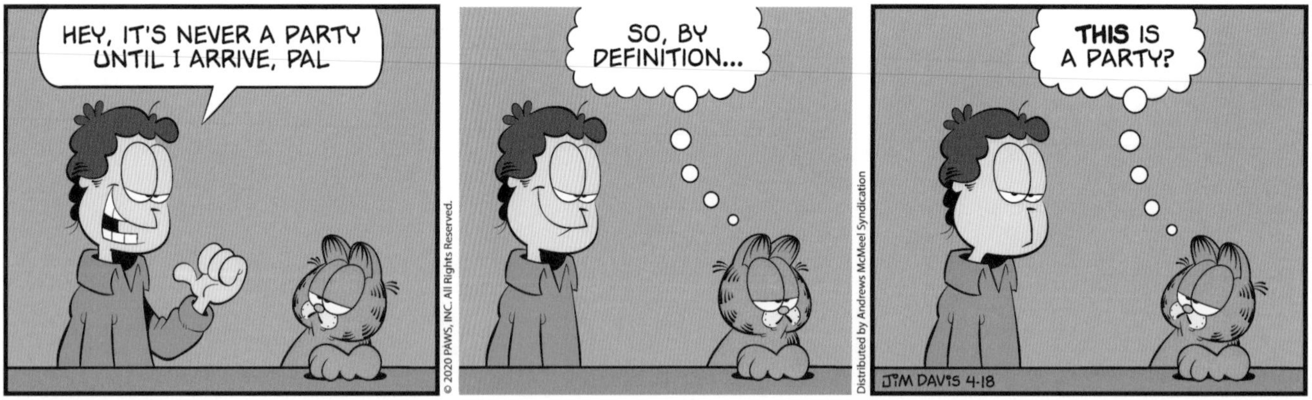
HEY, IT'S NEVER A PARTY UNTIL I ARRIVE, PAL
© 2020 PAWS, INC. All Rights Reserved.
SO, BY DEFINITION...
Distributed by Andrews McMeel Syndication
THIS IS A PARTY?
JIM DAVIS 4-18

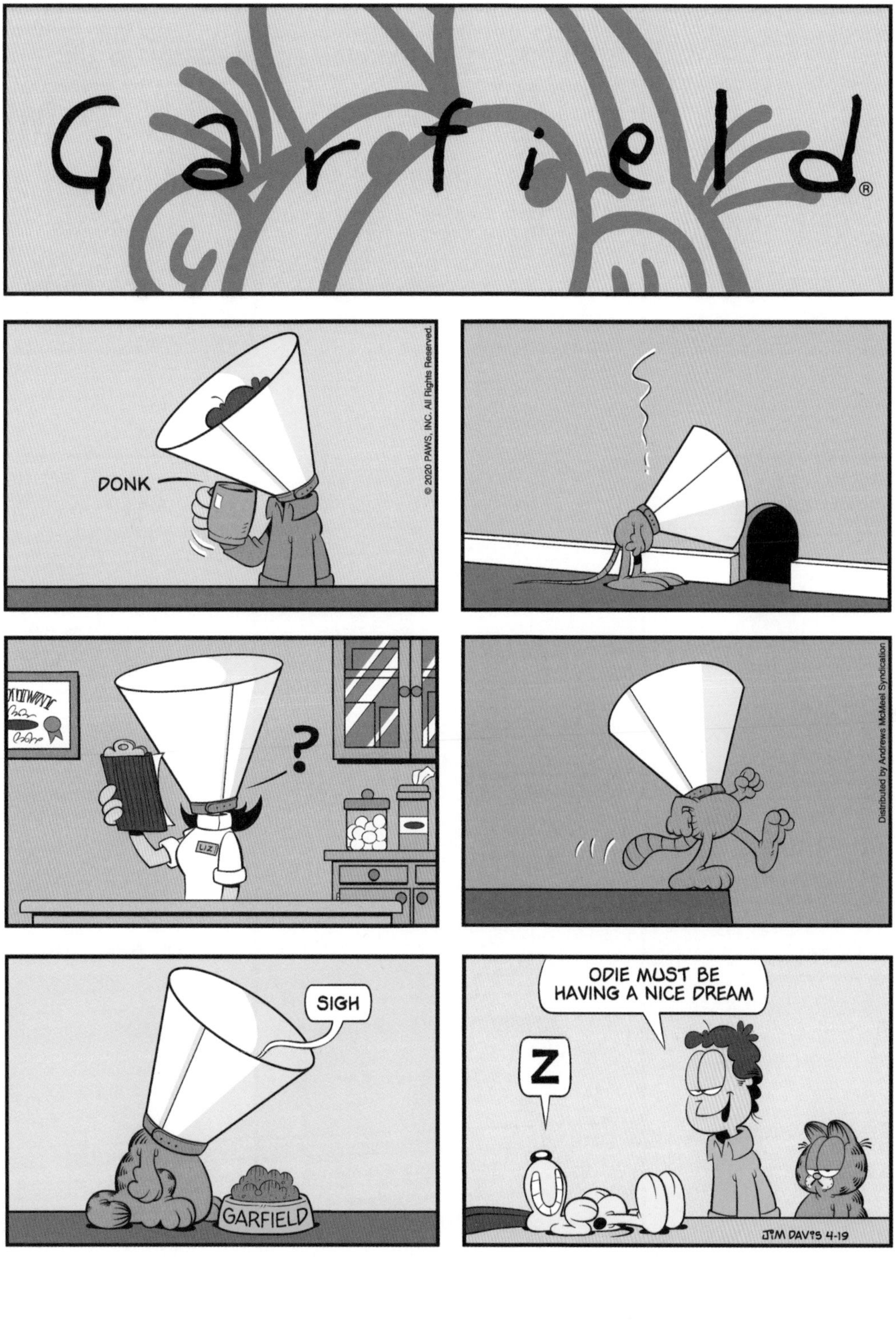
Garfield®
© 2020 PAWS, INC. All Rights Reserved.
DONK
LIZ
?
Distributed by Andrews McMeel Syndication
SIGH
GARFIELD
Z
ODIE MUST BE HAVING A NICE DREAM
JIM DAVIS 4-19

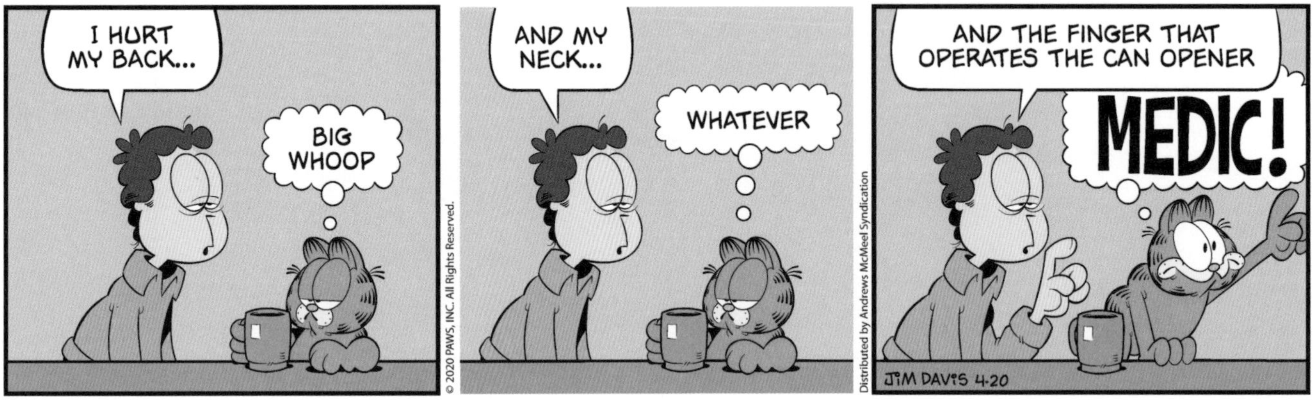
I HURT MY BACK...
BIG WHOOP
AND MY NECK...
WHATEVER
AND THE FINGER THAT OPERATES THE CAN OPENER
MEDIC!
© 2020 PAWS, INC. All Rights Reserved.
Distributed by Andrews McMeel Syndication
JIM DAVIS 4-20

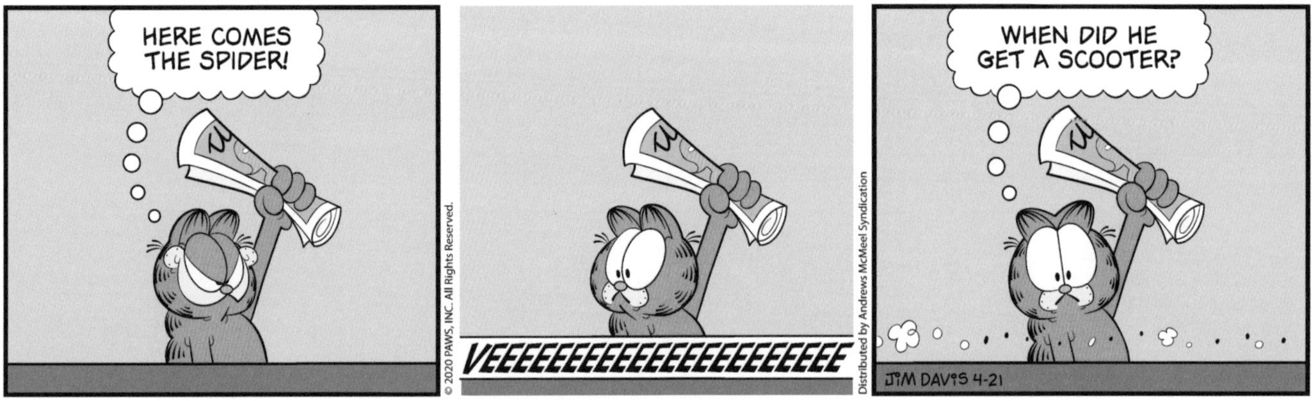
HERE COMES THE SPIDER!
VEEEEEEEEEEEEEEEEEEEEEE
WHEN DID HE GET A SCOOTER?
© 2020 PAWS, INC. All Rights Reserved.
Distributed by Andrews McMeel Syndication
JIM DAVIS 4-21

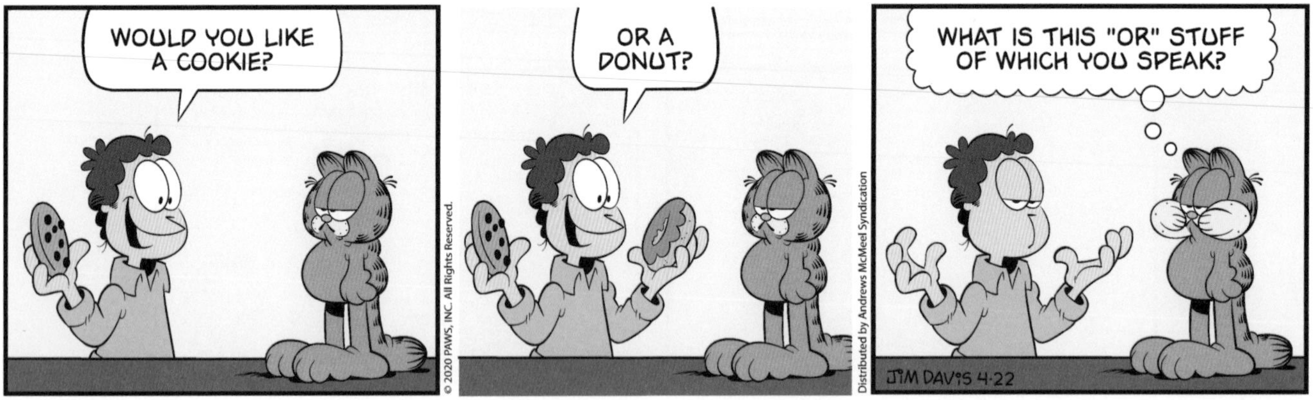
WOULD YOU LIKE A COOKIE?
OR A DONUT?
WHAT IS THIS "OR" STUFF OF WHICH YOU SPEAK?
© 2020 PAWS, INC. All Rights Reserved.
Distributed by Andrews McMeel Syndication
JIM DAVIS 4-22

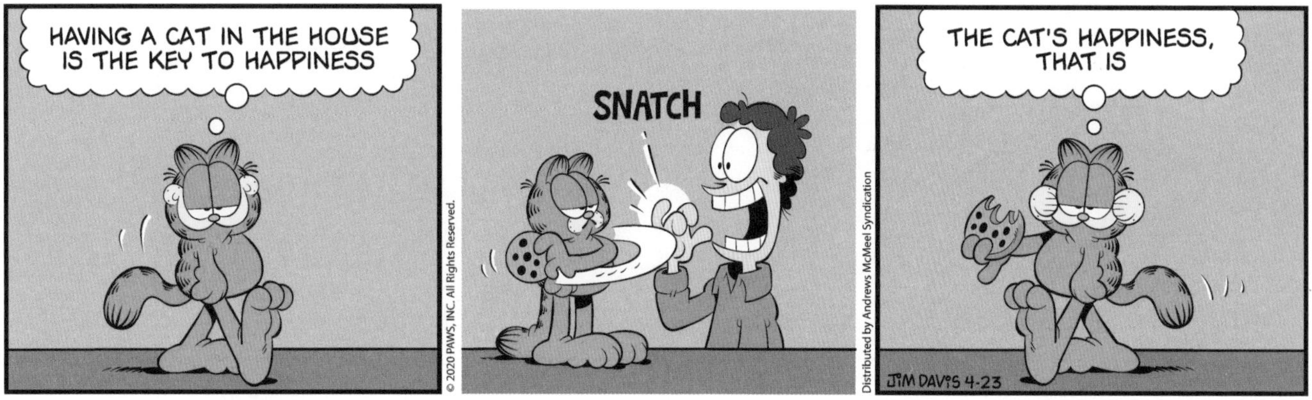
HAVING A CAT IN THE HOUSE IS THE KEY TO HAPPINESS
SNATCH
THE CAT'S HAPPINESS, THAT IS
© 2020 PAWS, INC. All Rights Reserved.
Distributed by Andrews McMeel Syndication
JIM DAVIS 4-23

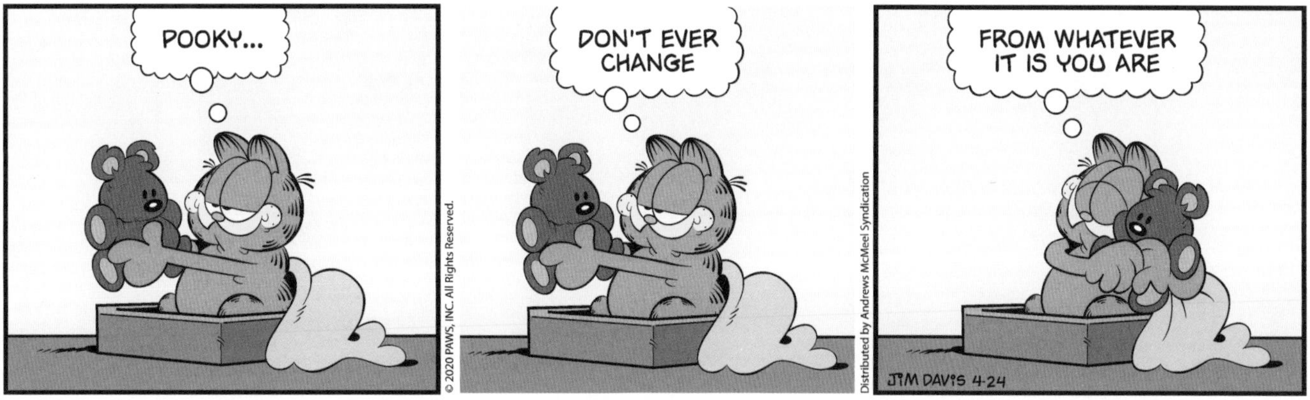
POOKY...
DON'T EVER CHANGE
FROM WHATEVER IT IS YOU ARE
© 2020 PAWS, INC. All Rights Reserved.
Distributed by Andrews McMeel Syndication
JIM DAVIS 4-24

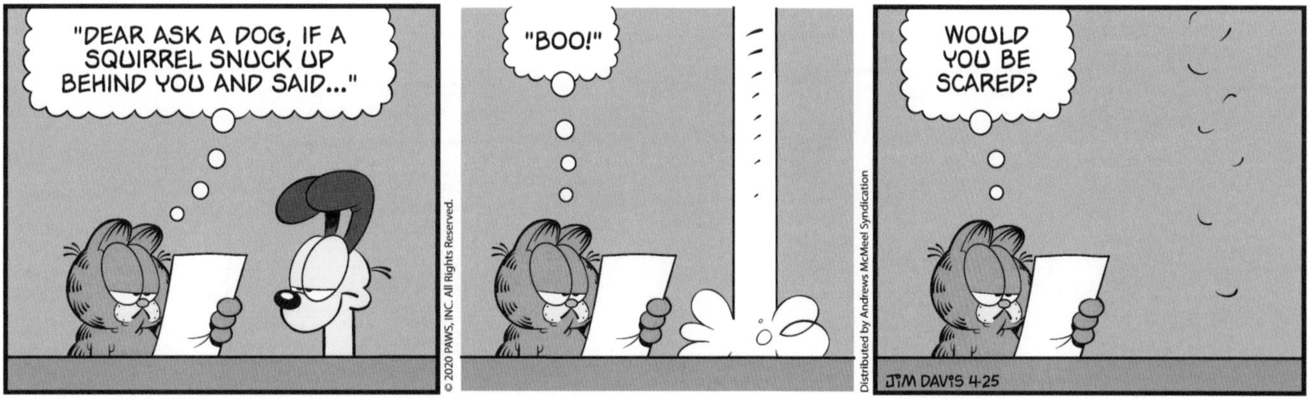
"DEAR ASK A DOG, IF A SQUIRREL SNUCK UP BEHIND YOU AND SAID..."
"BOO!"
WOULD YOU BE SCARED?
© 2020 PAWS, INC. All Rights Reserved.
Distributed by Andrews McMeel Syndication
JIM DAVIS 4-25

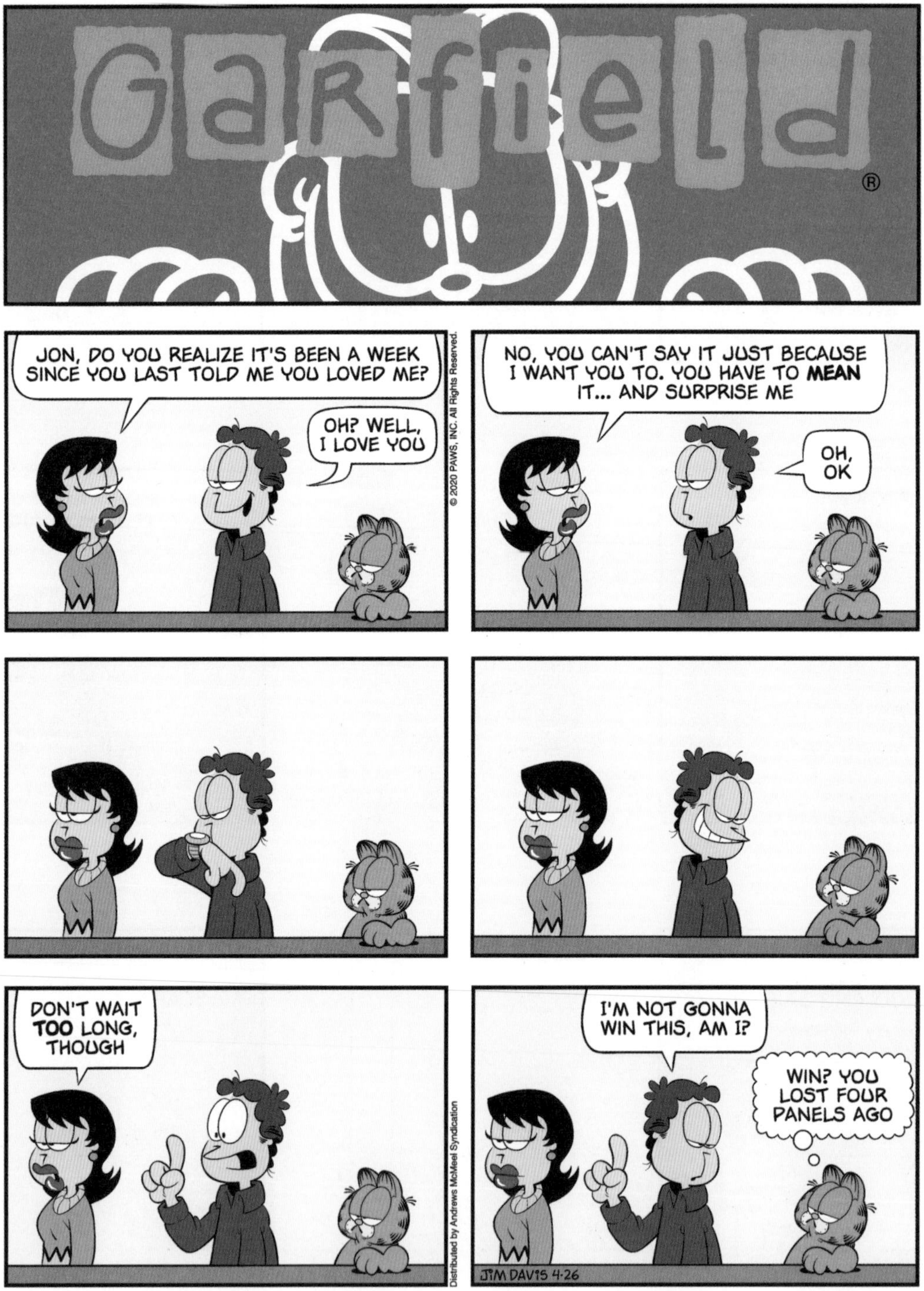
Garfield
JON, DO YOU REALIZE IT'S BEEN A WEEK SINCE YOU LAST TOLD ME YOU LOVED ME?
OH? WELL, I LOVE YOU
© 2020 PAWS, INC. All Rights Reserved.
NO, YOU CAN'T SAY IT JUST BECAUSE I WANT YOU TO. YOU HAVE TO **MEAN** IT... AND SURPRISE ME
OH, OK
DON'T WAIT **TOO** LONG, THOUGH
Distributed by Andrews McMeel Syndication
I'M NOT GONNA WIN THIS, AM I?
WIN? YOU LOST FOUR PANELS AGO
JIM DAVIS 4·26

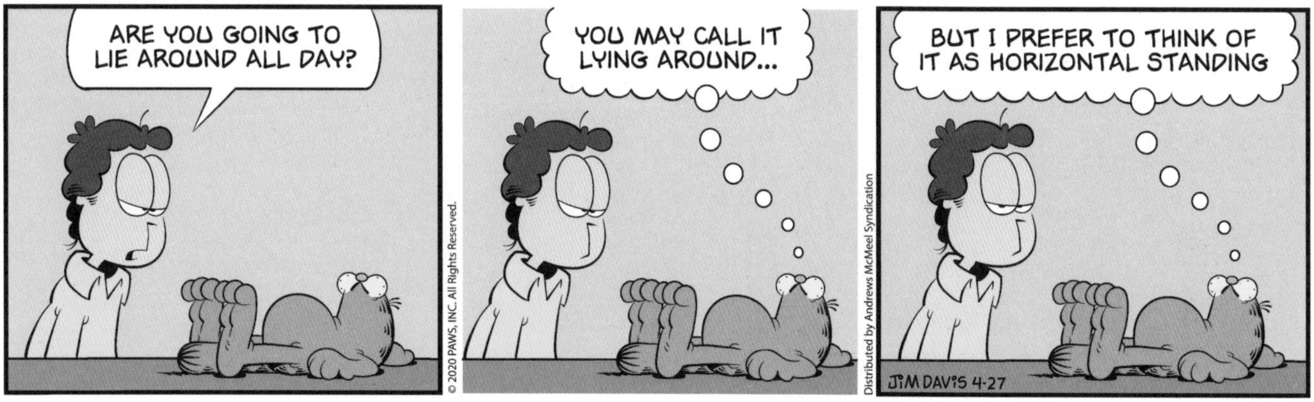
ARE YOU GOING TO LIE AROUND ALL DAY?
YOU MAY CALL IT LYING AROUND...
BUT I PREFER TO THINK OF IT AS HORIZONTAL STANDING
© 2020 PAWS, INC. All Rights Reserved.
Distributed by Andrews McMeel Syndication
JIM DAVIS 4-27

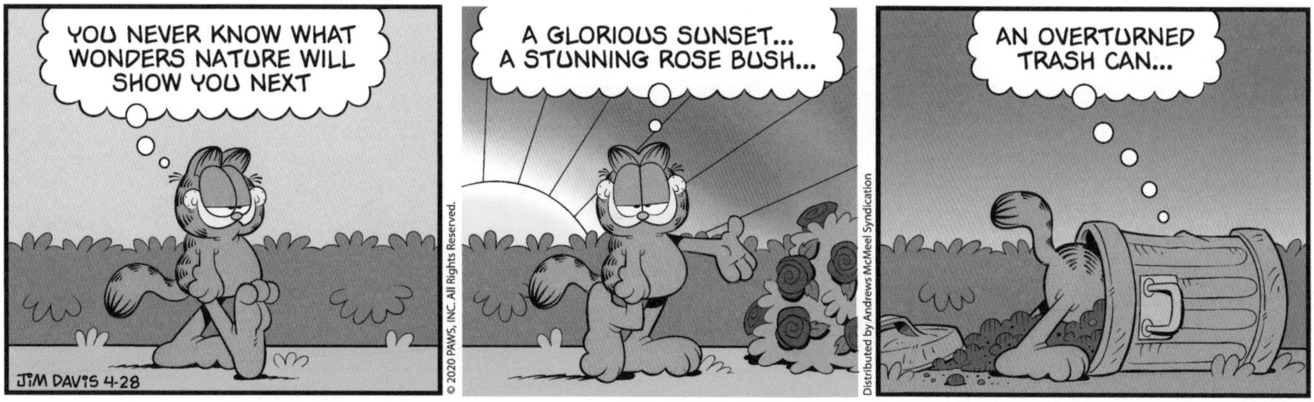
YOU NEVER KNOW WHAT WONDERS NATURE WILL SHOW YOU NEXT
A GLORIOUS SUNSET... A STUNNING ROSE BUSH...
AN OVERTURNED TRASH CAN...
JIM DAVIS 4-28
© 2020 PAWS, INC. All Rights Reserved.
Distributed by Andrews McMeel Syndication

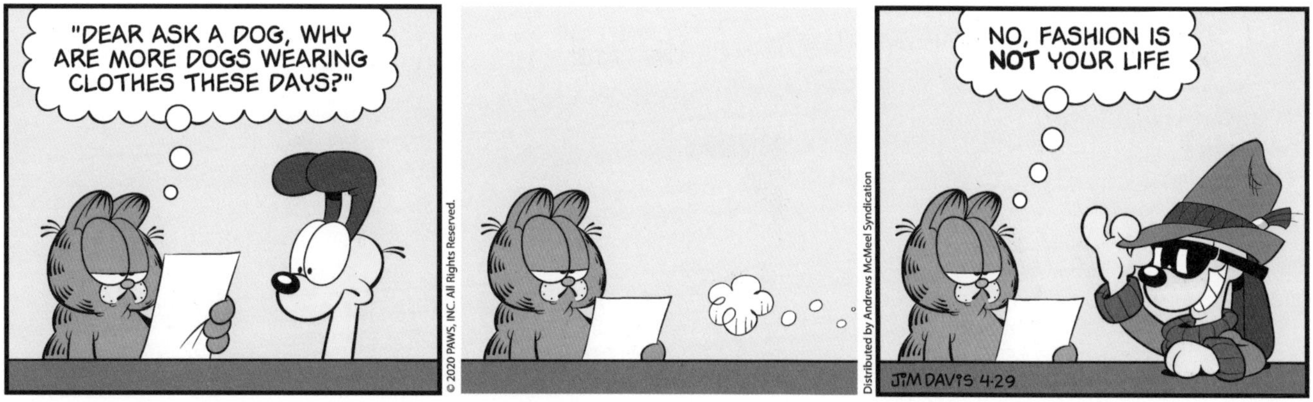
"DEAR ASK A DOG, WHY ARE MORE DOGS WEARING CLOTHES THESE DAYS?"
NO, FASHION IS **NOT** YOUR LIFE
© 2020 PAWS, INC. All Rights Reserved.
Distributed by Andrews McMeel Syndication
JIM DAVIS 4-29

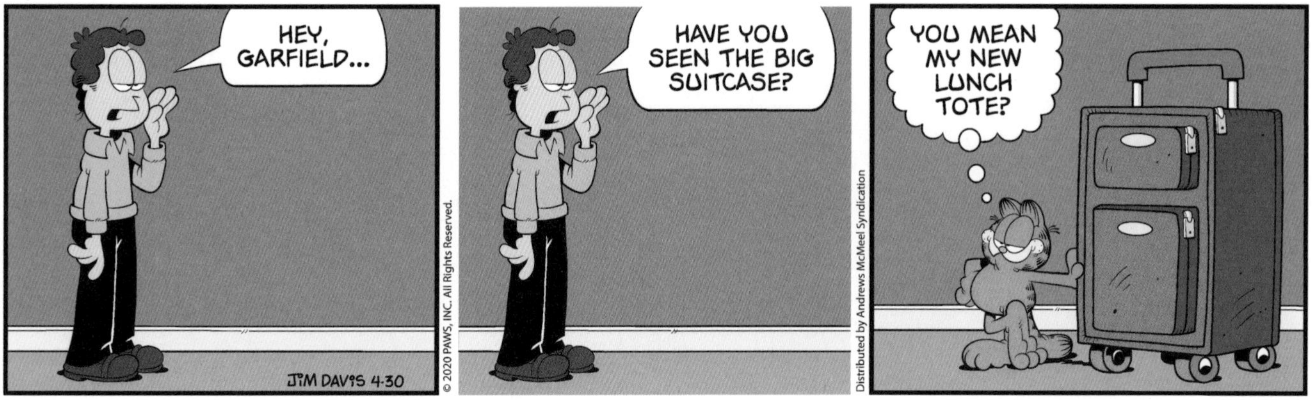
HEY, GARFIELD...
JIM DAVIS 4-30
HAVE YOU SEEN THE BIG SUITCASE?
YOU MEAN MY NEW LUNCH TOTE?

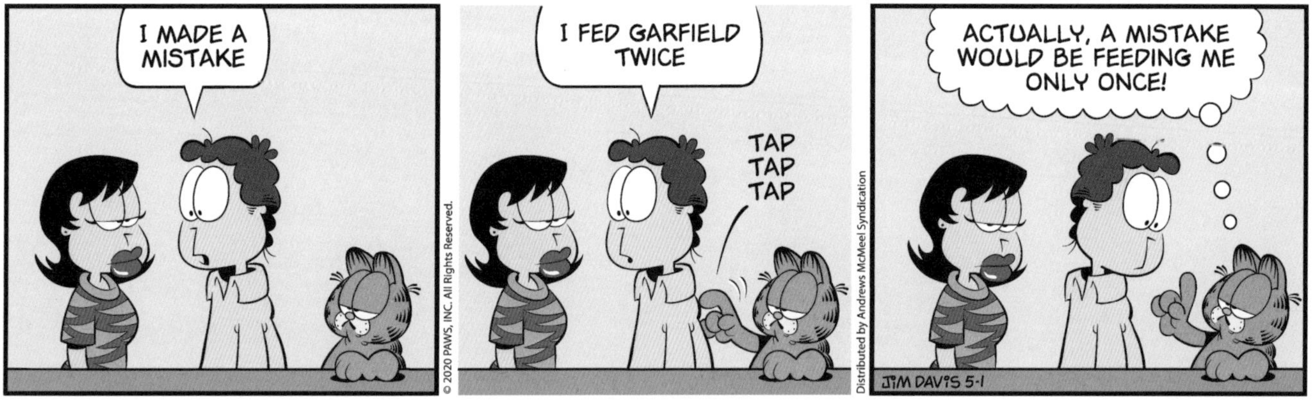
I MADE A MISTAKE
I FED GARFIELD TWICE
TAP TAP TAP
ACTUALLY, A MISTAKE WOULD BE FEEDING ME ONLY ONCE!
JIM DAVIS 5-1

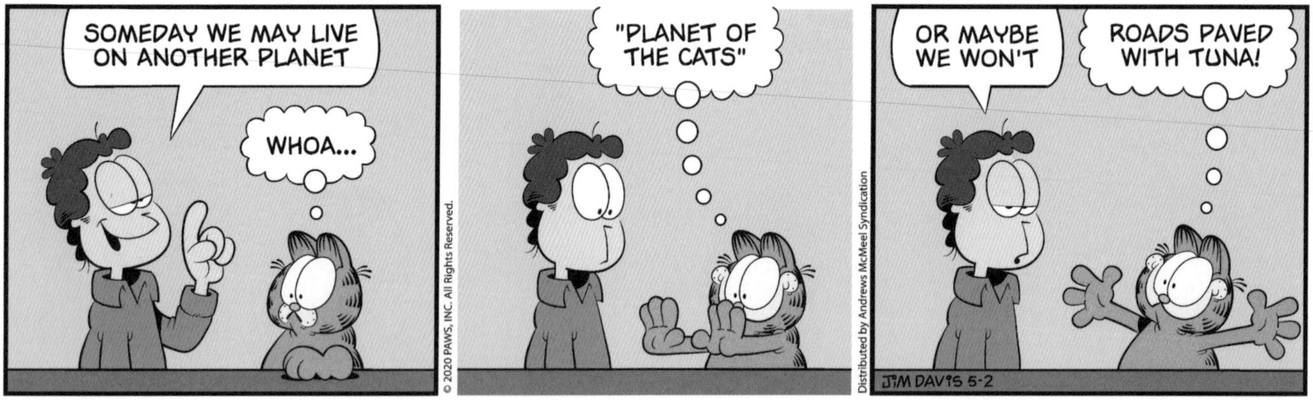
SOMEDAY WE MAY LIVE ON ANOTHER PLANET
WHOA...
"PLANET OF THE CATS"
OR MAYBE WE WON'T
ROADS PAVED WITH TUNA!
JIM DAVIS 5-2

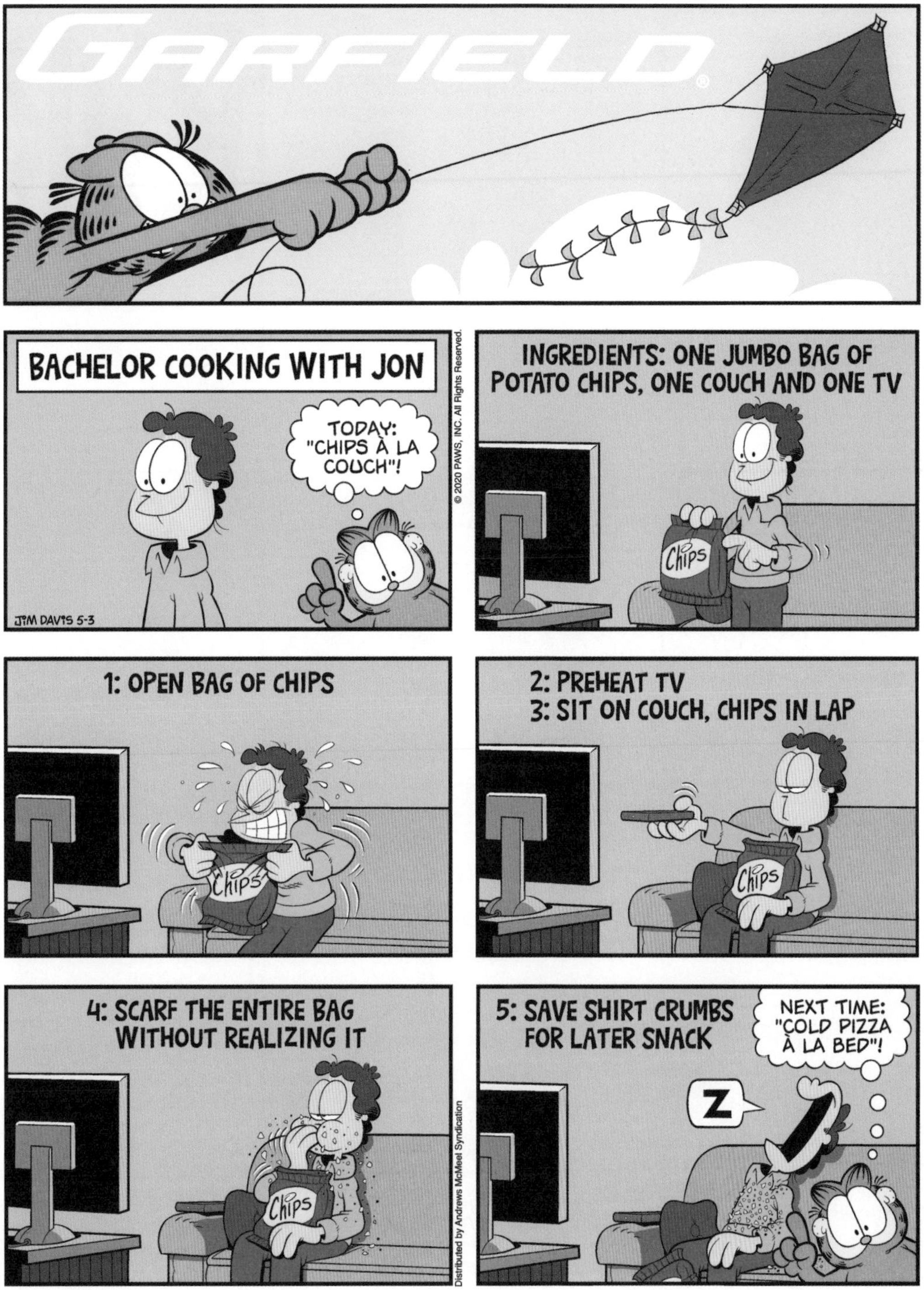
GARFIELD®
BACHELOR COOKING WITH JON
TODAY: "CHIPS À LA COUCH"!
JIM DAVIS 5-3
© 2020 PAWS, INC. All Rights Reserved.
INGREDIENTS: ONE JUMBO BAG OF POTATO CHIPS, ONE COUCH AND ONE TV
CHIPS
1: OPEN BAG OF CHIPS
CHIPS
2: PREHEAT TV
3: SIT ON COUCH, CHIPS IN LAP
CHIPS
4: SCARF THE ENTIRE BAG WITHOUT REALIZING IT
CHIPS
Distributed by Andrews McMeel Syndication
5: SAVE SHIRT CRUMBS FOR LATER SNACK
Z
NEXT TIME: "COLD PIZZA À LA BED"!

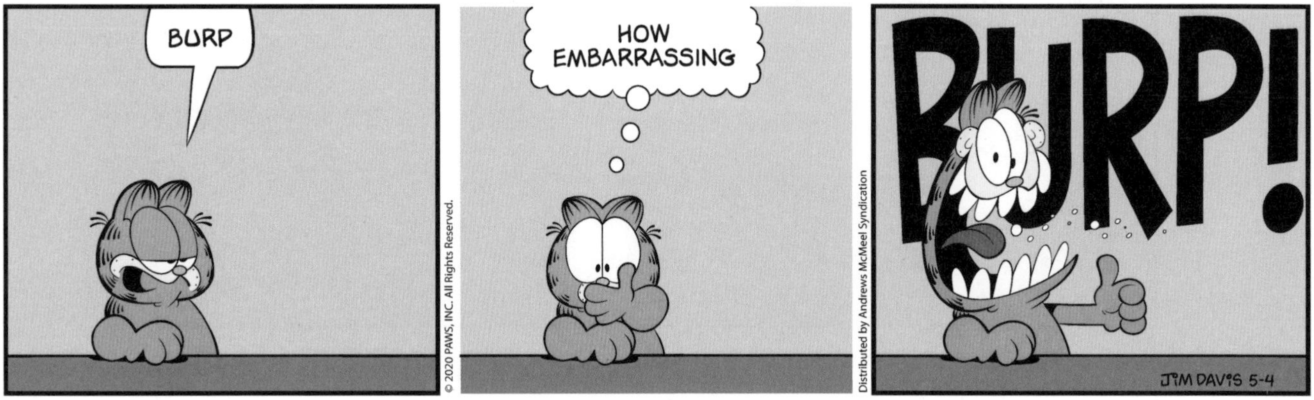
BURP
HOW EMBARRASSING
BURP!
© 2020 PAWS, INC. All Rights Reserved.
Distributed by Andrews McMeel Syndication
JIM DAVIS 5-4

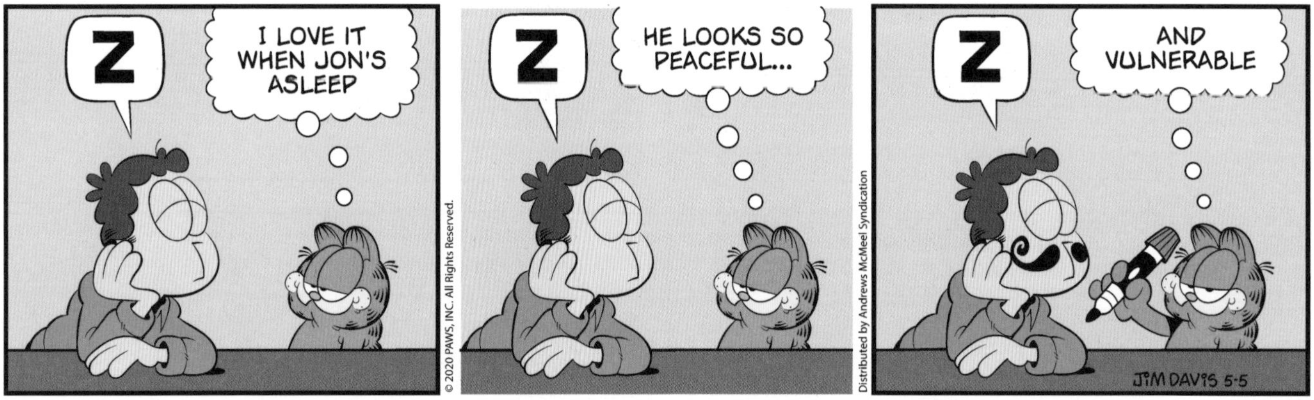
Z
I LOVE IT WHEN JON'S ASLEEP
Z
HE LOOKS SO PEACEFUL...
Z
AND VULNERABLE
© 2020 PAWS, INC. All Rights Reserved.
Distributed by Andrews McMeel Syndication
JIM DAVIS 5-5

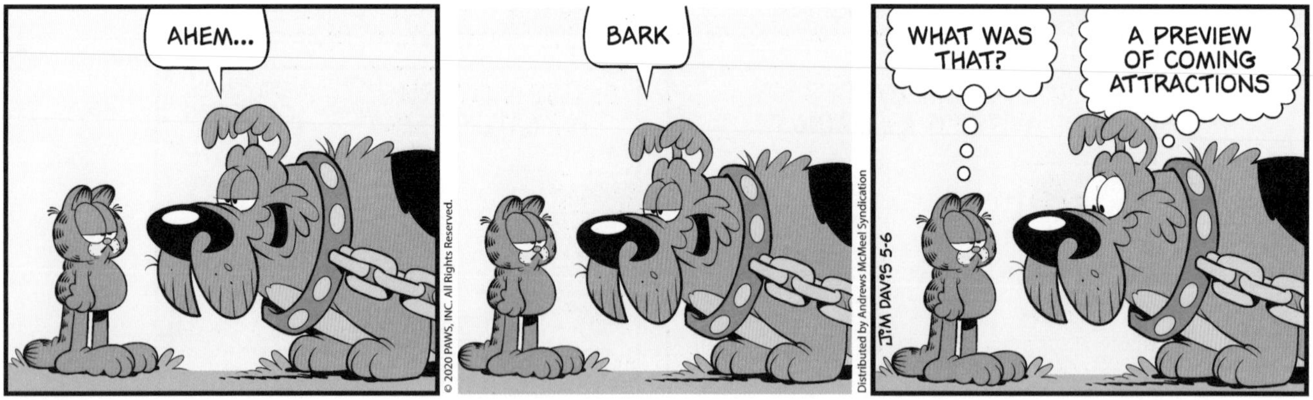
AHEM...
BARK
WHAT WAS THAT?
A PREVIEW OF COMING ATTRACTIONS
© 2020 PAWS, INC. All Rights Reserved.
Distributed by Andrews McMeel Syndication
JIM DAVIS 5-6

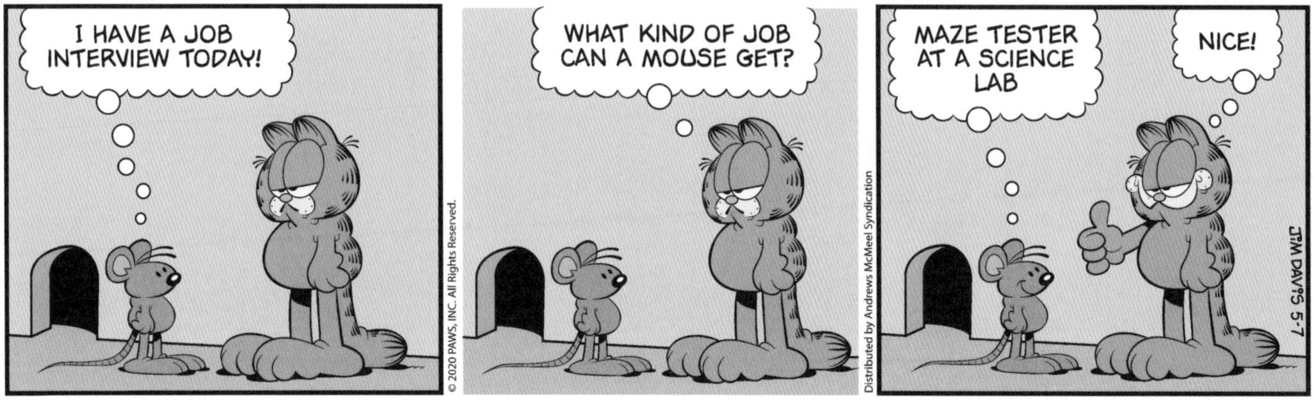
I HAVE A JOB INTERVIEW TODAY!
WHAT KIND OF JOB CAN A MOUSE GET?
MAZE TESTER AT A SCIENCE LAB
NICE!
JIM DAVIS 5-7
© 2020 PAWS, INC. All Rights Reserved.
Distributed by Andrews McMeel Syndication

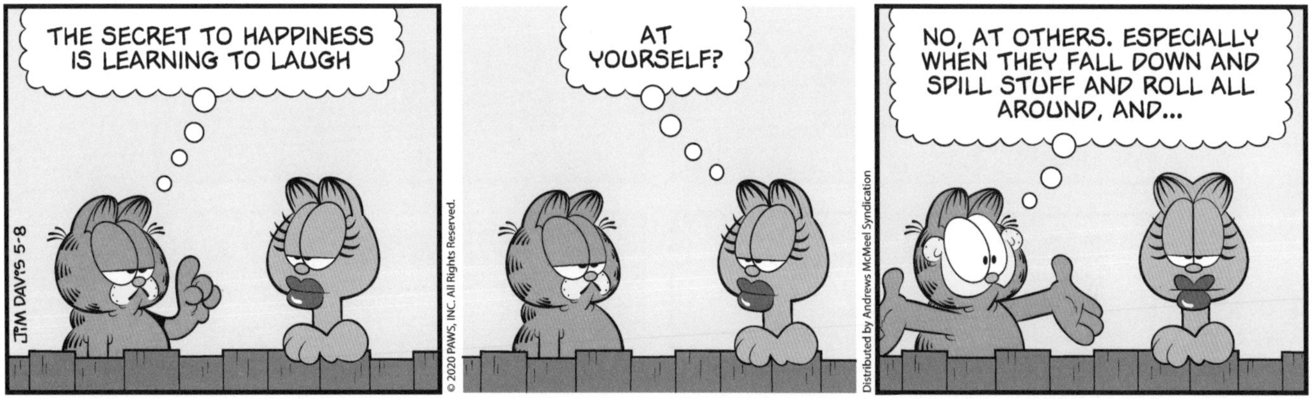
THE SECRET TO HAPPINESS IS LEARNING TO LAUGH
AT YOURSELF?
NO, AT OTHERS. ESPECIALLY WHEN THEY FALL DOWN AND SPILL STUFF AND ROLL ALL AROUND, AND...
JIM DAVIS 5-8
© 2020 PAWS, INC. All Rights Reserved.
Distributed by Andrews McMeel Syndication

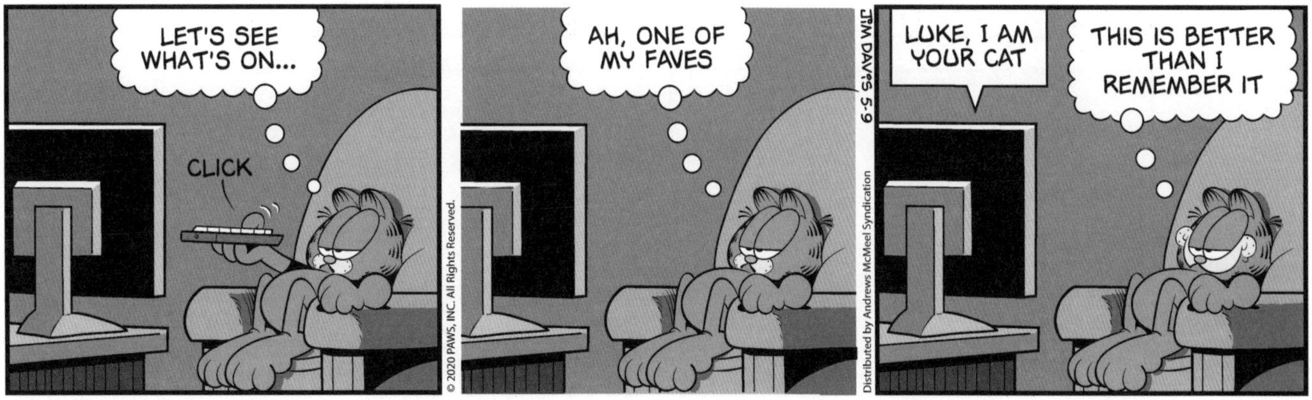
LET'S SEE WHAT'S ON...
CLICK
AH, ONE OF MY FAVES
LUKE, I AM YOUR CAT
THIS IS BETTER THAN I REMEMBER IT
JIM DAVIS 5-9
© 2020 PAWS, INC. All Rights Reserved.
Distributed by Andrews McMeel Syndication

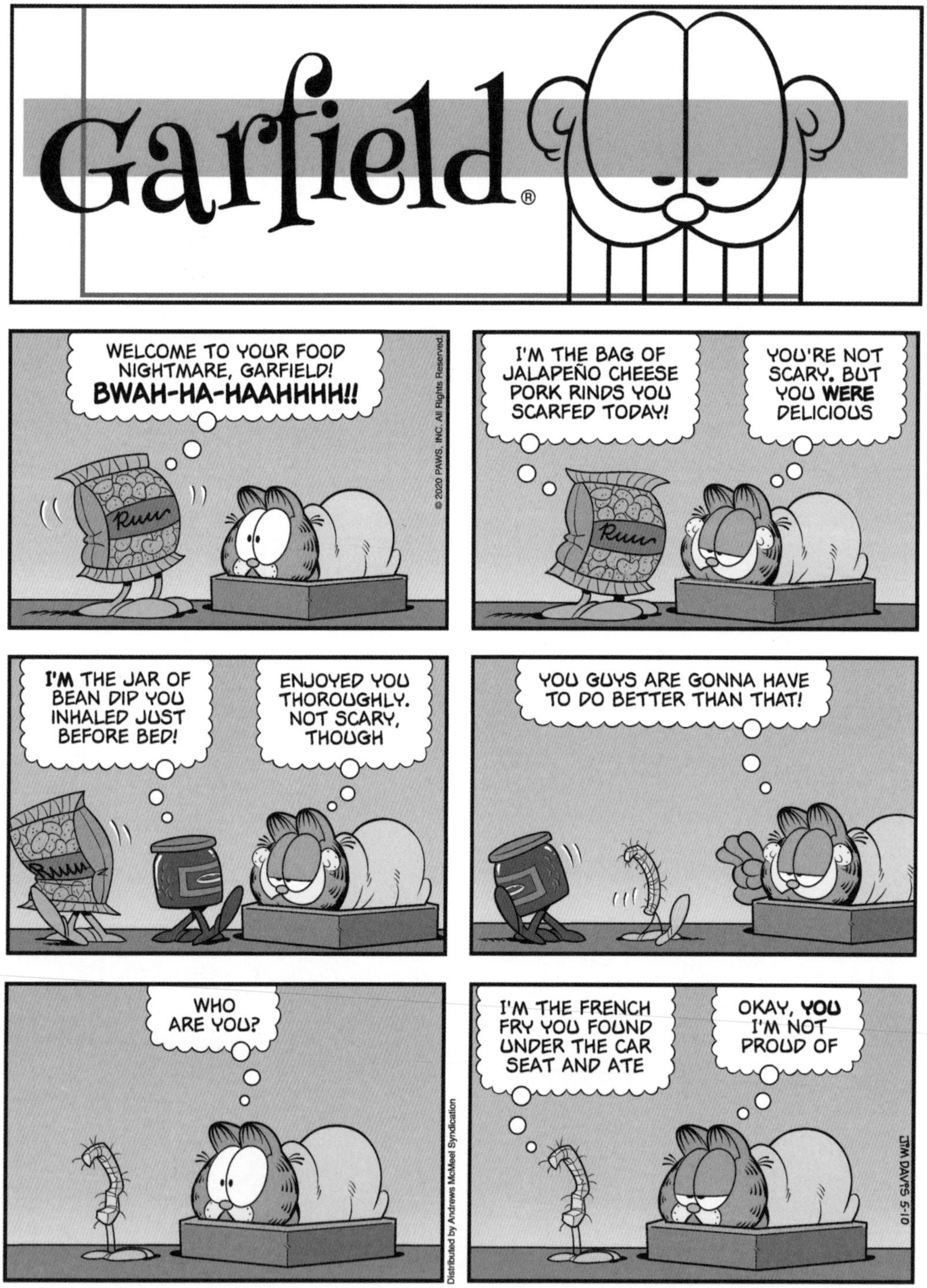
Garfield®
WELCOME TO YOUR FOOD NIGHTMARE, GARFIELD! BWAH-HA-HAAHHHH!!
© 2020 PAWS, INC. All Rights Reserved.
I'M THE BAG OF JALAPEÑO CHEESE PORK RINDS YOU SCARFED TODAY!
YOU'RE NOT SCARY. BUT YOU WERE DELICIOUS
I'M THE JAR OF BEAN DIP YOU INHALED JUST BEFORE BED!
ENJOYED YOU THOROUGHLY. NOT SCARY, THOUGH
YOU GUYS ARE GONNA HAVE TO DO BETTER THAN THAT!
WHO ARE YOU?
Distributed by Andrews McMeel Syndication
I'M THE FRENCH FRY YOU FOUND UNDER THE CAR SEAT AND ATE
OKAY, YOU I'M NOT PROUD OF
JPM DAVIS 5-10

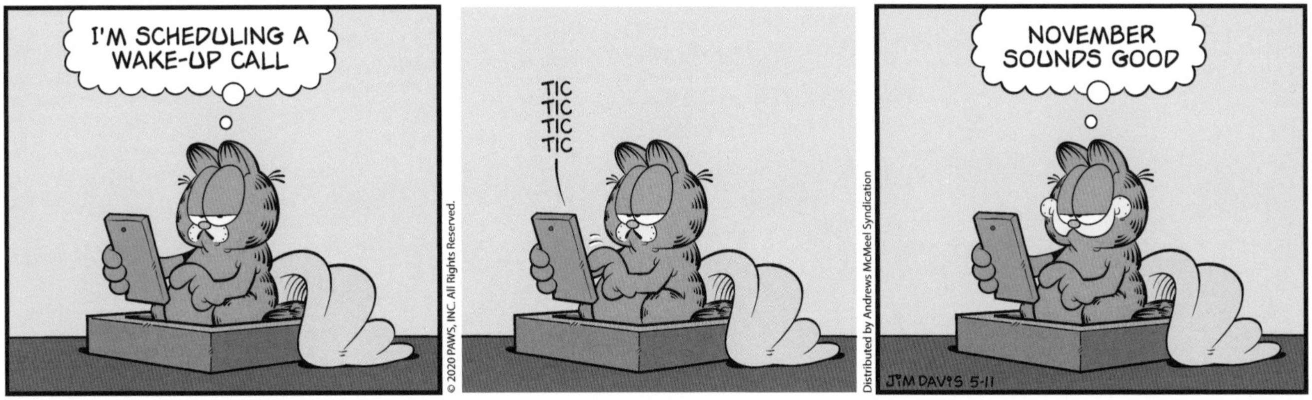
I'M SCHEDULING A WAKE-UP CALL
TIC TIC TIC TIC
NOVEMBER SOUNDS GOOD
© 2020 PAWS, INC. All Rights Reserved.
Distributed by Andrews McMeel Syndication
JIM DAVIS 5-11

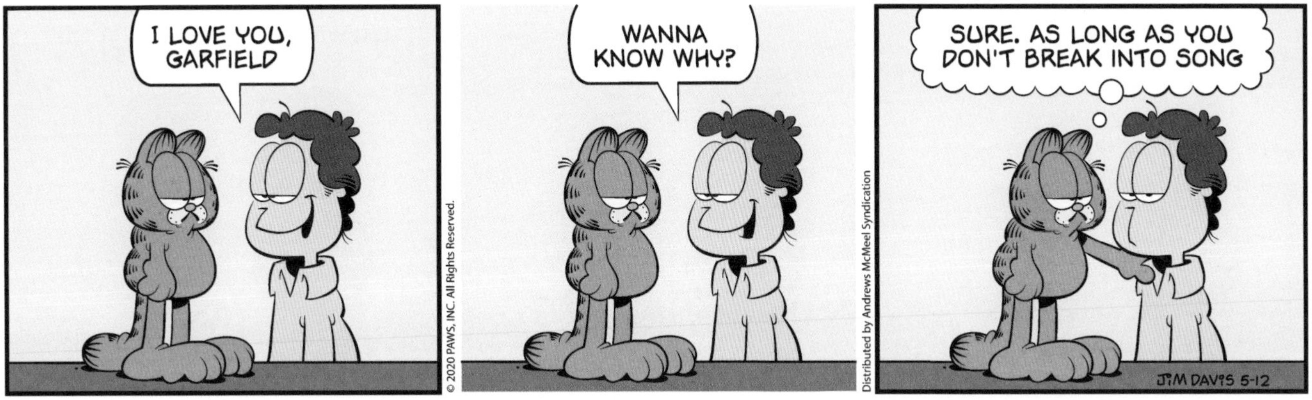
I LOVE YOU, GARFIELD
WANNA KNOW WHY?
SURE. AS LONG AS YOU DON'T BREAK INTO SONG
© 2020 PAWS, INC. All Rights Reserved.
Distributed by Andrews McMeel Syndication
JIM DAVIS 5-12

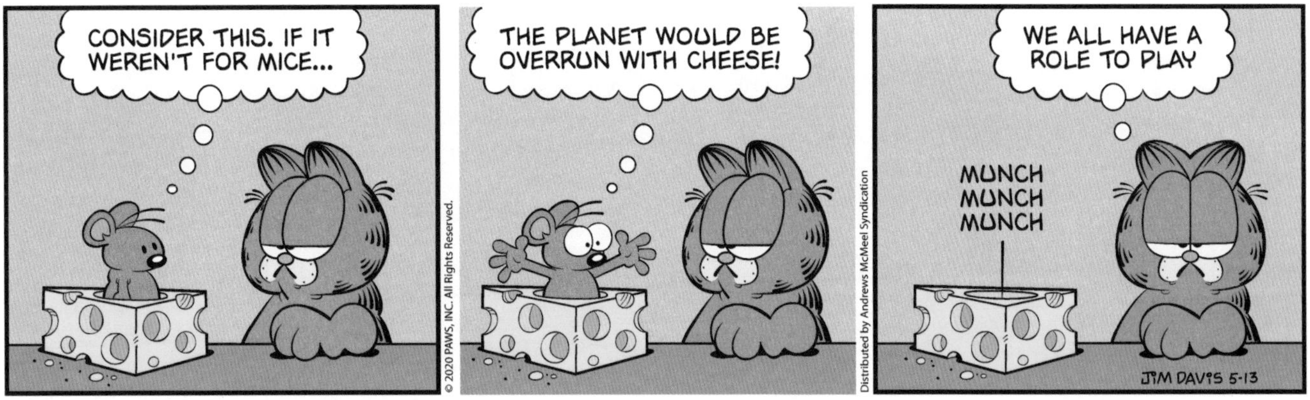
CONSIDER THIS. IF IT WEREN'T FOR MICE...
THE PLANET WOULD BE OVERRUN WITH CHEESE!
MUNCH MUNCH MUNCH
WE ALL HAVE A ROLE TO PLAY
© 2020 PAWS, INC. All Rights Reserved.
Distributed by Andrews McMeel Syndication
JIM DAVIS 5-13

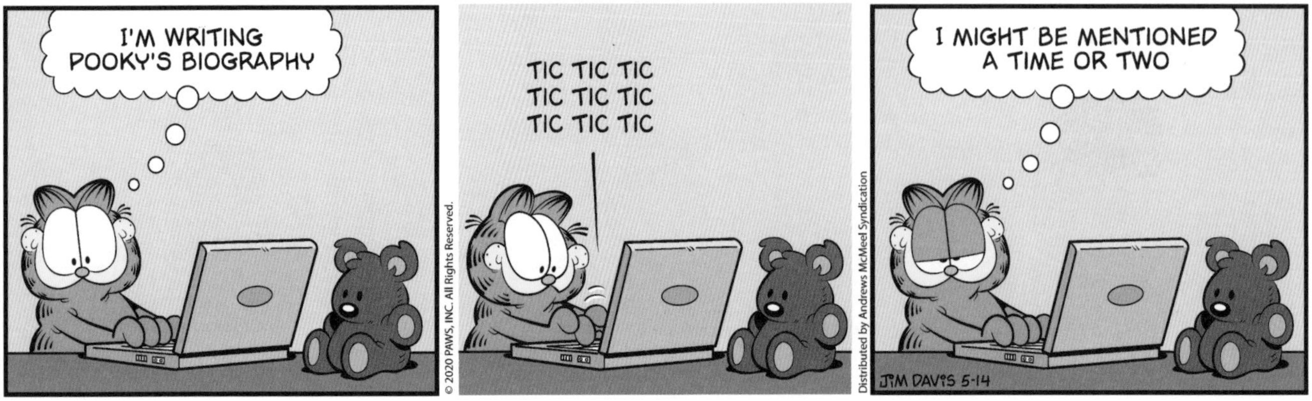
I'M WRITING POOKY'S BIOGRAPHY
TIC TIC TIC TIC TIC TIC TIC TIC TIC
I MIGHT BE MENTIONED A TIME OR TWO
JIM DAVIS 5-14
© 2020 PAWS, INC. All Rights Reserved.
Distributed by Andrews McMeel Syndication

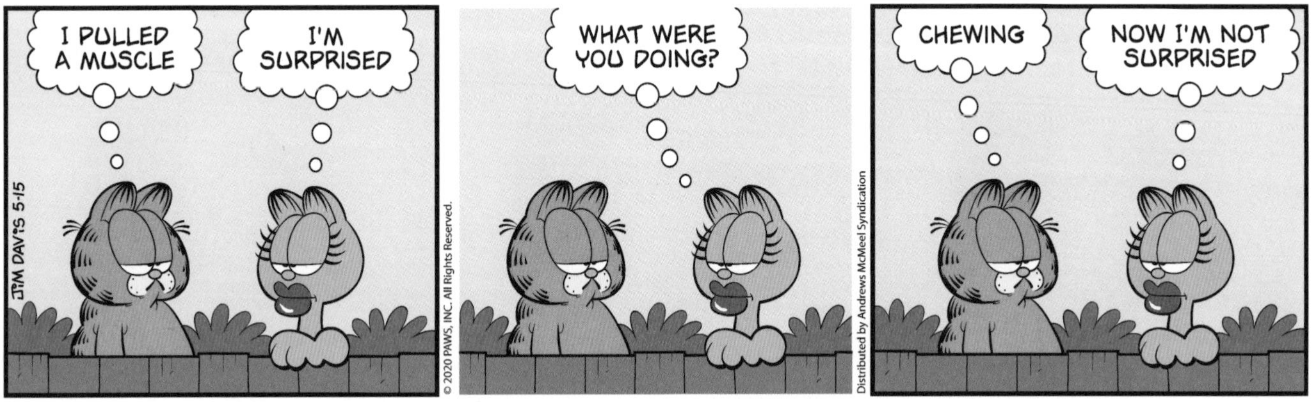
I PULLED A MUSCLE
I'M SURPRISED
WHAT WERE YOU DOING?
CHEWING
NOW I'M NOT SURPRISED
JIM DAVIS 5-15
© 2020 PAWS, INC. All Rights Reserved.
Distributed by Andrews McMeel Syndication

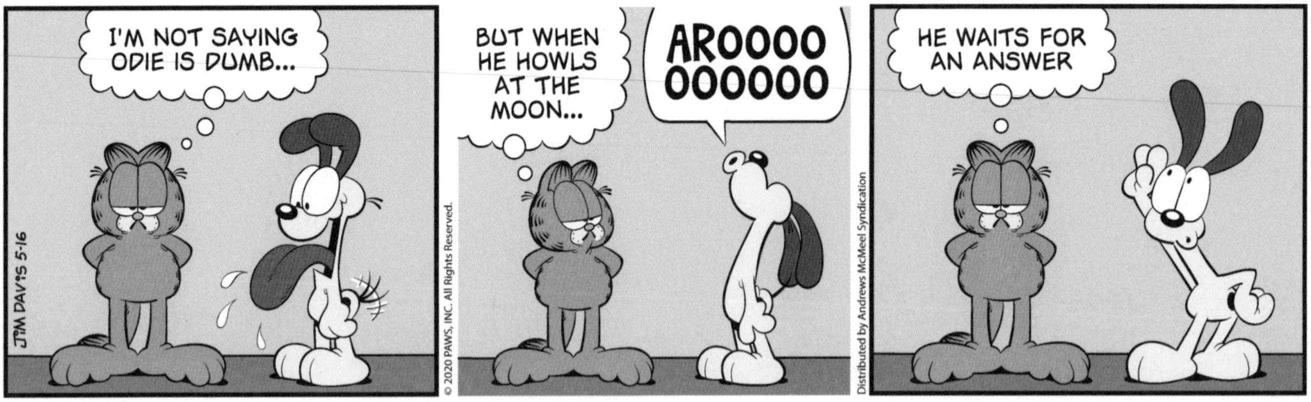
I'M NOT SAYING ODIE IS DUMB...
BUT WHEN HE HOWLS AT THE MOON...
AROOOO OOOOOO
HE WAITS FOR AN ANSWER
JIM DAVIS 5-16
© 2020 PAWS, INC. All Rights Reserved.
Distributed by Andrews McMeel Syndication

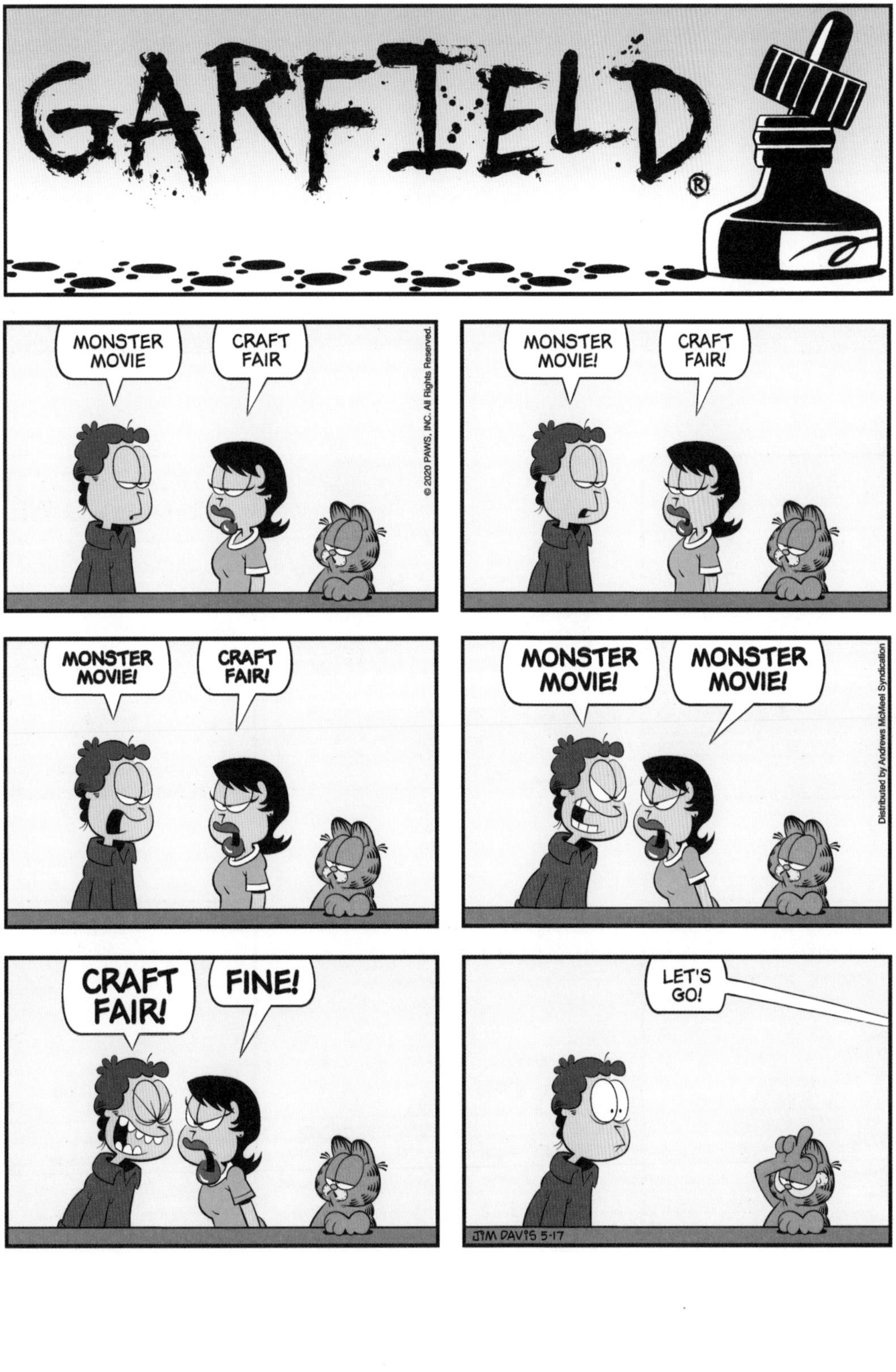
GARFIELD®
MONSTER MOVIE
CRAFT FAIR
© 2020 PAWS, INC. All Rights Reserved.
MONSTER MOVIE!
CRAFT FAIR!
MONSTER MOVIE!
CRAFT FAIR!
MONSTER MOVIE!
MONSTER MOVIE!
Distributed by Andrews McMeel Syndication
CRAFT FAIR!
FINE!
LET'S GO!
JIM DAVIS 5-17

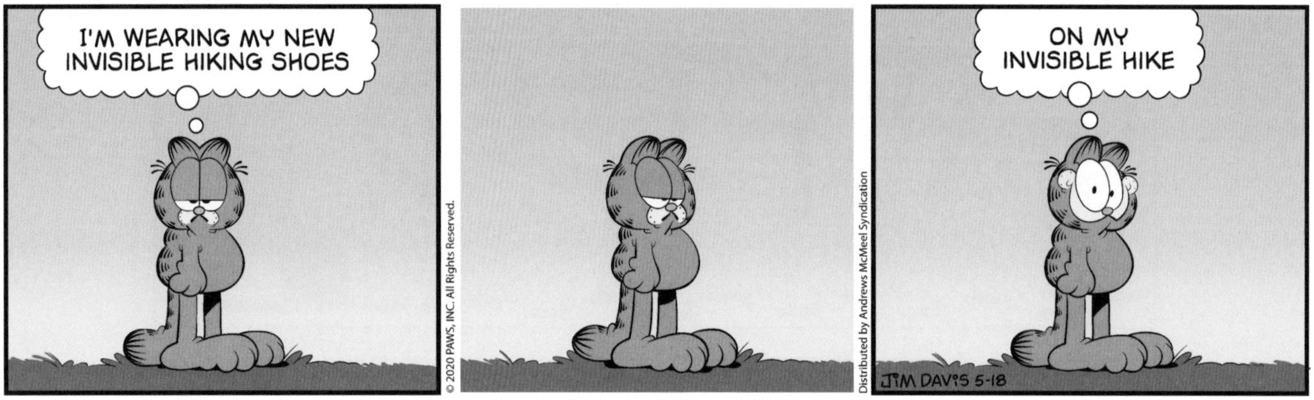
I'M WEARING MY NEW INVISIBLE HIKING SHOES
ON MY INVISIBLE HIKE
© 2020 PAWS, INC. All Rights Reserved.
Distributed by Andrews McMeel Syndication
JIM DAVIS 5-18

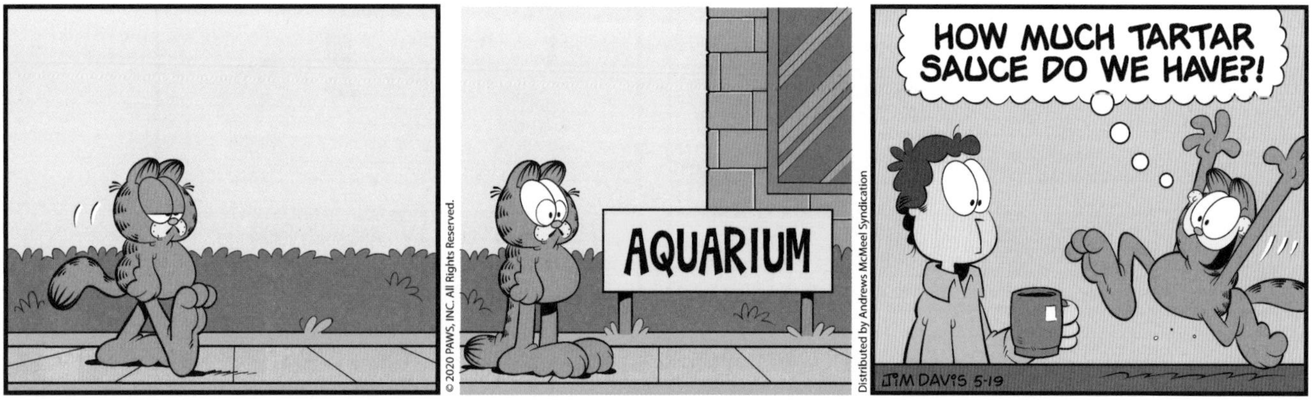
AQUARIUM
HOW MUCH TARTAR SAUCE DO WE HAVE?!
© 2020 PAWS, INC. All Rights Reserved.
Distributed by Andrews McMeel Syndication
JIM DAVIS 5-19

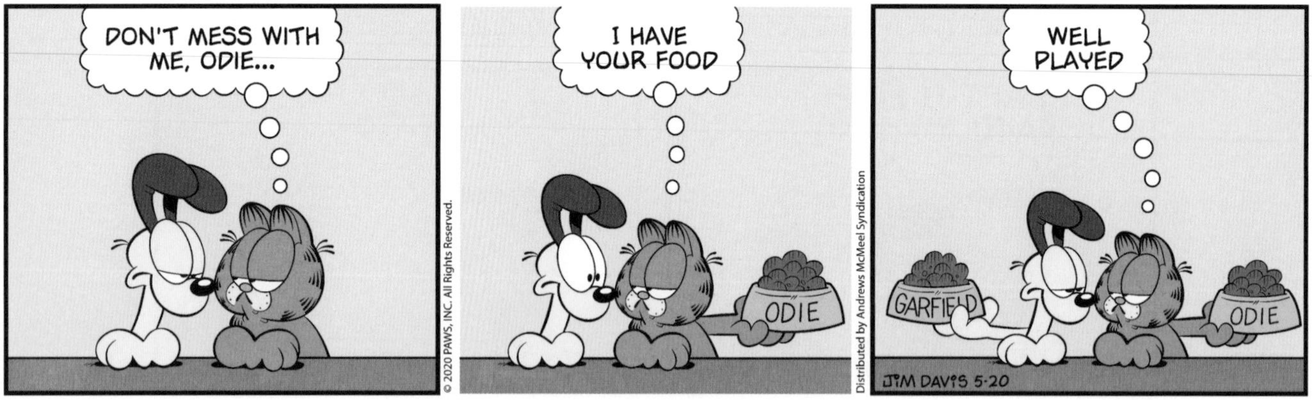
DON'T MESS WITH ME, ODIE...
I HAVE YOUR FOOD
ODIE
WELL PLAYED
GARFIELD
ODIE
© 2020 PAWS, INC. All Rights Reserved.
Distributed by Andrews McMeel Syndication
JIM DAVIS 5-20

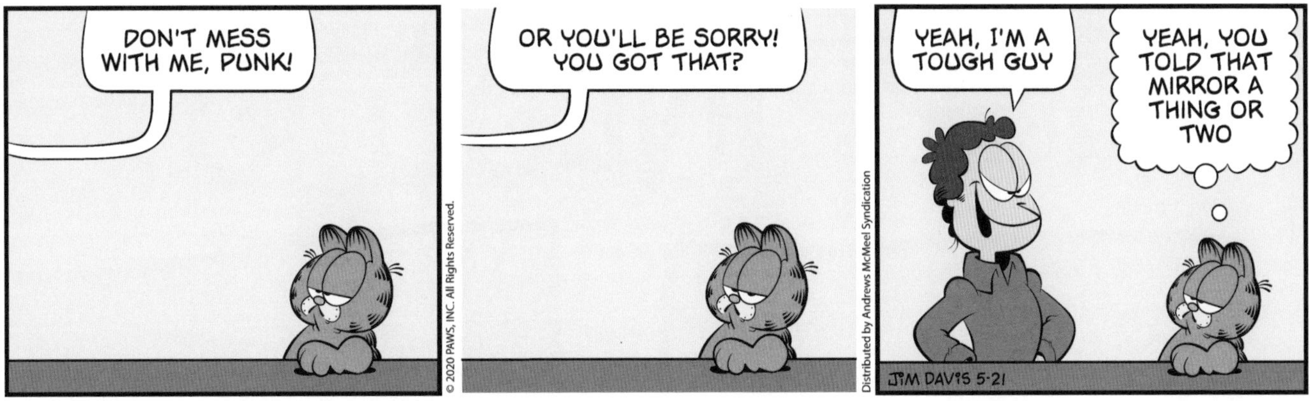
DON'T MESS WITH ME, PUNK!
OR YOU'LL BE SORRY! YOU GOT THAT?
YEAH, I'M A TOUGH GUY
YEAH, YOU TOLD THAT MIRROR A THING OR TWO
JIM DAVIS 5-21
© 2020 PAWS, INC. All Rights Reserved.
Distributed by Andrews McMeel Syndication

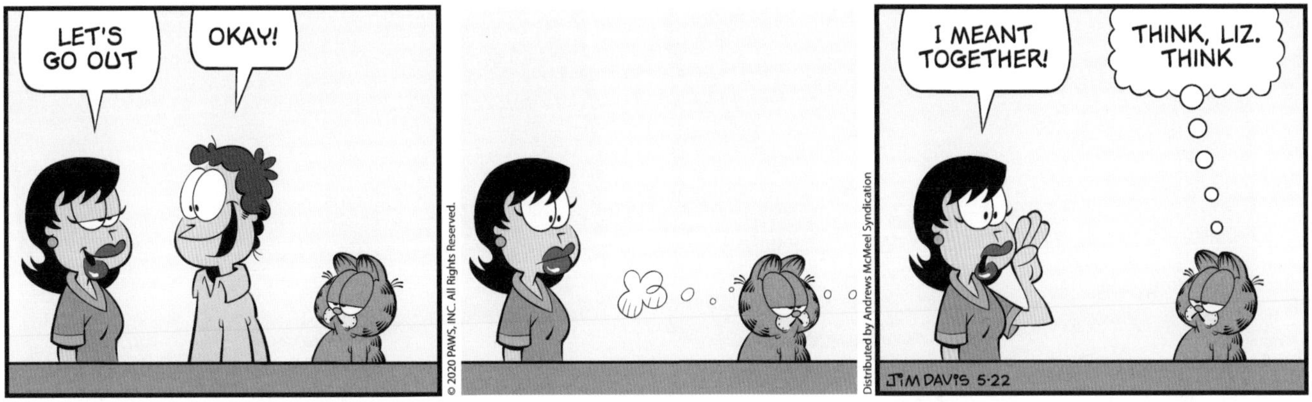
LET'S GO OUT
OKAY!
I MEANT TOGETHER!
THINK, LIZ. THINK
JIM DAVIS 5-22
© 2020 PAWS, INC. All Rights Reserved.
Distributed by Andrews McMeel Syndication

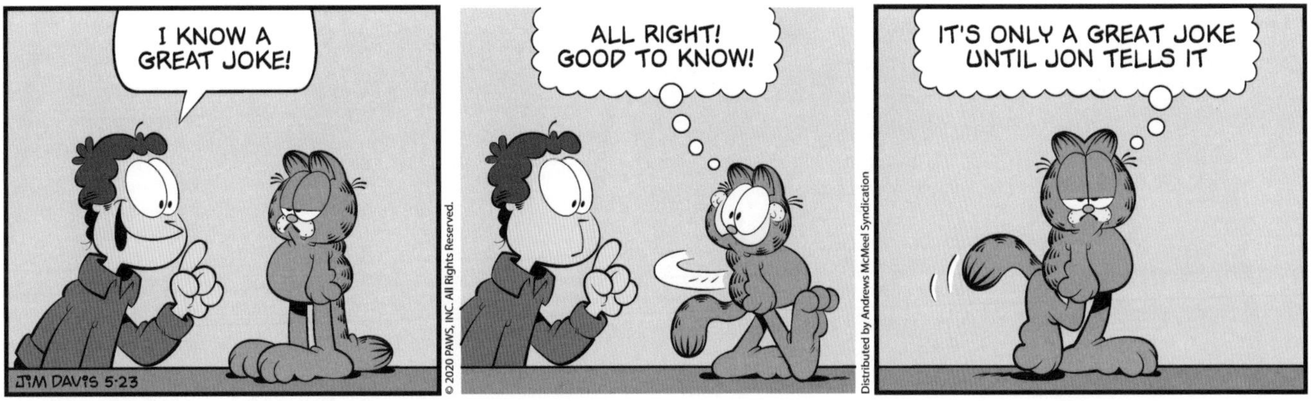
I KNOW A GREAT JOKE!
ALL RIGHT! GOOD TO KNOW!
IT'S ONLY A GREAT JOKE UNTIL JON TELLS IT
JIM DAVIS 5-23
© 2020 PAWS, INC. All Rights Reserved.
Distributed by Andrews McMeel Syndication

HAPPINESS IS...

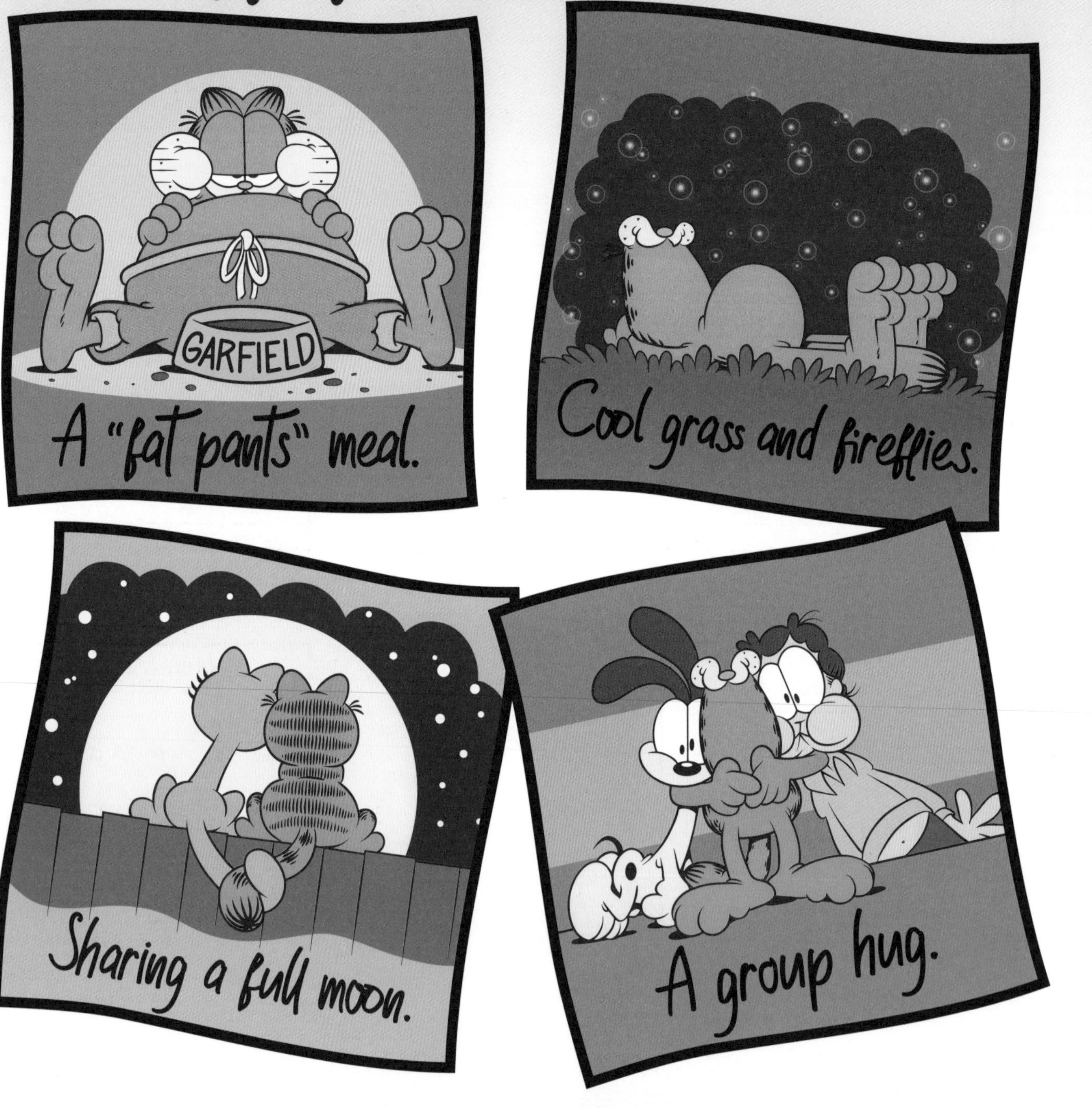
GARFIELD
A "fat pants" meal.
Cool grass and fireflies.
Sharing a full moon.
A group hug.